REFLECTIONS ON DE GAULLE

Political Founding in Modernity

Will Morrisey

UNIVERSITY
PRESS OF
AMERICA

LANHAM • NEW YORK • LONDON

Copyright © 1983 by

University Press of America,™ Inc.

4720 Boston Way
Lanham, MD 20706

3 Henrietta Street
London WC2E 8LU England

Printed in the United States of America

ISBN (Perfect): 0-8191-3096-6
ISBN (Cloth): 0-8191-3095-8

Library of Congress Catalog Card Number : 83-1225

TO MRS. ROSE M. MORRISEY

ACKNOWLEDGEMENTS

This book owes its beginning to Kenyon College. Professor William V. Frame, my adviser and teacher, introduced me to the study of de Gaulle and encouraged me to continue that study after graduation. Professor Philip N. Marcus gave me as much of the foundation of political thinking as an undergraduate is likely to accept; in the intervening years he has been consistently helpful and generous.

Professors Harry M. Clor and Robert H. Horwitz guided me in my first study of political philosophy, "ancient and modern," as they would not hesitate to add. Professor Horwitz's many kindnesses during those years and since them were and are much appreciated.

I met Professor Paul Eidelberg at Kenyon. His books on statesmanship deserve the gratitude of all who encounter them.

Outside of Kenyon, Professor Leo Raditsa of St. Johns College, editor of the *St. Johns Review,* subjected my chapter on *Le fil de l'épée* to meticulous and discerning scrutiny. The anonymous reader for University Press of America made useful criticisms, and the staff at the Press answered my questions with courtesy and professionalism.

My mother, Mrs. Rose M. Morrisey, worked to provide the means for my education. This book is dedicated to her.

PERMISSION TO QUOTE

I acknowledge, with gratitude, permission to quote from the following copyright material:

Aristotle: *The Basic Works of Aristotle,* translated by W.D. Ross, (Oxford: Oxford University Press, 1934); reprinted by Random House, New York, 1941.

Clausewitz, Carl von: *On War,* edited and translated by Michael Howard and Peter Paret. Copyright (c) 1976 by Princeton University Press.

De Gaulle, Charles: *The Edge of the Sword,* translated by Gerard Hopkins, (London: Faber and Faber, Ltd., 1960).

Memoirs of Hope, translated by Terence Kilmartin, (New York: Simon and Schuster, 1970).

War Memoirs, translated by Jonathan Griffin and Richard Howard, (New York: Simon and Schuster, 1956, 1959).

Lenin, V.I.: *Collected Works,* (New York: International Publishers, 1929).

Machiavelli: *The Art of War,* translated by Ellis Farnsworth, Indianapolis: Bobbs-Merrill Company, 1965).

Morrisey, Will: "De Gaulle's *Le fil de l'épée,*" *St. John's Review,* Winter 1981.

Nietzsche: *Basic Writings,* edited and translated by Walter Kaufmann, (New York: Random House, Inc., 1966).

The Portable Nietzsche, edited and translated by Walter Kaufmann, (New York: Viking Penguin Inc., 1954, 1982).

Plato: *The Dialogues of Plato,* translated by Benjamin Jowett, (Oxford: Oxford University Press, 1929).

Tocqueville, Alexis de: *Democracy in America,* translated by Henry Reeve, Francis Bowen, and Phillips Bradley, (New York: Random House, 1945).

CONTENTS

PREFACE

The war of books between modernity and tradition frequently becomes more than book-ish. It still consumes intellectual, ethical, and physical lives — as it has since the Renaissance. This book contains an examination of one incident in this war: an attempt, in modernity, to found a regime whose principles are not entirely modern.

The examination proceeds from the perspectives of textual interpretation and political thought. Rather than starting from abstract 'first principles,' as some philosophers would, I consider that point where principles and practice intersect.

Each of the book's five parts begins with a chapter of textual interpretation. One or more chapters concerning political thought follow them; these contain reflections on themes intimated by de Gaulle. The book moves from a discussion of modernity and tradition in the First Part to discussions of epistemology and ethics in the Second Part, the relation of ethics to the domains of war and politics in the Third Part, political founding in the Fourth Part, civic education in the Fifth Part. Readers who remember this structure will not find the material diffuse.

Separating textual interpretations from reflections on themes of the texts being interpreted achieves at least two things. It diminishes writer's temptation to construct (as distinguished from reconstruct) texts in order to fit theories. It simultaneously guards a writer from any tendency to construct theories to fit texts.

The chapters of textual interpretation belong to a traditional genre, the commentary that starts at the beginning and proceeds to the end of the text being interpreted. The chapters of political thought themselves contain textual interpretations, but only impressionistic ones. These juxtaposed impressions of the teachings of political philosophers and other writers yields a complex of dialogues — between those writers, de Gaulle, the writer, and the reader. In any dialogue each must contribute by completing thoughts others fail to express. Perhaps the most important contributor of all is the reader, the dialogues' silent partner.

FIRST PART

CHAPTER 1

LA DISCORDE CHEZ L'ENNEMI (1924)

The Great War, as it was called, broke Europe. Of those who survived, the thoughtful tried to discern meaning, or the lack of it, in what had happened and in what was left. Old men see endings; what Ludendorff, Foch, and Pershing wrote surprises no one. But obscure survivors, young men during the war, also saw an ending; the novels of Duhamel and Remarque, corrosively anti-nostalgic, are retrospective all the same. Not the least of the casualties was the sense of an equilibrium between past and future.

Charles de Gaulle, six years after the Armistice, was too young to write an apologia and too tough to write a horror story. He knew what Duhamel and Remarque knew; wounded several times, he spent much of the war in several of the Kaiser's prison camps. He did not choose to discuss his suffering, or that of others. All his life he found suffering, especially his own, uninteresting. Instead, de Gaulle wrote a history of the war meant not so much as a history as a manual of leadership. While de Gaulle never suggests that identical situations recur, he does insist on the existence of regularities that a writer or teacher can present in order to simplify history — without omitting the events that matter, or reshaping them to fit patterns.

La discorde chez l'ennemi: discretion causes the young French officer to analyze failures of German leadership; two centuries before, a much greater French writer commented on France by imagining Persian society. Fiction gave Montesquieu flexibility, the chance to elaborate many parallels. De Gaulle, using history, recent history, allows himself no more than a few hints. Nonetheless, because he whets them on history, those hints have sharp points for men who pride themselves on realism. The military, for example.

$$*\qquad\qquad *\qquad\qquad *$$

De Gaulle works with the best primary sources available to him in the early 1920's: parliamentary records, German newspapers, the memoirs of the principal German civil and military leaders. Although the latter are apologetic, "it is possible," he writes in his preface, "comparing some to others, juxtaposing the theses they maintain, grouping their affirmations and negations, to discern at the very least the principal vicissitudes and to form a judgment on the action of the personalities." By "the principal vicissitudes" de Gaulle means those "acts of the drama" that "appeared most charged with consequences, with regard to the direction and the upshot of the war," and that "appear to be the most characteristic of the spirit and behavior of the personalities who were in the conflict." "The drama" is one of de Gaulle's characteristic metaphors, and an appropriate one; tension, of which drama is one species, presupposes energy and order, the two poles of the Gaullist world.

Before discussing these directive events, de Gaulle describes the character of the men responsible for them. He finds four virtues in the German military (not civil) leaders, virtues so striking that defeat "did not diminish [the leaders'] fame": audacity, spirit of enterprise, will to succeed and vigor in the management of means. He also finds three faults: "taste for inordinate enterprise," "the passion to expand, regardless of risk, their personal power," and "contempt for the limits outlined by personnal experience, good sense [le bon sens] and law" — leaving us to notice that the faults are extreme forms of the virtues. Moreover, "far from combatting in themselves, or at least concealing these faults, the German leaders considered them as forces, raised them systematically"; this excess, in turn, was "like a crushing weight" on the directive events of the war.

If, to oversimplify, certain events caused defeat and certain personalities caused those events, what caused the personalities? De Gaulle avoids detailed speculation, which would lead him from his subject, and contents himself with a suggestion:

> Perhaps one will find in their operations the imprint of the theories of Nietzsche on the Elite and the Overman, adopted by the military generation that conducted the recent struggle and who attained the age of maturity and fixed its philosophy toward the end of the century.
>
> The Overman, with his exceptional character, the will for power, the taste for risk, the contempt for others . . . appeared to these passionate *ambitieux* as the ideal they must attain; they decided willingly to be part of that formidable Nietzchean elite who, in pursuing their own glory, are convinced it serves the general interest, who contemptuously constrain "the mass of slaves," and do not delay before human suffering, if not saluting it as necessary and suitable.

This extremist and individualistic ethic leads to a "philosophy of war [that] can soon render vain the most violent efforts of a great people" — who, far from being slaves, "sometimes constitute the most universal and the surest guarantee of the destinies of *la Patrie.*"

Not that de Gaulle is a democrat. This book is for would-be military leaders, not those they command.

> This study will attain its purpose, if it contributes, in its modest measure, to bringing our military leaders of tomorrow, according to the examples of their victorious models in the recent war, to molding their *esprit* and their character after the rules of classical order. It is in them that they will imbibe that sense of equilibrium, of what is possible, of measure [*la mesure*] which, alone, render durable and fruitful the works of energy.

Nietzschean will-to-power and individualism, by themselves, fail. Judged on its own terms, the German worship of success does not succeed. Energy needs stability, order, to attain its ends, and to maintain them. And stability precludes radical individualism made general.

To discover some of the truth in the various self-serving accounts of the war, de Gaulle will juxtapose them, then assess what he sees, using his own judgment — as any historian must. But that would only present the Germans in their terms and in terms of what de Gaulle hopes is his good sense: a foreign standard and a private one. In 1922, a twenty-one year old esthetician named André Malraux told the Parisian art world that "The Greek genius will be better understood by the opposition of a Greek statue to an Egyptian or Asiatic statue, than by knowing one hundred Greek statues." De Gaulle, never a denizen of the Left Bank, nonetheless had the same intuition. To Nietzschean individualism he opposes French balance:

> In the French-style garden, no tree seeks to choke the others in its shade, the flower-beds put up with being delineated geometrically, the pond does not aspire to be a waterfall, the statues do not pretend to assert themselves alone for admiration. A noble melancholy is liberated sometimes. Perhaps it comes of the sentiment that each element, isolated, would have been able to shine more. But that would have been to the detriment of the whole, and the stroller is pleased with the rule which imprints on the garden its magnificent harmony.

Here is a standard neither German nor private, a standard by which de Gaulle can appeal to other Frenchmen. Genuinely unmodern, de Gaulle's alternative to the ultra-modernity of Nietzsche (as understood by turn-of-the-century German officers) originates in seventeenth-century France and, beyond it, in Rome and in ancient Greece. His quaint-sounding use of what Ruskin called the "pathetic fallacy" — the *bon sens* of ponds, the deference of flower-beds — is probably a deliberate evocation of tradition, as is the conventional image of France as a garden.

The garden is more than the sum of its parts; ideally, so is France. Both attain unity by a pervasive rule. But unity for what?

Previously, de Gaulle emphasized success. A unified effort directs energy well; it wins, whereas individualistic backstabbers win battles but lose wars. This emphasis should not surprise us, for de Gaulle is a soldier writing for other soldiers. Moralizing won't impress. But even a military man can wonder about what he defends. His country, of course — but is it worth defending? De Gaulle thinks France worth defending, for two reasons. "Magnificence" is the more obvious; the garden pleases he who sees it whole. The ideal France, and the real one when the French act well, is beautiful.

To this esthetic worth de Gaulle adds ethical worth. The nobility of the melancholy the stroller feels and perceives originates in self-restraint, in subordinating one's ambitions to something else, something better. (Here is where de Gaulle's use of the "pathetic fallacy" helps him; he can blend the esthetic pleasure that the garden prompts with an ethical motif). Magnificent harmony presupposes success; it has survived. It includes many individuals who, taken together, are more beautiful and good than they might have been alone. Magnificence, moderation and harmony grace classical political thought, and they grace de Gaulle's.*

For my purposes, the preface to *La discorde chez l'ennemi* is the most important part of the book, containing some of the most instructive pages de Gaulle wrote. The bulk of *La discorde chez l'ennemi* contains his account of the five events or "vicissitudes" which, more than any others, caused the German defeat. De Gaulle orders them chronologically:

— "the indiscipline of von Kluck who, from 2-5 September 1914, created favorable conditions for our Marne offensive and provoked our victory";

— Grand-Admiral von Tirpitz's "obstinate struggle with Chancellor of the Empire Bethmann-Hollweg", an attempt to force the latter to declare unrestrained submarine war which, when it succeeded, provoked the United States to take arms;

— Germany's inability to establish sole command of the Central Powers;

— "the crisis of government, henceforth incurable, provoked in Berlin, in 1917, by the intrigue of Ludendorff", who wanted to sack Bethmann-Hollweg and seize absolute power;

— June 18, 1918: the beginning of the "abrupt and complete moral overwhelming of a valiant people."

Each of the five chapters concerns one event, beginning with "The Disobedience of General von Kluck."

* *

Von Kluck's disobedience originated not with von Kluck, but with his immediate military ancestors. The German leaders of 1914, particularly Kaiser Wilhelm II, formed their strategic and tactical predispositions during the 1860's and '70's, when von Moltke constructed a unique system of command. Moltke, as High Commander of the Prussian armies, gave his subordinates only the most general orders, "admitting, *a priori,* that they will find [specific plans] better and more quickly than he, in the current of changes in the situation." He expected them "to coordinate their efforts themselves." With two consequences: Moltke did not maintain proper means of acquiring information, and the means of transmitting orders between headquarters and the armies were "neglected outright." "All the more reason for [the generals] to esteem their conceptions better justified than those from above."

By virtue of the system and its consequences, with regard to means of infor-

---

*This is not to characterize de Gaulle's political thought as entirely or even decisively classical. Magnificence, moderation, and harmony occasionally grace non-classical political thought.

mation and transmission, the army commanders of Moltke, in the course of victorious campaigns, acted, in decisive moments, by themselves and against the intentions expressed by the High Commander.

De Gaulle gives two examples: the battle at Koniggratz in 1866 and the battle at Metz in 1870. At Koniggratz Moltke chose a faulty battle-plan; bad communications had resulted in his receiving wrong information. The general of the First Army, Frederick-Charles, acted on his own, according to the circumstance he knew, and won. "All military Germany, in consideration of the victory, had only praise for the system."

Moltke did understand the situation at Metz, and instructed his generals accordingly. But, as previously, Frederick-Charles had a "totally personal conception of the situation," and did the opposite of what Moltke ordered. And it worked, because "the systematic inertia of Marshall Bazaine", the French commander, rescued the Germans. With such successes, "the system of Moltke found itself definitely consecrated."

Militarily, the 1914 German leaders followed the principles of Moltke; 'philosophically,' they followed those of Nietzche.

> It was from Nietzsche that the leaders, as all thinking Germany, imbibed their philosophy, adopting enthusiastically the cult of the Overman, [which] naturally disposed each one to think of himself as the center of the world, inclined to develop to the extreme his character . . . .

This brought perseverance and audacity; it also "exaggerated their independence and induced them to act by themselves in all cases." Moltkean institutions and 'Nietzschean' beliefs combined to justify insubordination. The method was successful and flattering.

In 1914, Colonel-General von Moltke, nephew of the strategist of Koniggratz and Metz, was the German High Commander. He was also "sick, and considered, rightly or wrongly, by his ambitious and troublesome lieutenants [General of the First Army, von Kluck, among them] as a man of the background," a man with a famous name, only. On September 2 the Imperial Headquarters was in Luxembourg, at some remove from the battle-line. Until then, the younger Moltke and von Kluck pursued identical strategies. But aerial reconnaissance and "certain other means of information" revealed a different arrangement of French troops than had been supposed. Moltke sent new orders. Von Kluck, "like the illustrious ancestors of 1866 and 1870, neglect[ed] the directive of the leader," believing, "in conscience, that he judg[ed] the situation better than one can judge it in G.Q.G., and that he [had] the duty to act according to his own inspiration." He told Moltke that, "and Moltke never reacted. Such is the power of the past." Eventually, on September 4, Moltke sent another order; von Kluck persisted.

During the Battle of the Marne, "the strategical surprise of von Kluck was complete. The whole disposition of German troops proceeded to pay for this surprise by an irremediable defeat." De Gaulle's dry humor underlines what he knows his readers know: that the victory on the Marne saved France.

> German military history, bowing to national pride, was compelled not to discern, in the study of victories, the mistakes committed, to never draw warnings. What succeeded against a Benedek or a Bazain, a Joffre rendered fatal.

Fatal, because "in war, apart from several essential principles, there is no universal system, but only circumstances and personalities." Imitation fails; "this obsession, this superstition of the past" loses battles. Is de Gaulle glancing at his own colleagues in 1924, servants of old methods that 'won' the Great War? Years later, de Gaulle's critics derided his "chauvinism," his rootedness in the past, forgetting his lifelong opposition to any complacent patriotism. In the 1930's he attacked another "universal system": the French reliance on the Maginot Line, stationary artillery. But as early as *La discorde,* he saw the beginnings of mental rigidity among the French military. His point was lost on them, as they studied old victories.

*

The second cause of German defeat was the "tenacious struggle between the government and the navy" over the intensification of submarine warfare. Grand-Admiral von Tirpitz, "essentially a Junker of 'old Prussia,'" had fought secretly with Chancellor Bethmann-Hollweg, "jurist and democrat," before the war. Bethmann wanted to reduce naval construction; Tirpitz, whose "entire life was consecrated to preparing for war against Great Britain," opposed that successfully. On August 2, 1914 they argued over the timing of the various declarations of war, Tirpitz ("already!" de Gaulle exclaims) saying that "the gravity of the hour constrains me . . . to leap over the limits of my prerogatives."

The moderate Falkenhayn, who replaced Moltke as High Commander after the Battle of the Marne, thought Tirpitz "troublesome and unrestrained." When the Grand-Admiral advocated an immediate naval battle with Britain, the General Staff refused. Tirpitz, "wounded at heart, then rendered vain all the effort of his life," launching "a harsh and tenacious campaign . . . against the Chancellor," insinuating that Bethmann feared England. He persuaded the Reichstag to propose a new program of naval construction, which Bethmann defeated. Then a new strategy occurred to him: submarine warfare.

Tirpitz wanted to build more submarines before challenging Britain's fine navy. But von Pohl, the leader of the General Naval Staff, "was ambitious, vain and jealous of Tirpitz," he advocated starting the submarine war immediately, to 'make History' with the first such battle. Bethmann, seeing this would ruin "his hopes of American mediation at a favorable moment," opposed it — and in his anti-Bethmannian passion, Tirpitz supported von Pohl! Delays and maneuvering: de Gaulle writes that we don't know "what game the Grand-Admiral played during the next several days." Bethmann saw the dangers, but "was of too mediocre character to resist forthrightly." This was in January; in late February the submarine war began. Tirpitz, after describing submarine war as premature less than a month before, had told the Emperor's Cabinet of its promise.

On May 7 the Lusitania incident caused "a veritable national choler in the United States." Bethmann persuaded the Kaiser to spare neutral ships; "to pour balm on Tirpitz's wounds" Wilhelm II "gave him an order of merit." This failed to soothe the Grand-Admiral, who led his followers against Bethmann's in the Reichstag, a controversy that "was communicated to the public." In August the *Arabic* was sunk; Bethmann had the German ambassador in Washington apologize to President Wilson, promise to indemnify the victims and to punish the submarine commander. Whereupon Tirpitz, with the support of the Reichstag, asked to be relieved of his duties. The Kaiser, instead of asserting the authority of the civil command over the military, made a deferential statement to the effect that he wanted to consult Tirpitz on all important military questions. Tirpitz understood the significannce of that, and withdrew his resignation. De Gaulle exclaims:

> Extraordinary retreat of the supreme power, incontestable proof of that crisis of authority, that was, in spite of certain appearances, the real moral cause of the defeat of the Empire!

In a couple of years, the military would control Germany.

The relations between Bethmann and Tirpitz now "had . . . the character of an overt and public hostility." Individuals and groups contended; the press, big business, even the Left called for another Bismarck. Ordinary Germans did not fear American intervention, believing the submarine fleet a sure defense. Erzberger wrote that "to my knowledge, it was the first time, in Germany, that the street interfered with politics." In Germany, perhaps: but Erzberger and de Gaulle, familiar with Greek and Roman history, to say nothing of Bonaparte's, surely know that militarism and democratization do not contradict one another.

General Pétain prompted the Germans to resolve the argument, temporarily. Falkenhayn had supported Tirpitz because he needed support for his plan to possess Belgium. The French forces at Verdun, under Pétain, caused sufficient trouble to make Falkenhayn moderate his ambitions. Without Falkenhayn's support, the submarine war was postponed indefinitely; Tirpitz became ill, asked for his discharge, and got it.

Less than two weeks later, Tirpitz found the strength to form a new political party, whose platform consisted of three 'planks': the dismissal of Bethmann, the annexation of Belgium and "pitiless" submarine warfare. This party did well at first, but German setbacks in the summer of 1916 "silenced the pan-Germanists and gave courage to the moderates," who still desired a negotiated peace treaty.

However, on August 29 the Kaiser, "at the height of anguish" over these reverses, removed Falkenhayn and made Hindenburg High Commander. Hindenberg enjoyed popular respect, owing it not only to his successes on the Eastern Front, but to the "disinterestedness of his character, his profound calm, and to that obscure consciousness of the oppressed masses, that he was a sensible and piteous man as well as a resolute leader." De Gaulle may think of Hindenburg as a German Pétain; he is the only German whose character de Gaulle praises (Bethmann, usually judged worthwhile, lacked forthrightness). Pétain, de Gaulle's most powerful defender in the 1920's, recommended this book to all young French officers.

Whatever the accuracy of such a parallel, de Gaulle sees a problem. He has described the German military as Moltkean and Nietzschean; Hindenburg was not. He explains this anomaly in a footnote:

> Marshall Hindenburg was not part of the lawless [or unrestrained: "*effrenee*"] generation, that victorious Prussia formed on the morrow of 1870, and of which Ludendorff was the prototype. The Marshall had received his intellectual formation, constituted his philosophy and finished his military apprenticeship before 1866. A more fervent cult of duty, a greater moderation of judgment, a better-developed moral sense, an almost religious taste for "service" distinguished, in our opinion, Hindenburg from the younger Prussians, more vain, more selfish also — more in the current, moreover, of their age — who surrounded him in the G.Q.G.

De Gaulle's Hindenburg is a saint of the civic religion (the real Hindenburg had something of that quality, as well). No other German in *La discorde chez l'ennemi* is so nearly French.

Civic virtue has its rewards:

> One is astonished at the rapidity and the ease with which reeling Germany righted itself at the end of 1916, and repaired its compromised situation. The prestige of Hindenburg suffices to explain it.

Note that prestige comes from the public's recognition of virtue. Not especially virtuous itself, it nonetheless defers to the virtue of others — or so one may infer from de Gaulle's account.

Bethmann foresaw that the military

> . . . were going to exercise a moral dictatorship, next to which the rights of the civil power would amount to little. But he had to choose between their supremacy and the defeat of the Empire.

His belief that Hindenburg and Ludendorff, "men of the Eastern Front," did not want to attract additional enemies like America, Holland, and Denmark smoothed the Chancellor's dilemma markedly. Hoping to interpose Hindenburg between himself and Tirpitz, he told the High Commander that G.Q.G. was running the war, thus signalling "in advance, the capitulation of the civil power before the military authority . . . ."

As Germans recovered their confidence, the Tirpitz faction redoubled its attacks on Bethmann. In December, President Wilson said that he still wanted to mediate, a statement that delayed the submarine campaign for a while. But Tirpitz continued his agitation in the Reichstag, and even the Socialists waffled, lacking "the courage to condemn outright submarine warfare."

Tirpitz won — not by propaganda, but for a reason having nothing to do with military needs. Hindenburg became annoyed by Bethmann's politics, especially by the Chancellor's support of Polish independence. The "jurist and democrat" displeased the High Commander by being juridical and democratic. The United States, governed by a man who made much of such qualities, took exception to Marshall Hindenburg's new submarine blockade and declared war early in 1917.

The conflict between Tirpitz and Bethmann "finally was resolved in the worst manner, at the worst moment." In the next two months the Soviet revolution occurred and the French spring offensive was checked. At this moment the Germans could have seized "an advantageous peace" — had they not alienated their one skilled negotiator.

De Gaulle admires Hindenburg's "grandeur" and "moral courage" for, unlike Tirpitz and Ludendorff, the High Commander took responsibility for his mistake. Nonetheless, "History will doubtless blame him for having used his incomparable authority to violate a grand principle," namely, that of the subordination of military to civil authority. In doing otherwise, the German military "unleashed in the nation a furious and mortal tempest."

*

Before dealing with that internal tempest, de Gaulle backtracks, discussing an instance of disunity concurrent with the Tirpitz-Bethmann struggle: Germany's failure to impose its authority on its allies — notably, the Austro-Hungarian Empire.

The uncooperativeness of the old emperor, Franz-Josef, originated in neither senility nor envy, de Gaulle insists. Franz-Josef had always disliked Wilhelm II; when, early in the war, the Kaiser tried to deceive him about alleged German successes in battle, Franz-Josef never forgave him. Still, he refused to indulge in vindictiveness:

> In spite of the mortal perils that war alongside Germany caused for his Empire, despite the unskillfulness of the people in Berlin, he never tolerated the mentioning of a separate peace. Those whims originated in Vienna on the day of the death of Franz-Josef.

The Germans also blundered on the military level. The Austro-Hungarian Chief of the General Staff, Marshall Conrad von Holtzendorf, was a good, disinterested soldier who understood the importance of cooperation. But the Austrians didn't respect the German military leaders, and the two countries had never cooperated in a military campaign before 1914.

In the war's first months, Hindenburg and Conrad failed to coordinate their activities during an offensive against Russia; they lost. "Both had the character to recognize their errors," and planned a new, unified offensive in late 1914. It succeeded. Unfortunately, then-High Commander Falkenhayn oppugned those on the Eastern Front, especially Hindenburg, for whom he had a personal dislike.

After defeats at Ypres and on the Yser, Falkenhayn recognized that there would be no quick victory in the West. He nonetheless committed minimal forces to the East, partly because he was unsure of French intentions, mostly because his personal feelings, arising from an "arbitrary and egoistic" character, precluded his doing so. This decision offended Hindenburg and Conrad, and the latter's hostility had "most grave consequences."

9

In August 1915 Falkenhayn rejected the latest of Conrad's plans to attack Russia. Hindenburg went ahead anyway, with few troops, and failed. De Gaulle asks, "In what measure was the distinctness of [Falkenhayn's] judgment obscured by the jealousy produced by the glory of a rival?" The Serbian campaign occasioned another quarrel between Falken-Hayn and Conrad; "the Central Powers did not utilize . . . the lessons of 1914 and 1915," could not unite, and did not succeed.

Since late November 1915, Falkenhayn had prepared the Verdun offensive, while telling Conrad that there was little chance of activity on the Western Front. Conrad proposed attacking Italy, and when Falkenhayn stalled the Austrian commander suspected dissimulation. He matched it, secretly preparing an Italian campaign. The Russians, perhaps feeling neglected, attacked the Germans in June 1916. Falkenhayn refused to postpone the Verdun offensive, which went badly for him. He directed his anger at the Austrians.

On June 8 the two men sat down, argued, compromised. Falkenhayn agreed to reinforce the East with troops he'd planned to use in the West, admitting the error of "his vain Western offensive." This was insufficient. Conrad's political enemies accused him of incapacity; "in Vienna as in Paris, in Berlin as in Petersburg, we had, in 1916, the irrational taste for change." Irrational, but understandable because, as de Gaulle allows, citizens of all the countries involved had wearied of suffering after two years of war.

Conrad's political troubles gave the Germans the chance to seize command of the allied armies. After Verdun and after Rumania's declaration of war on Austria-Hungary, Wilhelm II replaced Falkenhayn with Hindenburg (despite his envy of the latter, which equaled Falkenhayn's). Conrad, faced with the command of Hindenburg and Ludendorff, "had the intelligence and moral merit to accept the proposition."

After two years and one month, then, the Central Powers achieved unity: too late for Austria-Hungary, whose forces were "materially and morally defeated" by then. On November 2 Franz-Josef died, and the young Emperor Charles wanted to break political ties with Germany, shake off Hindenburg's command.

Germany almost won the war, anyway. Had Austria-Hungary been in a position to contribute, the Germans might have won. De Gaulle doesn't write that; he doesn't have to. His readers also know that the "irrational taste for change" in 1916 wasn't the only parallel between Germany and France. The Western allied commands injured themselves in much the same way. If they did not lose the war because of it, they also had reinforcements from the United States, as Germany did not. French self-restraint is an ideal de Gaulle would see the next generation of officers approach; it was not so much a reality during the Great War as de Gaulle, perhaps for discretion's sake, pretends.

*

De Gaulle repeats: by spring 1917 Hindenburg and Ludendorff had reestablished the German position on both fronts. The German leaders were confident: the United States had entered the war but wouldn't send troops for a year; the Soviet revolution had paralyzed the major opponent in the East; the April French-English offensive was stopped.

The public, though, was "coming to a point of lassitude, such that success no longer excited their enthusiasm"; they wanted peace. Hindenberg and Ludendorff moved to reassure them — constraining the press, suppressing leftists in the Reichstag, and so forth. Chancellor Bethmann disagreed with these policies. He advocated a rapid peace settlement and universal suffrage. Hindenburg and Ludendorff decided to provoke his fall.

They had support:

> Conservatives hated [Bethmann's] liberalism in the interior, Pan-German-
> ists suspected his moderation and his desires of reconciliation with Europe.

Socialists and progressives found him too feeble *vis-à-vis* military authority . . .

No party forgave him for his stand on submarine warfare . . . .

Such are the problems of a moderate in an extreme situation, amongst extremists. Bethmann had supporters, however, not the least considerable of whom was the Kaiser. Bethmann never disturbed Wilhelm II's "superficial authroitarianism"; Bethmann might negotiate an honorable peace, the Kaiser hoped; Bethmann, above all, was a counterweight to Hindenburg and Ludendorff. In the Reichstag the Catholic Centrist, Progressive Left and Social-Democratic parties defended Bethmann. But it was Erzberger, a leader of the moderates, who brought the Chancellor down — with Ludendorff's help.

Erzberger, according to de Gaulle, was an *"ambitieux"* — an intelligent one — a good negotiator and propagandist. His three ambitions were to a peacemaker, to become the next Chancellor, to found a parliamentary regime. Knowing that his eloquence and parliamentary adroitness could never overthrow the Kaiser, he supported Ludendorff. Each man expected to dominate the other after he got what he wanted.

In a parliamentary battle that summer, the Right allied itself with the Left in opposition to Bethmann, hoping for the dictatorship of Tirpitz or Hindenburg. Bethmann "had the naiveté to think that he could disarm the opposition and persuade Erzberger"; when he failed, he offered his resignation to the Kaiser, who refused it. Hindenburg and Ludendorff believed that Bethmann had suggested that the Kaiser lecture them on the evils of political intriguing. Ludendorff suggested that Hindenburg resign in protest — which he did, provoking "immense and profound popular emotions." The Germans, "this romantic people," attached "a religious character" to Hindenburg's person.

Enter the Kaiser's son, with his desire to "manage his future crown," consistent with the "traditional spirit of opposition in his family." He consulted party leaders, all of whom now wanted to sack Bethmann. The Kaiser adopted a face-saving plan to recall Hindenburg and to extract a resignation from Bethmann.

That was done on July 12; on July 13 Ludendorff and the other military leaders appointed Michaelis, "an experienced and conscientious functionary," to the Chancellorship — thus jettisoning Erzberger less than twenty-four hours after he became unnecessary. The effects of Ludendorff's intriguing lasted:

> . . . under the ferment of the ambitions of Erzberger, Germany, over-whelmed by suffering, had searched confusedly for the end of the ordeal, toward moderation and democracy. The powerful will of Ludendorff was known to have prompted the birth, to have exploited and to have ended this crisis, in a fashion that served his designs . . . . [Ludendorff] had enlarged again his power and prestige . . . . But he had, at the same time, diminished the necessary authority of the Government of the Empire, and his success bent the instrument with which he intended to extract a better yield.

Ludendorff strengthened himself at the expense of the civil institutions that were, ultimately, the means of his power. "Germany docilely allowed itself to be conducted by Ludendorff," as long as he brought victories. When battlefield reverses came, Germany "wavered, suddenly in an irreparable disequilibrium, deprived of the indispensable supports needed to set it right"; when Germans needed "to see their military and civil leaders in their places, to feel, solid on its bases and in its proportions, the edifice of their authority" they found those leaders out of place, their authority unstable. "The sudden collapse of a strong and valiant people serves as testimony to the vengeance of outraged Principles."

De Gaulle ended the third chapter, on submarine warfare and the internal warfare over it, with the same lesson. Always a republican, though never an egalitarian, de Gaulle knows that military men tend toward impatience with civilians. Tensions between the military and the political leaders increase in wartime; France, with its relatively stable republican regime, did

11

not lack them. It is an idea "our military generation of tomorrow" might well have impressed upon it, in de Gaulle's judgment. Some forty years later, he instructed the Algerian *putschists* similarly, if more forcefully.

*

The final cause of Germany's defeat — sequentially and consequentially — was "the ruin of the German people," or, to use the more precise if less emphatic contemporary word, their 'demoralization.' 1918 began well for them; "never since the famous days of August 1914 had all Germany found itself better unified in hope, more resolute to vanquish." Count Hertling, who became the Chancellor after Michaelis resigned, was pleased by the new year's military successes. Ludendorff promised "a complete and rapid victory." On March 22 they began an offensive: in June they won a battle on the Marne, and Germans' hopes were "stretched to the extreme."

Then their armies were checked, just slightly. The press tried to disguise it, but it "produced a profound impression." "It was on this day that signs of nervousness began to appear, then sickness, then inquietude, which marked some fissures in the confidence and some weakness of the will." Other discomfiting incidents occurred: Ukraine, an important source of food at this time, had a mediocre harvest; submarine commanders reported fewer victims; von Kuhlmann, the man Hertling appointed to deal with foreign policy, said publicly that there might be no military solution (Ludendorff sacked him); the Socialists dissented. Despite battlefield successes and propaganda, Germans no longer believed in victory. They were not surprised when the Western powers stopped their defensive on July 15.

As yet they did not think they'd lose. Most Germans believed the French lacked the materiel, the initiative and the decisiveness to start a counteroffensive. The July 18 counter-offensive, therefore, did as much emotional as military injury.

> A sort of moral stupor seized all at once an authoritative and prideful sovereign, a government, so far tenacious, a docile political world, a confident and resolute military command, an obedient and courageous soldiery. This stupor, as if due to a fatal blow of a magic wand, annihilated with one blow the qualities of war of the German people, and magnified its faults.

At the "moment to galvanize effort" the Germans quarreled and intrigued. The military leaders "had deprived the government of authority and credit." The result was "a moral flabbiness, which will remain the wonder and the lesson of History."

Reverses followed, and "the Government of Berlin was shown incapable of fixing and pursuing distinct, defined, moderate policies that would permit it to group around itself the masses, to reassure the Allies, to diminish the *élan* of the enemies." Instead, the government's only actions were "sterile hesitations, provoking everyone." Partisans and journalists acted no better: "at the hour of peril, the political parties redoubled their furors and inflamed their passions"; the press, explaining away incorrect predictions, lost its usefulness "at the same moment when it became indispensable." If, years later, de Gaulle lacked respect for the parties and lacked that reverence toward the press desired by many journalists, his scepticism had some basis other than idiosyncrasy or prejudice.

All this provoked "the most complete moral confusion" among ordinary Germans. The German states had united only a few decades earlier; in each region, rumors of betrayals by other regions arose. Severe rationing induced pillaging. There was an influenza epidemic.

> As always, in moments of trouble and anguish, the folly of pleasure was unchained. The cinemas, concerts, theaters rejected the world . . . . Germany paraded vice in broad daylight.

Germans "abandoned themselves to destiny, defeated in advance at heart." "Each one knew, at the end of August, that the first grave incident, political or military, would definitely bring, in this discouraged country, an insurmountable national panic." The capitulation of their ally, Bulgaria came in September.

More resignations — including Ludendorff's — more partisan maneuvering, more surrenders by allies: "nothing, no one, could rally [the Germans] or induce them to make supreme sacrifices." The masses became as selfish as their leaders. In October "the life of pleasure became most ardent again" as Germans went on a buying spree. The rulers, who "no longer represented a ruined people," could not refuse the hard terms of the armistice.

*   *   *

De Gaulle wrote no conclusion. His book ends abruptly, as did the war. Perhaps his silence invites each reader to think his own conclusion. Such a conclusion, written, would take another chapter; here, I will only summarize.

La discorde chez l'ennemi is a manual for French military leaders in the form of a historical analysis and evaluation of the German military leaders during the 'Great War.' De Gaulle carefully suggests parallels between German and French errors.

On most of book's pages de Gaulle narrates the five "vicissitudes" that caused the German defeat. The military leaders' inability to cooperate — with each other, with civilian leaders, with allies — lost battles, both military and diplomatic. Moreover, exalting military over civilian authority endangered the military and the country. A student of de Gaulle's book might reflect that normally, if the military fails in a battle, the government survives, although some members of it may not. Military authority (insofar as it is military) rests on immediate success, whereas governments have a wider base, which includes military force, but also includes civil institutions, ethics, customs, law. By undercutting governmental authority Tirpitz, Hindenburg, and Ludendorff left no stable institution, only themselves. When their strategies failed, Germans had nothing but their own passions to govern them. The account of the fifth "vicissitude" shows the effect: the ordinary Germans, like their leaders finally refused to make the sacrifices of self that war requires. With one difference: the selves of ordinary people are animated less by ambition than by escapist pleasure.

In his preface de Gaulle suggests a reason for the leaders' failure. They were disciples of Nietzsche, and shared the Overman's virtues (audacity, enterprise, determination, vigor) but also his faults. They had no sense of limits; too individualistic and power-hungry, they lacked self-control or, rather, control of selfishness. This contrasts with the French sense of *la mesure* which, according to de Gaulle, young officers may find in the "victorious models of the recent war." Not always, however, as he well knows: de Gaulle prefers to offer an idealized depiction of Frenchness by means of his "French-style garden." The *telos* of the garden is "magnificent harmony," an esthetic and ethical quality upheld by self-restraint. French classicism succeeds when the German success-philosophy fails and, unlike the latter, it should succeed.

De Gaulle's classicism is not an apology for immobility. He emphasizes the importance of circumstances; that may be why he wrote a history and not an essay. "Apart from several essential principles, there is no universal system, but only circumstances and personalities." Louis XIV *and* Montesquieu. *La discorde chez l'ennemi* concerns the problem of diversity-in-unity, of avoiding both tyranny and faction.

The 'Great War' did not turn de Gaulle into a pacifist — a 'realist' with bad nerves. It convinced him that the French military, which overstepped its place during the Dreyfus Affair, needed reminding of what it was for and what it could do. His book reveals a man who looks at politics with interest and with acumen, but who avoids making political suggestions. Is this discretion (a measured avoidance of overstepping one's place) or simply the result of the belief that the French have not yet lost their distinguishing *espirit?*

13

CHAPTER 2

MODERATION (NIETZSCHE CONTRA PLATO):
REFLECTIONS ON *LA DISCORDE CHEZ L'ENNEMI*

De Gaulle sees clearly when he teaches that Nietzsche's Overman, as conceived by the German military, would make a bad general. The military virtue of the spirit of enterprise, unmoderated, becomes the taste for inordinate enterprise. The military virtues of audacity and the will to succeed, unmoderated, become the passion to expand, regardless of risk, one's personal power. The military virtue of vigor in the management of means, unmoderated, becomes contempt for the limits outlined by personal experience, good sense and law. With immoderation comes the Overman's contempt for others, characteristic of an "elite who, in pursuing its own glory, is convinced it serves the general interest, who contemptuously constrain 'the mass of slaves,' and does not delay before human suffering, if not saluting it as necessary and suitable." If one defines prudence as the part of wisdom that has to do with measuring, hence with moderation (without moderation one has no reason to measure; infinitude reigns), one observes that military virtues tend toward the destruction as well as the preservation of the political order, that prudence and moderation inhere in that order, having to do with its being political. Hindenburg, the only German military leader de Gaulle praises, had five characteristic virtues; the virtue de Gaulle regards as central was prudence (the others were disinterestedness, calm, pity, resolution — all but the last un-Nietzschean). But even Hindenburg violated the "grand principle" of political moderation, the subordination of the military to the civilian authority; he thereby "unleashed in the nation a furious and mortal tempest." Because military power is based on civilian power as much as civilian power is based on military power (Bethmann's removal reflected the latter fact; he was removed in part because the military thought he impeded their activity, believed he made the nation more difficult to preserve), the military ruined themselves indirectly by ruining the politicians; when military authority declined (and military authority, separated from politics, depends on battlefield success), no other authority remained. Deprived of the prudence and moderation characteristic of the best political and military leaders, the people "wavered, suddenly in an irreparable disequilibrium"; "the folly of pleasure was unleashed." Appetites were the only rulers that remmained: the people's counterpart to the unrestrained spiritedness of the elite. The war was lost and new leaders revolutionized the political order.

Beyond prudence, wisdom also entails self-knowledge. The German military leaders believed their vices virtues. De Gaulle's stated purpose is to contribute to bringing tomorrow's French military leaders to mold "their *esprit* and their character after the rules of classical order," because equilibrium, prudence and *la mesure* "alone render durable and fruitful the works of energy." Equilibrium, prudence and *la mesure* are characteristically French; de Gaulle wants tomorrow's French military and political leaders to know themselves, to become themselves, ethically and politically.

Frenchness is a neoclassical garden, wherein one sees a "magnificent harmony" and a "noble melancholy" (noble because moderate, but also noble because there is a nobility in the potential Overman, who is rendered melancholy by restraint). Frenchness, like the great neoclassical garden at Versailles, is a public thing, as is consonant with its non-individualism. It is therefore more than the sum of its parts; the individuals who comprise it are more beautiful, good and successful than they would have been alone, although they are individually less glorious.

Military virtues are a part of Frenchness, but they cannot be identical to it. War is no harmony. In war, circumstances count more than in a well-ruled garden. The tension between political order and military disorder is not superficial. Further, militarism and democratization seem to resemble one another: both are inharmonious, tempted by immoderation. If military leaders overcome their (as it were) natural disorderliness by cultivating the virtues of disinnterestedness, calm, prudence, pity and resolution they achieve prestige; the people, if uncorrupted, are deferential, not democratic. If the military leaders in turn defer to the political leaders, refrain from using their prestige to overthrow them, the political order endures, fruitfully.

*

During Nietzsche's 'middle period,' when he is said to have most nearly approached a kind of rationalism, he sometimes praised convention. In *The Gay Science* he writes that "the eruption of madness" has been and is "the greatest danger" for mankind, that the *"law of agreement"* is "man's greatest labor so far." He goes so far as to assert that "what is needed is *virtuous stupidity,* stolid metronomes for the slow spirit, to make sure that the faithful of the great shared faith stay together and continue their dance." In an unpublished note written in 1887 he observed:

> Hatred of mediocrity is unworthy of a philosopher: it is almost a question mark against his *'right* to philosophy.' Just because he is the exception, he must protect the rule, and he must encourage self-confidence in all the mediocre.

Unpublished, indeed: Nietzsche's writings rarely encourage self-confidence in all the mediocre (although in practice they encouraged it in the likes of his reverent sister and the pious Gast). Zarathustra's nausea (as distinguished from hatred) is more characteristic:

> What? Does life require even the rabble? Are poisoned wells required, and stinking fires and soiled dreams and maggots in the bread of life?
> Not my hatred but my nausea gnawed hungrily at my life. Alas, I often grew weary of the spirit when I found that even the rabble had *esprit.* And I turned my back on those who rule when I saw what they now call ruling: higgling and haggling for power — with the rabble.

And in *Ecce Homo: "Nausea* over man, over the 'rabble,' has always been my greatest danger." Zarathustra must overcome his extreme sentiment by an extreme means: by overcoming human nature — more precisely by overcoming that in human nature which nauseates him.*

To do so he cultivates himself in solitude, away from the modern political order. **But to overcome human nature in others as well as in himself he must affect others. Nietzsche's published writings therefore contain many attacks on moderation, which in modernity only perpetuates mediocrity, "though it be called moderation." "Aristotelianism of morals"

---

*Nietzsche's historicism is not, then, crypto-democratism, as Dannhauser charges (*Nietzsche's View of Society,* Cornell University Press, Ithaca and London, 1924, p. 153 ff.). While it is true that Zarathustra, unlike Socrates, addresses the people voluntarily, he soon learns that this is a mistake. While it is true that Zarathustra loves man, "what I love in man is that he is an overture and a going under," a prelude to the Overman. Those who would preserve man as he is are "the Overman's greatest danger" [*Thus Spoke Zarathustra,* Walter Kaufmann trans., in *The Portable Nietzsche,* p. 399]. Hence the critique of pity. "In man *creature* and *creator* are united: in man there is material, fragment, excess, clay, dirt, nonsense, chaos; but in man there is also creator, formgiver, hammer hardness, spectator divinity, and seventh day: do you understand the contrast? And that *your* pity is for the 'creature in man,' for what must be formed, broken, forged, torn, burnt, made incandescent, and purified — that which *necessarily* must and *should* suffer? And *our* pity — do you not comprehend for whom our converse pity is when it resists your pity as the worst of all pamperings and weaknesses?"

**"To live alone one must be a beast or a god, says Aristotle. Leaving out the third case: one must be both — a philosopher" [Nietzsche's *Twilight of the Idols,* "Maxims and Arrows," sec. 3, in *The Portable Nietzsche,* p. 467].

merely 'tunes down' the irrationalism of men, makes it harmless to the people. To want to render a thing harmless reflects fear: "public spirit, benevolence, consideration, industriousness, moderation, modesty, indulgence and pity," far from being virtues, reflect the herd's fear of the truly noble. True philosophers live *"imprudently,"* risking themselves, playing what is called "the wicked game." Against moderation (which he calls immoderation toward the passions) and other herd-virtues, Nietzsche would strengthen spiritedness.

Live dangerously: Nietzsche's way of writing reflects that famous counsel. A scholar has observed that traditional writers wrote superficially edifying and uncontroversial books that shock the discerning few, but that Nietzsche practices "a reverse esotericism" whereby what shocks is often more noticeable than what is stated with delicacy. This immoderate style contrasts with the Socratic/Platonic irony that Nietzsche represents as an act of resentment against the world.* But Nietzschean affirmation does not *simply* affirm everything; there is also that in man which must be overcome. To overcome one must affect, and Nietzsche, who decries the morality underlain by fear, wants new philosophers who lead. "And only those inspiring dread can lead"; perhaps Nietzschean rhetoric, his reverse esotericism, is intentionally dread-inspiring.

There is more. I suspect that Nietzsche wants the people to wreck themselves and be wrecked. Zarathustra knows that "your ears do not want to accept" his teaching on good and evil.

> . . . . it harms your good people, you say to me. But what matter your good people to me? Much about your good people nauseates me; and verily, it is not their evil. Indeed, I wish they had a madness of which they might perish . . .

Incapable of belief (famously: God is dead) only capable of temporary self-preservation, the dappled and motley people must burn: "Hourly, they are becoming smaller, poorer, more sterile — poor herbs! poor soil! and *soon* they shall stand there like dry grass and prairies — and verily, weary of themselves and languishing ever more than for water — *fire!*" Pillars of fire must precede the great noon of the Overman.

Those quick to insist that such passages are metaphorical, that the apocalypse Nietzsche strives for is 'spiritual' not physical, rightly protest the vulgarization of Nietzschean doctrines effected by the Nazis, among others. But in so 'spiritualizing' Nietzsche they themselves commit what Nietzsche would surely regard as a vulgar error. These triumphant tamers of the dead lion would make Nietzsche acceptable to 'decent' men, even to gentle American college students. A man who would annihilate old beliefs and create the new when those old beliefs are public spirit, benevolence, consideration, industriousness, moderation, modesty, indulgence and pity — the beliefs with which, he asserts, the vulgar defend themselves by corrupting the strong — can hardly fear that small thing, the real war, with its physical annihilation of masses of people. Nietzsche always insists on what he calls historicity, and history reveals that such

---

*The "morality of mediocrity is hard to preach: after all, it may never admit what it is and what it wants. It must speak of measure and dignity and duty and neighbor love — it will find it difficult to *conceal its irony.* — " [*Beyond Good and Evil, Basic Writings of Nietzsche,* p. 402]. Nietzsche charges the esoteric writers with concealing their herd-orientation, not an anti-herd orientation. Zarathustra: "You have served the people and the superstition of the people, all you wise men — and not truth . . . . [T]hat is why your lack of faith was tolerated: it was a joke, and a circuitous route to the people." "It was ever in the desert that the truthful have dwelt, the free spirits, as masters of the desert; but in the cities dwell the well-fed, famous wise men [e.g., Socrates] — the beasts of burden. For, as asses, they always pull the people's cart" [*Zarathustra, The Portable Nietzsche,* pp. 214-216]. Nietzsche believes that the truly wise today are anti-political. Solitude is not merely a reaction to modernity, but to any circumstance in which the life of the city claims precedence over the life of solitary wisdom.

17

revaluations frequently cause real bloodshed.* Mere pacifists are as vulgar as mere bellecists. Because "all truths that are kept secret become poisonous," Nietzsche writes bluntly, knowing — insisting — on his responsibility for the consequences.

> Not every word belongs in every mouth. These are delicate distant matters: they should not be reached for by sheeps' hooves.

They were, and Nietzsche had to know that they would be. So much the worse for the sheep.

> Those who can breathe the air of my writings know that it is an air of the heights, a *strong* air. One must be made for it. Otherwise, there is no small danger that one may catch cold in it.

A rare understatement. World wars — physical and spiritual — don't make Nietzsche flinch. Nietzsche is the philosopher of *thymos*.**

Nietzschean rhetoric serves Nietzschean politics. In his early writings Nietzsche eschewed politics, especially modern politics, for what he called culture: the unity of artistic style in every expression of the people's life, especially in its highest examples. "Culture owes its peaks to politically weak ages." Among the best "statesmen" of such an age were the pre-Socratic Greek philosophers, who refrained from examining the irrational basis of their culture and thus allowed it to flourish. (One might wonder: did Nietzsche not indulge in the vice of the mediocrities condemned in *The Use and Disadvantage of History for Life,* who compare ancient things to contemporary things at the expense of the latter? For Nietzsche's conception of Greece's "tragic age," drawn from Homer and the pre-Socratics, does not include the probability that mediocrity flourished as much then as later.***)

In later writings Nietzsche preferred to merge politics and culture (a distinction Plato might not have made so sharply to begin with; in this sense, Nietzsche revives the classics). He would achieve "great politics." Great politics has nothing to do with the "civic mediocrity" with which Euripides (and, by implication, Socrates) corrupted and reflected the corruption of the Athenian nobility. "All community makes men — somehow, somewhere, sometime 'common.'" Although Nietzsche agrees with Plato that courage is a virtue, he replaces wisdom with "insight" (the former has the unfortunate connotation of "prudence," to say nothing of its association, in Plato, with the apprehension of the illusory ideas), justice with sympathy,**** and moderation with solitude. (Nietzsche would reply to de Gaulle that the people might well defer to 'leaders' of disinterestedness, calm, prudence, pity and resolution, for such leaders are already *of the people.)* These virtues will flourish with great politics, and great politics can arise when the modern political order is *in extremis.* Perhaps, Nietzsche speculates, the increasing menace of Russia will provoke the unification of Europe's will "by the means of a new caste that would rule Europe," eliminating the divisive nationalisms, democratic and dynastic.

---

*"To be sure, one should not yield to humanitarian illusions about the origins of aristocratic society (and thus of the pre-supposition of this enhancement of the type 'man'): truth is hard." The truth is that barbarians of superior physical and 'spiritual' strength conquered "weaker, more civilized, more peaceful races" or "mellow old cultures." [*Beyond Good and Evil,* in *Basic Writings of Nietzsche,* p. 391]. Warning: that does not mean that 'history' will necessarily 'repeat itself'; it only means that it may, and that Nietzsche accepts that possibility.

**To be the philosopher of *thymos* is more than to be a man of *thymos.* Plato's guardians are men of *thymos.* The Overman is more than a spirited lion; he is the child of the third metamorphosis.

***If one replies that a culture is to be judged by its highest examples, but then argues, as Nietzsche does, that the pre-Socratics were better philosophers than Socrates because they served the health of their culture, the argument is circular.

****"And how should there be a 'common good'! The term contradicts itself: whatever can be common can be of little value" [*Beyond Good and Evil,* in *Basic Writings of Nietzsche,* p. 243].

Following the teaching of Book VIII of Plato's *Republic,* but giving it a distinctively modern application, Nietzsche predicts that Europe's ongoing democratization involuntarily cultivates tyrants — "taking that word in every sense, including the most spiritual." As cosmopolitanism lowers the masses, causes them to become more slavish, the few "will have to turn out stronger and richer than before — thanks to the tremendous manifoldness of practice, art, and mask." Nietzsche seems to synthesize the Platonic philosopher and the anti-Platonic tyrant in his portrait of these new philosophers, achieving a class of philosopher-tyrants. Using religion as a social bond, the new philosophers will rule selected disciples or "brothers"; they will nominate kings (as the Brahmins did) who will rule the people. Thus the new philosophers will obtain "peace from the noise and exertion of *cruder* forms of government, and purity from the *necessary* dirt of all politics" — even of great politics. (Nietzsche doesn't bother to suggest details; the man who detested systematic philosophizing would hardly attempt to produce its poor relation, the political program.) This civic religion will give some of the ruled the opportunity to rise, by "asceticism and puritanism," above their plebeian origins, perhaps to enter the class of kings. And the civic religion will give contentment to the ruled, ennoble their obedience, 'justify' their life. All of this resembles a *more* 'ideal' (less human) Platonic 'republic,' *actualized,* but with a major difference: it will fight wars gladly. "The concept of politics will have merged entirely with a war of spirits . . . ." Spirit is also will, and the will of the new philosophers will put "an end to that gruesome dominion of nonsense and accident that has so far been called 'history.'" Democracy, as the political order or regime most ruled by chance, is 'history' *in extremis.**

Spirit-as-will is "the life that itself cuts into life: with its own agony it increases its own knowledge." It is distinct from language, which has to do with our "social or herd nature," our non-individualistic translation into consciousness of our "altogether incomparably personal, unique, and infinitely individual" actions. It is then also distinct from reason, which Nietzsche subordinates to will. The Socratic or Platonic attempt to judge life is fruitless because life's value is inestimable. Truth can be approached if not apprehended by 'enlarging one's perspective, by the accumulation of passions, 'intellectual' and other, directed at the thing one would 'know'; the Overman's superiority inheres in his largeness. The weapon of dialectic wounds truth, thereby reflecting the plebeian's resentful attempt to defeat the noble. Nietzschean philosophizing is a kind of moral reductionism; one explains a philosopher's metaphysics (epistemology, ontology, cosmology) by his moral aims, and morality is irrational. Nietzsche replaces the Platonic ideas, known by reason, with the will to power, known by — what? By itself, perhaps: its human, then post-human form attaches itself to its cosmic form.** Nietzsche's historicism is not a historicism in Marx's sense, but a means of returning to genuine nature: that which Marx and others would escape (for resentment is anti-nature). Nature is the "*primordial fact* of all history."

Nature is immoderate — "Dionysian," not "Apollonian." Life (Nietzsche seems to use the words "nature" and "life" synonymously) "is *essentially* appropriation, injury, overpowering of what is alien and weaker; suppression, hardness, imposition of one's own forms, incorporation and at least, at its mildest, exploitation"; "life simply *is* will to power." Moderation, as traditionally understood, compromises life. Nature is "wasteful beyond measure [*beyond measure*], indifferent beyond measure, without purposes and consideration, without mercy and justice . . . ." In opposing this nature in order to live, man — if he opposes it wilfully, not tamely — imitates nature, even partakes of it. That is the significance of Nietzsche's affirmation of eternal recurrence: to joyfully *will* all history, all the things of

---

*It is in this sense that the 'pacifist' interpreters of Nietzsche may be right. After the period between Nietzsche's time and the Overman's great noon, wars may be philosophic wars, not physically violent. But Nietzsche is even less specific than other great prophets.

**Hence the Overman's largeness. His soul includes many more drives or passions than a human soul. Nietzsche to Burckhardt: "at bottom I am every name in history."

this earth, is finally, somehow, to become and overcome them by the comprehensiveness, inclusiveness, of one's own soul; the most extreme individualism merges with the most extreme anti-individualism.

Individualism finally dominates this merging.

> . . . [A]t the bottom of us, really 'deep down,' there is, of course, something unteachable, some granite of spiritual *fatum,* of predetermined decision and answer to predetermined selected questions. Whenever a cardinal problem is at stake, there speaks an unchangeable 'this is I . . .'

As the Calvinist demands that we love the God who predetermines our lives, Nietzsche demands that we love this "piece of *fatum*" and not resentfully attempt to negate it by judging it according to some fictional (non-existent) standard. Moreover, the Overman's comprehensive soul is no giant ragbag of all that has been or is. A truly powerful soul eschews the unselective affirmation of the merely eclectic, all-too-human "higher men." The immensity that bespeaks true power requires the artful organization of the many phenomena; the Overman's cosmos-affirming individuality is a hierarchy — the result of assimilation, not mere collection.

With the overcoming of the mediocrity called moderation, one can develop a moderation of excellence. Zarathustra: "One ought to hold on to one's heart; for if one lets it go, one soon loses control of the head too." Pity is a bad immoderation insofar as it is directed at the human-all-too-human. Nietzschean moderation is a moderation-by-tension, not a moderation of tensions; the conflicting drives balance each other — a balancing which yields their mutual intensification, not slackening. Zarathustra gives a rare caution:

> Will nothing beyond your capacity: there is wicked falseness among those who will beyond their capacity. Especially if they will great things! For they arouse mistrust against great things.

Was Nietzsche's madness evidence of "wicked falseness"? Perhaps: Nietzsche claimed he was *also* a decadent.

*

A principal source of the neoclassical French garden is the Platonic philosophy Nietzsche attacked. To Plato, moderation is "a certain kind of order and mastery of certain kinds of pleasures and desires" whereby the better, distinctively human, nature rules the worse. Rules: moderation has a political aspect; it is a precondition of justice. (Justice, too, is a kind of measuring, apportioning, as seen in Aristotle's *Nichomachean Ethics.*) Accordingly, each of the three classes in Plato's ideal *politeia* has its kind of moderation. For the many, moderation is temperance (ruling the bodily pleasures) and obedience to the guardians. For the guardians, moderation is temperance, obedience to the rulers, and the ruling of certain pleasures of the soul (not listening to some poetic modes, for example: hence the famous training in "music"). For the philosopher-kings, moderation is only the necessary consequence of being ruled by the rational *eros* that loves the "ideas" or "forms." Moderation, Socrates tells his interlocutors, "is like a kind of harmony."

> . . . it's unlike courage or wisdom, each of which resides in a part [of the soul and in a part of the *polis*], the one making the [*polis*] wise and the other courageous. Moderation doesn't work that way, but actually stretches throughout the whole, from top to bottom of the entire scale, making the weaker, the stronger, and those in the middle . . . sing the same chant together.

The musical imagery is no accident. A scholar has observed that in the *Republic* the Greek word *metrion,* which means measured (from which the English word "meter" derives: a word associated with a measure of length in both geography and poetry) is "frequently equivalent to *sophrosyne,"* the word for temperance and moderation. De Gaulle's *la mesure,* being an esthetic *and* ethical idea, reminds us that Plato also associated esthetics and ethics; right esthetic taste leads to (but does not guarantee) right ethics — that is, the development of right character. Moderation is a virtue that contributes to the soul's health, beauty and good condition. (One might wonder if Nietzsche ever truly overcame his early attachment to Wagner's "Dionysian" music, although he surely repudiated Wagner's later musical and political activities.)

Plato's Socrates argues that immoderation ruins all arts. "For all these arts are on the watch against excess and defect, not as unrealities, but as real evils, which occasion a difficulty in action; and the excellence of beauty of every work of art is due to the observance of measure." Between excess and defect is the Platonic standard, in the art of politics as well as in the other arts. (Those who fault Plato for his 'absolutism' ignore this.) Without the mean, "everything is overthrown." To Nietzsche's claim that individual and political health is the moderation arising from the balanced tension of opposing irrational drives, Plato's Socrates might reply that the guardians' souls should be "tuned to the proper degree of tension and relaxation."

Nietzsche's intention is precisely to see that "everything is overthrown," not to guard but to overcome. Plato would reply that this overcoming is an attempt to will beyond one's capacity. Nietzsche, the philosopher of *thymos,* knows that moderation alone tends toward paralysis, but finally ignores the fact that courage alone tends toward madness.* To counteract the rule of appetites, democracy, Nietzsche exalted the rule of the will to power, which *thymos,* the leonine virtue, prepares. He thus circumscribed reason's power, associating it also with democracy; in this he could have cited the use of reason by such philosophers as Hobbes and Locke, for whom reason acts as scout for the appetites. He preferred to attack Plato's Socrates, for whom reason, Nietzsche claims, was a weapon at the service of resentment. But to borrow Nietzsche's objection to Darwin's theory of evolution, this seems to have been more asserted than proved. And the circumscription of reason may actually damage the will in the guise of liberating it. "[W]hen the feeling of pleasure or pain is most intense, every soul of man imagines the objects of this intense feeling to be the plainest and truest: but this is not so, they are really the things of sight." The Nietzschean illusion produces the great tension that ends in madness — a broken will, not the playful child of the "third metamorphosis." Plato denies that man can be overcome.

*

Historicism claims that man can and must be overcome. The potential for vulgar historicism exists in any political order insofar as it yearns for success. The military, whose authority derives mostly from success or hoped-for success in preserving the political order and the lives of those within it, has a larger potential for historicism than do politicians, who more easily achieve glory in a lost cause. The people also seem to have a noticeable potential for historicism, impatient as they are for successful protectors (if not for Platonic guardians). This was surely true in Germany. The military lost its authority when it no longer succeeded; the press lost its authority not when it reported events inaccurately (it did that habitually) but when it predicted wrongly. The Germans "abandoned themselves to destiny"; in this instance, destiny was appetite, "the folly of vice." Vulgar historicism seems to yield immoderation. Or perhaps it is its reflection.

Historicist politics in this century, whether of the 'left' or of the 'right,' owes much to vulgar historicism, can perhaps be defined as vulgar historicism. Communism — whether

*Cf. *Statesman, The Dialogues of Plato,* Benjamin Jowett translation, Oxford at the Clarendon Press, 1964, Volume III, p. 525, 307b.

Leninist, Stalinist or Maoist — and Nazism found success in immoderation, in extreme demands and extreme actions. Historicism itself need not be immoderate; whether or not Tocqueville was a real historicist, he was a moderate. But Tocqueville's democracy was a restrained democracy rarely seen by Plato and condemned by Marx and Nietzsche: a democracy obedient to non-democratic limits. By the First World War that democracy was imperiled. De Gaulle, a republican, saw the peril, and moved to guard France by educating France's future military leaders.

SECOND PART

CHAPTER 3

LE FIL DE L'ÉPÉE (1932)

In 1927, French political and military leaders believed defensive security safer than any strategy of counter-attack. Had not the aggressive, 'Bergsonian' strategy failed in the Great War? The fashionable pacifism of the day provided sentimental buttressing for this cathedral, a place for humanitarian worship.

The flock was not free of heretics. Marshall Pétain dissented, with discretion; he had a less-cautious protegé who could be sent out for the riskier acts of sacrilege. Major Charles de Gaulle, at Pétain's insistence, was allowed to read three lectures to higher-ups at the École Superieure. Being higher-ups, they doubtless found the young officer's subject provocative:

> The more he spoke, the more uncomfortable and angry the professors in the front row became. For de Gaulle's theme was the vital role of leadership, and the picture he painted of the leader was at once a criticism of his superiors, a justification of himself and a veiled but unmistakable tribute to the Marshall.

Pétain, who introduced each lecture, must have enjoyed himself. De Gaulle's career was not advanced, and a repeat performance at the Sorbonne later that year provoked not even resentment — only indifference. These lectures were, to use a German's word, untimely.

Later, de Gaulle revised his lectures, added a 1925 article on military doctrine and a new essay on the relationship of the military to politics, publishing them in 1932 under the title *Le fil de l'épée*. Few cared to read the apologia of an obscure man. Twelve years later the man was no longer obscure, and the second edition sold well. It turned out to be not only an apologia but, as Stanley Hoffmann has written, "a self-portrait in anticipation." De Gaulle became the leader he had imagined. He omitted the first edition's dedication to Marshall Pétain, who had since become an embarrassment.

*   *   *

He kept the Forward's epigraph: *"Être grand, c'est soutenir une grand querelle."* Translators who use the Shakespearean original —

> Rightly to be great
> Is not to stir without great argument . . . .
> (*Hamlet, Act IV, sc. iv*)

miss de Gaulle's concision and forcefulness. De Gaulle's Hamlet uses fewer words and speaks of action, not inaction. He is what Hamlet in this speech aspires to be: one who acts.

> O, from this time forth,
> My thoughts be bloody, or be nothing worth!

Le fil de l'épée contains such thoughts, aimed at pacifistic souls, especially those in the military. De Gaulle omits the second half of Hamlet's sentence:

> Rightly to be great
> Is not to stir without great argument,
> But greatly to find quarrel in a straw,
> When honour's at the stake.

For de Gaulle, the object of contention — France — is not trivial, although honor is indeed at the stake, along with survival.

He begins:

> Incertitude marks our epoch [as it marks Hamlet]. So many denials [*démentis:* also "disappointments" or "contradictions"] of conventions, previsions, doctrines, so many trials, losses, deceptions, so many scandals also, shocks, surprises have shaken the established order.

The military, being part of that order, suffers from "melancholy"; de Gaulle observes that this is usual after a period of effort, as the examples of Vigny and Vauvenargues show. But usualness consoles no one; everything in "the ambiance of the times appears to trouble the conscience of the professionals." The masses, having endured "the cruelties of force," "react with passion" against it. A "mystique" arises, which not only causes men to curse war but "inclines [them] to believe it out of date [*périmée:* also, "no longer valid"], to such a degree as one wishes that it was." Men try to exorcise this "evil genie," war, with imprecations; "to inspire the horror of sin, a thousand painters apply themselves to representing [war's] ravages." They evoke "only the blood, the tears, tombs, not the glory with which people consoled their sorrows." They deface "History's" traits "under the pretext of effacing war," thus attacking the military order "at its root." Balance: fundamental to *La discorde chez l'ennemi*, it reappears in *Le fil de l'épée*. Without it the legitimacy of the military dies. In *La discorde chez l'ennemi* the German military disregarded it; in *Le fil de l'épée* it threatens France within France.

De Gaulle finds this ambiance "only too easily explicable"; it is

> . . . the instinct of preservation of enfeebled Europe, which senses the risks of a new conflict. The spectable of a sick man who shakes his fist at death can leave no person unfeeling.

He also discerns a rhetorical strategy. Those who would establish an "international order" — obviously, he refers to the League of Nations and its publicists — *in the name of the people* (who are, de Gaulle remarks tartly, "temporarily made wiser"), need "a vast collective emotion" to do it. "Now one does not rouse crowds other than by elementary sentiments, violent images, brutal invocations." De Gaulle does not lack rhetorical skill, either; he accuses the internationalists of the same sort of rhetoric that they decry. He reminds them of other sentiments:

> Without disavowing any hope [except the one under discussion?] where do we see that the passions and the interests wherefrom armed conflict emerges silence their exigencies, that anyone renounces willingly what he has and what he desires, that men, finally, cease to be men?

Given human nature, internationalists cannot depend on voluntary consent when building a peaceful world order; if such an order appears, it will appear because someone imposed it. And one imposes nothing so ambitious without the aid of the military force internationalists decry. "Whatever direction the world takes, it will not dispense with arms."

De Gaulle goes beyond the negative, force-as-necessary-evil argument: "Without force, in fact, can one conceive of life?" Only in an "immobile world." Force is the "resource of thought, instrument of action, condition of movement."

> Shield of masters, bulwark of thrones, battering-ram of revolutions, one owes to it, turn by turn, order and liberty. Cradle of cities, scepter of empires, gravedigger of decadences, force gives the law to the people and regulates their destiny.

With Nietzsche, de Gaulle sees force as that which, by causation, pervades and unifies the world. He may not see it as the only such thing. Force underlies both order and liberty, for example, because it can serve both masters and revolutionaries. But order and liberty are distinguishable; they have to do with ends, not only with means. De Gaulle does not present force as an end. It is a resource, shield and battering-ram — it enables and regulates but does not prescribe. What does?

In truth, the military spirit, the art of soldiers, their virtues, are an integral part of the capital of humans. One sees them incorporated in all phases of History . . . . For finally, can one understand Greece without Salamis, Rome without the legions, Christianity without the sword, Islam without the scimitar, the Revolution without Valmy, the League of Nations [!] without the victory of France? And then, this abnegation of individuals to the profit of the *ensemble,* this glorified suffering — of which one makes troops — corresponds *par excellence* to our esthetic and moral concepts: the highest philosophical and religious doctrines have not chosen another ideal.

Actually, some have — as de Gaulle knows very well. Of the two religions mentioned here (coincidentally, he places them in the middle of the list, paired as if equivalent), Christianity does not, precisely, teach self-abnegation for the glory of the *ensemble* so much as self-abnegation for the glory of God — and force is not the way one goes about it. But de Gaulle will return to that.

Returning to the contemporary world, de Gaulle contends that if French military strength declines, that decline would imperil *la patrie* and "the general harmony." In this, he broadens the parallel teaching in the preface of *La discorde chez l'ennemi,* perhaps for the benefit of internationalists and pacifists. Good or bad, if "power escapes the wise, what fools will seize it, or what madmen?" In the end, responsibility involves power. "It is time that the military retake the consciousness of its preeminent role, that it concentrate on its object, which is, simply, war." To do this, "to restore the edge to the sword," it must "restore the philosophy proper to its state"; for de Gaulle, a "philosophy" both energizes and provides the ends energy, force, power serves.

Le fil de l'épée, then, contains a military "philosophy," not a 'philosophy of life,' although the one implies the other. The book has five chapters, of two, three, three and four sections, respectively: fifteen in all.

*   *

The first chapter's title — "The Action of War" — emphasizes de Gaulle's thesis that war, because essentially active, is not susceptible to what he calls *"a priori"* planning. Consonant with this, he uses an (undevout) Faustian epigraph: "In the beginning was the Word? No! In the beginning was the Action." Faust, like Machiavelli and Bacon, aspired to the domination of things, and this chapter's tension is that between the flow of events and those who would dominate them — Heraclitus versus Machiavelli, if you will.

"The action of war essentially comes to the character of contingency": the enemy's strength and intentions, the terrain, events, the direction, speed and manner of one's strike, men and materiel, atmospheric conditions. "In war as in life one can apply the [everything flows] of the Greek philosopher; what has taken place will no longer take place, never, and the action, whatever it may be, might well not have been or might have been different." He quotes Bergson (a friend of de Gaulle's family who had revived and metamorphosed Heraclitean metaphysics twenty years earlier) on the intelligence's discomfort when it attempts to seize what is not constant, fixed and definite, but mobile, unstable and diverse. Logic doesn't work there; to use it, de Gaulle writes, is like trying to catch water in a fishnet.

Intelligence does have its function: "elaborating in advance the givens of the conception, it clarifies them, makes them precise, and reduces the chance of error." It limits the problem and formulates hypotheses on how to deal with it; "in short, in the mind of the man who would act, [the intelligence] prepares the conception but does not produce it." According to de Gaulle's Bergson, the intuition does that. The intuition has "a direct contact" with "the realities," being "the faculty that links us most closely to nature." This is probably why the intuition gives us not only "profound perception" but the "creative impulse"; life (inconceivable without force) *produces,* and the intuition enables us to be productive.

> We participate in what it is possible to find there of obscure harmony. It is by instinct [de Gaulle uses "instinct" and "intuition" interchangeably] that man perceives the reality of conditions which surround him and that he experiences the corresponding impulsion.

Military inspiration is analogous to the artist's, and de Gaulle quotes Bacon: "It is man adding to nature." De Gaulle apparently means that man adds to external nature by linking himself with it. Man then draws upon its productive force, which is also an obscure harmony; this force, filtered through himself, reemerges in the world in order to master it. Alexander's "hope," Caesar's "fortune" and Napoleon's "star" were "simply the certitude of a particular gift putting them in a strict enough relation to realities to dominate them always." One might recall Bacon's observation — that to master nature one must know and use nature's laws. But Gaullist participation in nature may differ in the degree to which he thinks one may dominate or master reality or nature; unlike Bacon, de Gaulle promises no utopias brought by the advancement of learning. Human nature has limits, inspiration to the contrary. The most de Gaulle asserts is that such men give others "the impression of a natural force that will command events" — as Flaubert said of Hannibal (in *Salammbô*), "the indefinable splendor of those destined for great enterprises." Despite his assertion that such men can dominate realities, the examples he chooses are of men who could not dominate them "always," as he surely knows.

> The intelligence takes the "given" of instinct and "elaborates them, attributes to them a determined form, in fact a definite and coherent whole," like a person using a stereoscope.* This enables the military leader to set priorities, purposes, decide timing, placement, coordinate the various operations and their phases — to synthesize.

> This is why all the great men of action have been meditative. All possessed to the highest degree the faculty to retreat into themselves, to deliberate inwardly.

Some critics exalt instinct, claiming that there is no true art of war because chance alone determines battles. Speculative minds "lose the sentiment of the necessities of action," as did Socrates when he told Nichomachides that the popular assembly's choice of a leader was unimportant because a dishonest and incapable citizen would be no different than a skilful and conscientious leader. ("It is true," de Gaulle adds, "that the same Socrates, interrogated by Pericles on the causes of the indiscipline of the Athenian troops, held responsible their leaders, incapable of commanding them.") De Gaulle's allusion would be unimportant — the sort of decorative reference that military writers with literary training and/or pretensions seem to enjoy — were it not what may be an intentional distortion. In Xenophon's *Memorabilia,* Book III, chapter iv, Nicomachides complains that the assembly elected Anisthenes, a man without Nichomachides's military experience to be a general. Socrates does not argue that the choice of commanders doesn't matter, but that military experience doesn't matter. What counts is the ability to rule. Anisthenes managed a chorus successfully, although neither skilled in music nor in teaching choruses, because he found the best masters to do this work for him. A good commander need not command if he selects officers who can command. The difference between the private and the public is not one of kind, but of magnitude; he who succeeds at one should succeed at the other.

Xenophon's words could not be innocently misread as de Gaulle misreads them. A slip of

---

*Although de Gaulle writes that the intelligence *attributes* form to the "givens," it's important to recall that they are not inchoate, but possess "an obscure harmony" of their own. To what extent that harmony must match the form attributed to the givens by intelligence is not clear; obviously, there must be some relationship, or the battle-plan wouldn't work.

memory is just as unlikely, for de Gaulle's memory, which he trained since childhood, was nearly infallible when he wanted it to be. As if to prove it, he correctly recalls Socrates' remarks to Pericles (son of the famous Pericles), which occur in the following chapter of the *Memorabilia*. In fact de Gaulle has good reason to be forgetful; as we've seen and will continue to see, de Gaulle wants France to have a professional army. De Gaulle prizes military experience. His book is an attack on the notion that anyone who can rule well can rule an army. The last chapter, "Politics and the Soldier," contains a more subtle view of the relationship between politicians and soldiers than Xenophon's apparent teaching. De Gaulle cites it, perhaps as Bacon, in his *Essays,* cites the execution of Socrates under the oligarchy — to impress the ignorant and to stimulate those who are not ignorant.

The aside on Pericles refers to a conversation on how one may lead the Athenians so as to enhance the city's fame and to defeat their enemies. Notable among these enemies are the Boeotians, "who formerly did not dare, even on their own soil, to meet the Athenians in the field without the aid of the Spartans and the other Peloponnesians, [and] now threaten to invade Attica single-handed." The Athenians fail to elect good generals because the Athenians are overconfident, hence degenerate. They must be made to fear the Boeotians, and unite. At the same time, they must be incited to "regain their ancient spirit, glory, and happiness." To do this they must imitate the Spartans, who now dominate Greece. But more important, Athenian military affairs are commanded by "men who are greatly deficient in knowledge." Specifically, the Athenians, "if equipped with light arms," could "do great mischief to our enemies, and form a strong bulwark for the inhabitants of our country" if they occupied the mountains on the frontiers of Attica, especially those bordering on Boeotia. Pétain and de Gaulle, as early as the 1920's, thought that the Germans would attack France again. Without a contemporary Sparta to emulate, de Gaulle suggests that the military imitate the portrait of the ruler he draws, who is spartan, if not Spartan. France has no mountains on the German border, but in 1928 de Gaulle wrote an essay, "The Historical Role of French Places," which described the military uses French terrain had and could be put to. He praised fortifications but also insisted on the need for mobility — the combination of a strong, defensive bulwark and a maneuverable attack force that Socrates recommends.

Enough. It is only an aside, if a fascinating one. De Gaulle ends this essay on epistemology by noting that military men sometimes neglect the intelligence (this probably irritated the boys in the front row), especially when afflicted by the "depression of spirits" that follows a "great victorious effort." But more frequently they make the opposite error. The longing to "deduce the conception of known constants in advance" — what de Gaulle calls *"a priorism"* — "exercises a singular attraction over the French mind." The "speculative and absolute character" of such dogma "renders them seductive and perilous."

In section ii de Gaulle turns to the non-intellectual faculties of the leader. Pétain, he tells us, said that giving orders calls for the greatest effort of any part of an action. "In fact, the intervention of the human will in the chain of events has something irrevocable about it"; from this derives the military leader's responsibility, of "such weight that few men are capable of supporting it entirely."

> This is why the highest qualities of mind do not suffice. Without doubt, the intelligence aids, without doubt, instinct pushes, but, in the last resort, the decision is of the moral order.

An officer must act, and not conceal his incapacity by claiming that he has no specific orders to do something (as did Canrobert at Rezonville), or by looking after details only (as did Bazaine at Rezonville). The other extreme, the exaggeration of initiative "to the point of violating discipline and smashing the convergence of efforts," was exemplified by von Kluck at the Marne, and usually occurs in "the absence or the softness of the decisions of the superior echelon" — in the von Kluck incident, the weakness of the younger Moltke.

The mean between these extremes is "the spirit of enterprise," necessary if the leader will "win over the others." As he must, for any leader needs not only to know what he wants to do and to order it done, but to have the authority that ensures his men's obedience. Army discipline helps, "but it does not suffice for the leader to bind the executants by an impersonal obedience."

It is in their souls that he must imprint his living mark. To move the wills, to seize, to animate them to turn themselves toward the purpose that he has assigned them, to grow and to multiply the effects of discipline by a moral suggestion that surpasses reasoning, crystallizing around himself all that there is in their souls of faith, of hope, of latent devotion [what? no charity?], such is this domination.

Questions: What is the nature of this "moral suggestion that surpasses reasoning"? Does ethics surpass reasoning, too?

For the moment, de Gaulle only hints at answers. Preparation for war trains leaders; it can occur during war or during peacetime. Peacetime favors poor selection of officers in three ways. First, because they are hard to recruit: "the profound motive of the activity of the best and the strongest is the desire to acquire power," and the peacetime army offers ambitious men no place to command, slow advancement. De Gaulle resembles Nietzsche here, particularly in his broad definition of "power"; he writes that after 1815, when the French saw that there would be peace, those desirous of power — Thiers, Lamennais, Comte, Pasteur — went into politics, law, speculation, the arts, and not into the army. A Pasteur does not desire "power" in the vulgar sense — as did, for example, many German leaders of the Great War. If "power" is what the best men want, perhaps they are inspired by that 'Bergsonian' intuition mentioned earlier, which connects them to the forces of life.

Today, it is toward affairs that ambitions turn; money is, for the moment, the apparent sign of power [de Gaulle refuses to see it as a genuine sign of power — again, no vulgar sense of power here] and the French nourish willingly the conviction that international laws and *ententes* will succeed in preventing war.

Second, in peacetime military leaders select their successors by observing field exercises, which highlight superficial cleverness, the ability to grasp the immediate features of a situation and flexibility of mind, rather than real aptitude, the power of seeing the essentials of a situation and genuine understanding.

Third, "powerful personalities" often lack "that superficial seductiveness that pleases in the course of ordinary life." The mass may admit their superiority, but does not love them, and they are not chosen for advancement. Of all the young major's statements, this may be the one that most immediately angered his superiors. Not only is de Gaulle such a "personality," criticized for his arrogance, but he dares to suggest that his superiors are of the mass, men who recognize his excellence but will not reward it.

De Gaulle's conclusion is relatively bland. "Our times are little propitious to the formation and selection of military leaders" because the intensity of the Great War led to "a relaxation of wills, a depression of character," which led to "moral lassitude." War and soldiers are not thought well of.

*

We know something of Gaullist morality; Chapter Two, "Of Character," elaborates on it. De Gaulle's epigraph — "The smell of the world has changed" — comes from Georges Duhamel;to choose a sentence from one of the era's best-known pacifists probably amused de Gaulle, especially because he now writes on the 'spirit of the age.'

The French army has had "powerful life only by the effect of an ideal, issuing from the dominant sentiments of the epoch and drawing from that harmony its virtue and radiance."

This sounds like standard historicism, the sort historians in the nineteenth and twentieth centuries were and are fond of (if for no other reason than professional vanity). It also reminds de Gaulle's readers of his comments on how intuited realities are organized by the intelligence; ethics, it seems, comes from sentiment, not reason.

As de Gaulle rehearses his examples, this interpretation seems accurate. In the seventeenth century, Louvois's reforms unified the military so as to serve the interests of the sovereign, who was engaged in unifying the country. The Republican army of Hoche was possessed of a "rather ostentatious contempt for honors and rewards," an affectation that "went well with glory."

When de Gaulle comes to the state of things today, we detect a curious irony. De Gaulle has already noted that today's ambiance is anti-militaristic. Presumably, the army most consonant with 'the times' would be the army they have now: torpid, defensive, hard for de Gaulle to get promoted in. There have been improvements in institutions, equipment and, he admits, in military thinking, but they are insufficient. For "efficacity," the French army needs "a moral renaissance." The "rejuvenating ideal" of this epoch is "character," the "virtue of difficult times." The tension of the second chapter, evident in this second section, is that between reality and Reality, the ambiance as seen by most people and the ambiance de Gaulle presents, selected from the former.

"The man of character," the Gaullist leader, has recourse "to himself." "His impulse is to impose on action his mark . . .to make it his affair." "He has the passion to will, the jealousy to decide." Uninterested in profit, this "gambler . . . searches less for gain than to succeed, and pays his debts in his own money." If he loses he reacts not with sorrow but with "some bitter satisfaction." Hence

> . . . the man of character confers to action nobility; without him, [action is the] dismal blemish of the slave, thanks to him [it is the] divine sport of heroes.

He doesn't act alone. Subordinates assist him; their virtues are self-sacrifice and obedience. Counsellors and theorists help him plan. But his "character" is "the supreme element, the creative part, the divine point." If the realities perceived by intuition are creative and forceful, so is character. It is the ethical correspondent to the "obscure harmony" of nature.

> This property of vivifying the enterprise implies the energy to assume the consequences [is he thinking of Bergson's "spiritual energy"?] Difficulty attracts the man of character, for it is in gripping [the difficulty] that he realizes himself. But whether or not he vanquishes, it is an affair between it and he. Jealous lover, he never shares what it gives him, or what it costs him.

What it gives him is "the austere [or harsh: *"âpre"*] joy of being responsible." This paradoxical phrase epitomizes the Gaullist balancing of opposites in the domain of ethics. De gaulle here opposes Machiavellian success-philosophy; the *telos* of Machiavellian *virtù* has little to do with austerity. De Gaulle combines the individualism of such 'moderns' as Machiavelli and Bacon with the austerity of the 'ancients.' Enlargement and self-refinement in struggle and the austere joy of being responsible: one thinks of Nietzsche, or, perhaps, of Aristotle's great-souled man.

In peacetime the man of character has critics, "but in action, enough of criticisms!" In a passage reminiscent of Aristotle *(Nichomachean Ethics,* Book IV, chapter 3), de Gaulle writes:

> Reciprocally, the confidence of the small exalts the man of character. He feels himself obliged by this humble justice rendered to him. His firmness increases in measure, but also his benevolence, for he was born a protector. If the affair succeeds, he distributes advantage generously and, in the case of a reverse, he does not allow reproach to descend on any but himself.

Esteem and loyalty exchanged for security: to 'ancient' and 'modern' themes, de Gaulle adds a

31

'medieval' one: the (ideal) relationship of the vassal and his lord. With intuition, de Gaulle wrote, one "participates" in reality's creative force; with character, he might have added, one participates in the reality of other men, calls up their creative force, as well as one's own.

In ordinary times, the man of character's superiors often dislike him, calling him "arrogant and undisciplined" (de Gaulle writes from experience). "But when events become grave," he receives justice; "a sort of groundswell [Reality recognizing its own?] pushes to the first level the man of character." He "does not abuse" his moment, scarcely tasting "the savor of revenge, for the action absorbs everything." Not quite Aristotelian magnanimity — which eschews revenge because revenge is small and it is large, not because action preoccupies it — but de Gaulle's man of character comes nearer to achieving it than do most of the men of his time.

De Gaulle shows that "character" is not an exclusively military virtue, any more than intuition is. He finds it in Alexander, Richelieu, Napoleon, Bismarck and Clemenceau, but also in Galileo, Columbus, Boileau and Lesseps. He fails to list a religious leader (unless one would so characterize Cardinal Richelieu).

> . . . [T]he success of great men implies multiple faculties. Character, if accompanied by nothing, only gives daredevils and stubborn persons. But inversely, the highest qualities of mind cannot suffice.

Sieyès and Talleyrand were notable for their qualities of mind, but were not great men.

De Gaulle writes more against his 'time' than with it. In the third section of this chapter he 'reconciles' the 'time' with "character." The pre-1914 world, he observes, was an era of stability, economy and prudence. It is gone. Competition and technique "symbolize the new age." The postwar generation is adventurous and money-conscious. Initiative and self-reliance are its virtues. The army should 'reflect' this; more precisely, de Gaulle would have it 'reflect' a judiciously-selected portion of it. For he does not advocate money-consciousness in soldiers and, as he wrote (and will write again in the chapter's next-to-last paragraph), these are bad times for the military. The "dominant sentiments" of an epoch are really those among the popular sentiments that the man who would dominate his epoch selects — because they most resemble his own. There are epochs in which such a man cannot advance, and undominating men predominate. De Gaulle waits, writing books.

While it waits, the army will be paralyzed if its leaders smother initiative, along with "the taste to be responsible and the courage to speak plainly." De Gaulle wants "character" respected. Each individual should have responsibility on his own level — an idea that anticipates the "participation" he advocated in 1969. If "character" is respected, the army will have fewer regulations, get better results. Better men will adopt the military career, and continue in it, exercising the "capacity to act" that such men want.

"Prestige," the central chapter of *Le fil de l'épée,* consists of de Gaulle's final diagnosis of and prescription for the epoch's disease. Prestige is usually a matter of appearance only, but de Gaulle chooses a phrase from Villiers de L'Isle-Adam — "In his breast, to carry his own glory" — as the epigraph: a phrase that links prestige to character.

The postwar disease is authority's decay. Men are either reticent and unsure or overconfident and obsessed with forms.

> This decadence follows the decline of the moral, social, political order which, for centuries, held sway in our old nations. By conviction and by calculation, one has for a long time attributed to power an origin, to the elite rights that justify hierarchies. The edifice of these conventions has collapsed.

Deference fades; perhaps this is the other, bad, side of the taste for initiative de Gaulle noted before.

The crisis cannot last.

Men cannot, fundamentally, do without being directed. These political
animals have need of organization, that is to say of order and of leaders.

Ancient sources of authority no longer exist, but "the natural equilibrium of things will bring
others, sooner or later, better or less good, proper in all cases to the establishment of a new
discipline." Even as he dismisses the old, de Gaulle affirms something ancient: the idea,
discarded by Machiavelli and Hobbes, that man is a political animal, by nature and not by
convention. The "new discipline," of course, will be in large part conventional; still, it
responds to a natural requirement, and will be "better or less good" than its
predecessors — not 'historically relative,' simply.

De Gaulle sees the beginnings of the new discipline in "the individual value and
ascendence of some ones." Once, the mass accorded credit to a man's function in society, or
his birthright. Now it respects "those here who know [how] to impose
themselves" — dictators, technicians, athletes — men who owe success to their own efforts.
In the army today, rank has some importance, but "personal prestige" has more importance.

In section ii, the central section of the central chapter, de Gaulle writes frankly of prestige.
Prestige is "a sort of sympathy inspired in others," comprised of affection, suggestion, and
impression; it depends on "an elementary gift, a natural aptitude that escapes analysis." Not
dependent on intelligence, it is undefinable, although one can isolate "some constant and
necessary elements" of it.

Mystery is one of them; "one reveres little what one knows well." Mystery doesn't come
from isolation — the most isolated man is unknown, not mysterious — but from reserve,
which contributes to the sense that the man possesses a "secret," or a "surprise" with which he
can intervene at any time. "The latent faith of the masses does the rest."

Prestige incorporates an outer reserve also, one of words and of
gestures — "appearances, perhaps, but according to which the multitude establishes its
opinion." Great soldiers have always taken care to appear a certain way; de Gaulle reminds us
of Hamilcar in Flaubert's *Salammbô,* Caesar in his *Commentaries,* Napoleon. "Nothing
enhances authority more than silence"; for action, as we've seen, demands concentration, and
speech dissipates strength. There is a necessary correspondence between "silence and order,"
and de Gaulle quotes the Roman phrase, *Imperatoria brevitas.* Aristotle's animals are political
due to their capacity of speech — reasoned speech or logos. De Gaulle, with his intuitionism (a
distrust of verbal depictions of reality), apparently does not regard the natural order, including
human nature and the politics it necessitates, as verbally comprehensible. Politics becomes as
much the art of silence as the art of speaking, and rhetoric emphasizes brevity and symbolism
instead of elaboration and argument. Hence

There is liberated from such personages a magnetism of conficence and even
illusion. For those who follow them, they personify purpose, incarnate aspiration.

To become such a personification or incarnation, the ruler responds to "the obscure wish
of men" who are imperfect, who therefore "accept collective action with a view that it tends
toward something great." Whereas the great man realizes himself, as noted, by participating in
a difficult action, lesser men complete themselves by participating in a collective action, under
the direction of a great man. The ruler needs "the character of elevation," but

It is no affair of virtue, and evangelical perfection does not conduct the
empire. The man of action scarcely conceives of himself without a strong dose
of egoism, pride, hardness, ruse.

The tension of this chapter is that between means and ends. Ends, results, count; if he uses
these means for "realizing great things," the means will be forgotten because he satisfies "the
secret desires of all."

One can observe, in fact, that the conductors of men — politicians, prophets, soldiers — who obtain the most from others, identify themselves with high ideas . . . .

The prophets' centrality on the list suggests, perhaps, that they do not differ entirely from secular leaders, at least in their self-identification with "high ideas." In view of the assertion that this is a *self*-identification, one may wonder if such men are models of evangelical perfection, but at the least we can say that all of them incarnate ideas rather than arguing for them. "Whereas, sometimes, reason blames them" — for they are "renowned less for utility than for the extent of their work" — "sentiment glorifies them." De Gaulle is silent on the justification of that glorification. It is true that he discussed it in the previous chapter.

And de Gaulle retains an ethical seriousness that Machiavelli lacks in this, his most Machiavellian chapter. His exemplary leader does not 'enjoy himself.' Indeed, the suffering that comes of his solitude-among-men partly explains why some leaders "suddenly reject the burden." (Years later Malraux remembered this passage as he considered de Gaulle's final retirement.) De Gaulle completes this section with an anecdote: Bonaparte (he usually calls him Napoleon, but here, in a personal moment, his given name seems more appropriate), regarding "an ancient and noble monument," agreed with a companion who thought is sad — *"comme la grandeur!"* he added.

The third section of "Of Prestige" is the eighth of the book's fifteen sections, the central one. It extends the previous treatment of individual authority to the army. The ambiance of the time damages corporate as well as individual authority. "For recovering [*prestige*], the army has little need of laws, *réclamations* [demands for money], prayers[!], only a vast internal effort." "The military spirit" needs distance and reserve, as does the great man; such partial isolation contributes to prestige, because military rigor and cohesion have always impressed men.

Some current tendencies favor the development of military spirit. "Individualism is in the wrong" today:* trades unionize, political parties and sports are mass-oriented, as well; *la machinisme* has increased and the division of labor intensifies, leading to less eclecticism and fantasy; labor and leisure are equalized; standardization exists in education, housing and fashions.

As important as these tendencies may be, the army's self-esteem matters more. The military must not only appear firm; it must feel "confidence in itself and in its destiny." "The day the French nobility consecrated its ardor to defending its privileges rather than to conducting the State, the victory of the Third Estate was already certain." The military should not react to the public's anti-militarism as the eighteenth-century French nobility reacted to attacks by the bourgeoisie. It won't if it reminds itself, and the public, that anti-militarism is understandable, even good (men should not want to destroy each other) but inadequate. Foreigners envy French prosperity, and France's geography renders her vulnerable to invasion. The French need a shield.

And war is not purely evil. "The desires of conquerors" have brought riches, advances in science and art, "marvellous sources of wisdom and inspiration." "With what virtues [arms] have enriched the moral capital of men!" Courage, devotion and "greatness of soul" are among them. Armies have transported ideas, reforms and religions; "there would have been no Hellenism, no Roman order, Christianity [the central item on the list], Rights of Man, modern civilization but for their bloody effort." Pacifists and bellicists are both right:

Arms have tortured but also fashioned the world. They have accomplished the best and the worst, begetting infamy as well as the most great, by turns

---

*Earlier, de Gaulle wrote that individual initiatives were fashionable; the contradiction is less de Gaulle's than that of his 'time.' Again, we notice de Gaulle's selectiveness.

34

wallowing in horror or radiating in glory. Shameful and glorious, their history is the history of men.

The history of men, de Gaulle might have added, is not a matter of evangelical perfection, any more than rulership is. And he repeats: if an international order is to come, a military force will "establish and assure it."

It is not an exclusively 'pragmatic' argument. As with individuals, the army's greatness depends on virtue, if not on evangelical virtue. De Gaulle expresses this with a paradox: the army's pride would be worthless were it not accompanied by self-sacrifice. There is "a curious relationship, but incontestable, between the renunciation of individuals and the splendor of all." We saw it in *La discorde chez l'ennemi.*

Most contemporary Frenchmen give their energies to profit-making, and it's hard to find soldiers who don't imitate civilians. Here also, however, balance asserts itself; "in a fracas of bankruptcies, scandals and judicial prosecutions" "moral values" return "to the great daylight of public respect." With them, de Gaulle contends, the army's prestige will return, grounded as it is on ethics.

*

"In war, there are principles, but they are few," wrote Bugeaud, the unsuccessful defender of Paris in 1848. De Gaulle uses this remark as the epigraph for "Of Doctrine," which is the simplest, if not the shortest chapter of *Le fil de l'épée.* the doctrine outlined is strategic, not ethical, because war is not exclusively a problem of ethics.

Once more de Gaulle insists on the importance of circumstances. A statesman must fail, despite will, hardness, national resources and alliances, if he "does not discern the character of his times" — by now his readers know what de Gaulle means by that. The French military tends to ignore war's empirical character — the French military of the seventeenth century excepted. That was the age of Descartes's *Discours sur la Méthode,* Bossuet's *Discours sur l'Histoire Universelle,* Richelieu's "realistic *politique*" (de Gaulle gives it the central position), the "practical administration" of Colbert, the "objective strategy" of Turenne; in that century, the French mind "constrained itself by the rule of *mesure* and of the concrete." What one might call the Aristotelianism of French neo-classicism (more apparent in Bossuet, one should think, than in Descartes) was shared by Napoleon insofar as he avoided '*a priorism*' and adapted his strategy to circumstances. (As opposed to his Byronic propaganda, uncited by de Gaulle: "Circumstances! I make circumstances!") More often — in the eighteenth century and in the generation that fought Germany in 1870 — '*a priorism*' dominated French minds. De Gaulle criticizes attempts to construct a system applicable to all circumstances. These systems fail on the battlefield for strategic and ethical reasons. Circumstances overturn them, and they form the sort of character easily overturned by circumstances; too often, "a doctrine constructed in the abstract rendered blind and passive a leader who, in other times, had made proof of experience and audacity."

In the central section of "Of Doctrine," de Gaulle assesses the doctrine governing the French leaders in the Great War — what de Gaulle preferred to comment on obliquely in *La discorde chez l'ennemi.*

> Military thought turned toward the offensive. This orientation was salutary . . . . But the measure went too far.

French strategists propounded "an absolute metaphysic of action" modeled on Prussia's offensive drives in 1870. That worked against an inactive opponent; a mobile and resolute opponent does better against it, as the Great War demonstrated.

Colonel Pétain had objected to this doctrine of attack, arguing for the importance of circumstances and the need for maximum obtainable fire-support at the time and place of attack ("concentration of means" forms "the basis of execution"). He proved his thesis during the Battle of the Marne. His superiors persisted in advocating, and practicing, an attack-strategy; only after the failure of their "systematic audacity" during the April 1917 offensive did they relent. (In 1918, they postponed the offensive until the American reinforcements appeared, and they won.) De Gaulle's purpose in citing this history is clear. Regarding the present French military stance as too defensive, he has praised a military strategy of action, leadership. But critics would surely remark that the excessively attack-minded leaders in the Great War espoused the offensive, and that the present defensive strategy resulted from the failure of "systematic audacity." De Gaulle avoids that possible criticism by qualifying his argument, insisting that he does not advocate any *'a priori'* of attack or of defense.

De Gaulle turns to defense-strategy in the third section. The new doctrine may end in "abstract deductions and exclusive conclusions." Obviously an extension of Pétain's teaching on fire-power, it involves the use of such fire-power coupled with the siting of offensives only where the terrain best allows them. The problem is that this neglects other variables — most notably, the enemy, who may not decide to occupy the sites that French guns can most easily shoot at. Although de Gaulle has not seen a need for prayers, he permits himself an exclamation: "May French military thinking resist the ages-old attraction of the *a priori,* of the absolute and of dogmatism!" It should instead "fix itself in the classical order," the "taste for the concrete," the "gift of *mesure"* and the "sense of realities."

*

The tension of the fifth chapter is that of its title: "Politics and the Soldier" — specifically, that between politicians and soldiers. As did the fourth chapter, it concerns the practical question: *what* should leaders think and do?

Politicians and soldiers may, as the epigraph (from Musset) claims, "go two by two/ Until the world ends, step by step, side by side," but they rarely go amicably. In peacetime the politician has the dominant role; in wartime he shares it with the military leader, and interdependence is not friendship. Politicians and soldiers are different and not especially compatible men.

The politician attempts to "dominate opinion" — whether it be that of the monarch, the council or the people (the one, the few or the many) — because nothing is possible for him except insofar as he acts in the name of the sovereign. Pleasing and promising, not arguments, lead to advancement; "to become the master, he poses as servant . . . ." After acquiring power he must defend it — convincing prince or parliament, flattering passions, dealing with special interests. It is a precarious career in an unstable world.

Unlike the soldier's. His world has hierarchy, discipline, regulations. He advances slowly, but with slight worry of demotion. As de Gaulle knew only too well, the off-battlefield danger for a military man is stagnation, being 'posted' to nowhere and forgotten.

Hence they act differently. The politician reaches his goals by covering himself; the soldier is direct. The politician's eyes are far-sighted and beclouded because for him reality is complex, mastered only by calculation and ruse. The soldier is short-sighted but also clear-sighted because for him reality is simple, controlled by resoluteness. The politician asks, 'What will people say?' The soldier asks, 'What are the principles?' Predictably such men find one another distasteful.

Nor is this entirely bad. Soldiers who make laws alarm neighboring countries, and politicians who intrude into the army corrupt it with partisan doctrines and passions. Mutual interest suggests collaboration *and* separation: compromise.

Before elaborating on that suggestion, de Gaulle writes two sections on the difficulties of

36

enacting it. In peacetime the two 'sides' bicker (especially in regimes wherein public opinion matters). Arms cause expense, are therefore unpopular except among soldiers. Soldiers are "only too ready" to believe war may come, because wartime brings their chance for glory and advancement. Civilians, who have no reason to want war, who fear it, tend toward the opposite fault: refusing to think that another war approaches.

In wartime soldiers and politicians unite, initially. Later, if the war lingers, the civil government feels its own impotence, becomes frustrated. So does the public. Reverses of fortune yield recriminations. Perhaps most important, both soldiers and politicians are men who want power, and they don't want to share it. If one group succeeds in subordinating the other the destruction of the balance may ruin the country — as in 1793 and 1870, when the French politicians dominated the military and caused battlefield defeats, and in 1917 when the military undermined civilian authority in Germany.

A country avoids that not by hiring pleasant fellows to run the government and the army, but, paradoxically, by finding leaders who are not pliable or docile. "It is necessary that masters have the souls of masters, and it is a very bad calculation that excludes from power characters accused on the pretext that they are difficult." De Gaulle, for example.

Nor can the two groups separate entirely. As always, circumstances differ, sometimes from day to day — personalities, the phase of the war, and so forth. No *'a priori'* compartmentalization works. Purposes are separable, however. "The most just glory" a statesman can win follows his success in maintaining the "national will" during war. Soldiers should deal with the fighting.

In the fourth and last section de Gaulle explains the ethical and institutional bases for this balanced relationship between civil and military authorities. Although fluid, changing with circumstances, the relationship does not depend on "chance" to "inspire" leaders. It depends on the institution of a system that educates men of character to rule well. "Other epochs assured [this] by a social and political regime that mingled in the families and in the councils all the sorts of servants of the State": Roman patricians and Prussian nobles held both civilian and military posts; French nobles served in one branch or the other, but understood the problems of both. Too, the sovereign "personified all the powers, symbolizing their harmony." "Resulting from this perpetual osmosis was a reciprocal understanding between toga and arms that is no longer in the spirit of the times" — although it is in de Gaulle's 'spirit.' De Gaulle implies that parliamentarism lacks the unifying sovereign who would compel politicians and soldiers to think of shared ends, if only by symbolizing the harmony of all state powers.

Nonetheless, today's military leaders retain "the secret esteem of the strong for the strong." The man of character wants things his way and remains alone among subordinates. But as he protects helpful inferiors and attacks his enemies, he also esteems others of his kind; he may conceal this esteem, but he acts in accordance with it. Relations between great-souled equals are productively, not injuriously, tense. With classical moderation, unmentioned in this section but presumed by it, the secret esteem of the strong for the strong prevents self-defeat of the sort the Germans suffered in 1917.

De Gaulle now proposes an institutional basis for this *concordia discors*. He does not as yet propose a political revision for France. He suggests an educational reform:

> One could conceive, it is true, of a provident State wishing to prepare a
> political, administrative and military elite, by studies done in common, to direct,
> if such should be the case, the wartime effort of a nation.

De Gaulle's civic education would increase the accord between the two domains in wartime, clarify discussions and laws concerning military power in peacetime. It would not 'solve' the problem because the problem isn't susceptible to rules. It would help.

Intuition and character are not teachable. "One does nothing great without great men," the "*ambitieux*" of the first rank, "who want nothing of life but to imprint their mark on events and who, on the shore where they spend their ordinary days, dream only of the surge of History!" These are men who know that an illustrious military career must serve "a vast policy," that a statesmann "of great glory" defends his country.

*   *   *

De Gaulle's books always concern leadership — this book does most explicitly. Against the "incertitude" of his age and the "melancholy" of the army, de Gaulle attempts to restore the mental balance of his contemporaries by a defense of power (broadly defined) and of self-sacrifice (which is, paradoxically, self-enlargement and refinement).

In the first three chapters he begins with epistemology, and therefore metaphysics, moves to ethics, then to politics. In the fourth and fifth chapters he discusses more immediate things: military doctrine and educational reform. The book moves from the theoretical and timeless to the practical and immediate.

Gaullist epistemology reconciles, without blending, the 'flow of events' and the need to adjust to them with the attempt to dominate events. That attempt consists of a process whereby the leader intuitively perceives the nature of things (which is creative, forceful and has an "obscure harmony"), using his "intelligence" to give these data an applicable form. The intellectual process complements the ethical, decision-making faculty, the "spirit of enterprise."

Gaullist ethics reconciles, without blending, the 'spirit of the age' with "character," under the aegis of the will to power (broadly defined), which animates the best men. If intuition participates in reality, character participates in other men and in events; unlike intuition, however, it is itself creative, selecting certain aspects of "the ambiance of the times," 'the spirit of the age,' ordering and directing them. In doing that, the leader realizes himself in the struggle and feels "the austere joy of being responsible" — the joy of the great-souled or magnanimous man. Intuition and intelligence, with character, yield *grandeur*.

Gaullist politics reconciles, without blending, the means and the end. Authority's present disrepute cannot last, as men are by nature political animals. Prestige is what enables the man of character to rule. De Gaulle associates it with the use of words, but more with actions and with the personification of aspirations and purposes. The end of politics is *grandeur,* and the means are not those of evangelical perfection. Such means are nonetheless forgiven because they serve "the secret desires of all." War, which is not politics but shares some of the characteristics of politics, embodies the tension of means and ends in its extreme form, having both tortured and fashioned the world. As all products of human nature, perhaps as human nature itself, it is both shameful and glorious.

Gaullist military strategy depends on balance, *mesure.* It is anti-absolutist, for absolutism encourages either passive, complacent rulers blind to circumstances or overactive, overly aggressive rulers blind to circumstances. Gaullist civic education recondiles, without blending, the politician and the soldier. By nature different — the one speaks in order to gain power, the other acts in order to gain power* — their mutual will to power and consequent attempts to achieve it cause discord. But their natural similarity can cause the *concordia discors* that is Gaullist reconciliation; this similarity issues in the secret esteem of the strong for the strong. Too, they both serve the country, realizing themselves by self-sacrificing patriotism. If its members participate in common studies, this elite will suffer less discord.

---

*This raises the interesting question: What is de Gaulle, this book-writer? Implicit in the soldier was a politician; a remark that is obvious now, that should have been noticeable then.

De Gaulle concerns himself, on each 'level' of human life, with the problem of establishing a *concordia discors* that does not sacrifice but rather enhances the integrity of the participating elements. Similarly, by writing an apologia for the future as well for the past he links history to policy, after the Great War marked their break.

CHAPTER 4

CHARACTER AND MAGNANIMITY: REFLECTIONS ON *LE FIL DE L'ÉPÉE*

Character is "the virtue of difficult times"; it is "creative" and "divine" (by which — given his epistemology — de Gaulle means "natural"). It is the ethical correspondent to intuition, that which perceives nature's "obscure harmony." Creativity is harmony-making, and the man of character, by his nature, reinforces that in human nature which is harmonious. He is a ruler. To say that men are political by nature re-states the same insight, as political life is nature's harmonious aspect in man.

The man of character, "in gripping [the difficulty] . . . realizes himself" — that is, he fulfills his nature, which is that of the ruler. "Jealous lover, he never shares what [the enterprise] gives him, or what it costs him." The *eros*-imagery reminds us of Plato's tyrants and philosophers, but de Gaulle's *eros* is the *eros* of neither the tyrant nor the philosopher, for the man of character's reward is neither satisfied appetite nor satisfied reason; it is "the austere joy of being responsible," a ruler's joy.

The man of character, unlike a Nietzschean, protects lesser men. "Reciprocally, the confidence of the small exalts the man of character," and he "feels himself obliged by this humble justice rendered to him." Justice: character has a political quality because it brings prestige, involves other men. Prestige is "a sort of sympathy inspired in others," the ethical equivalent, on the part of ordinary men, of Bergsonian intuition. Although he does not share what the enterprise gives him or costs him, the man of character does "distribute advantage generously" if it succeeds, "and, in the case of a reverse, he does not allow reproach to descend on any but himself." Advantage, then, is not primarily what an enterprise gives to the man of character. Money doesn't interest him and even power is only a means to an end: self-realization. Revenge fails to interest him because "the action absorbs everything."

De Gaulle's man of character resembles Aristotle's great-souled or magnanimous man, described in Book IV, chapter 3 of the *Nichomachean Ethics*. Magnanimity, *megalopsychia*, characterizes he who "thinks himself worthy of great things, being worthy of them." Although such a man is an extreme "in respect to the greatness of his claims," he is genuinely moderate in the sense that he claims no more and no less than he deserves. He who claims more than he deserves is vain; he who claims less than he deserves is a man of *mikropsychia*, smallness of soul. Small-souledness is "both commoner and worse" than vanity is. (In Aristotle's Athens, centuries before modern individualism, this may have been so).

The greatest of external goods is honor — "that which we render to the gods, and which people of position most aim at, and which is the prize appointed for the noblest deeds." Hence the magnanimous man concerns himself with honors and dishonors. Such honors and dishonors accrue to virtue and vice. "And greatness in every virtue would seem to be characteristic" of the magnanimous man. He is courageous and just: "it would be most unbecoming for [him] to fly from danger, swinging his arms at his sides, or to wrong another . . . . for to what end should he do disgraceful acts, he to whom nothing is great?" He is also moderate "towards wealth and power and all good or [bad] fortune, whatever may befall him, and will be neither over-joyed by good fortune nor over-pained by [bad fortune]." Not even honor and dishonor shake his moderation:

> . . . at honors that are great and conferred by good men he will be moderately pleased, thinking that he is coming by his own or even less than his own; for there can be no honor worthy of perfect virtue, yet he will at any rate accept it since they have nothing greater to bestow on him; but honor from casual people and on trifling grounds he will utterly despise, since it is not this that he deserves,

and dishonor too, since in his case it cannot be just . . . . Hence [magnanimous] men are thought to be disdainful.

But "the [magnanimous] man despises justly (since he thinks truly), but the many do so at random." This is the nearest Aristotle comes to writing that magnanimity, "a sort of crown of the virtues," comprehends wisdom. Wisdom is the philosopher's chief virtue, and the magnanimous man is not a philosopher. He is, rather, a man of right opinion.

The magnanimous man's courage does not force him to "run into trifling dangers." "[B]ut he will face great dangers, and when he is in danger he is unsparing of his life, knowing that there are conditions on which life is not worth living." He never conceals his hatred or his love because he cares more for truth than "for what people will think." "[H]e is free of speech because he is contemptuous, and he is given to telling the truth, except when he speaks in irony to the vulgar."

The magnanimous man's justice reveals itself in his readiness to confer benefits and in his shame at receiving them; when the latter occurs, "he is apt to confer greater benefits in return." He tends to remember the benefits he has conferred and not those he has received, and "to hear of the former with pleasure, of the latter with displeasure; this, it seems, is why Thetis did not mention to Zeus the services she had done him, and why the Spartans did not recount their services to the Athenians, but those they had received." One of Aristotle's translators notes that Thetis actually begins her entreaty:

> Father Zeus, if ever before in word or action I did you favor among the immortals, now grant what I ask for.

(He might have added that what Thetis asks for is honor for her son: honor, the magnanimous man's reward.) The same translator notes that in 369 B.C., when the Spartans requested Athenian help against the Thebans, they reminded the Athenians of benefits the Athenians had received from them as well as those the Athenians had conferred. Another scholar wittily suggests that Aristotle's forgetfulness here reflects the forgetfulness of magnanimity, but I suspect that Aristotle hints that neither Zeus nor the Athenian democrats are magnanimous. It is true, of course, that the magnanimous man tends to forget, or overlook, wrongs done to him.

The magnanimous man's moderation reveals itself in his dignity "towards people who enjoy high position and good fortune," and in his refusal to show contempt for "those of the middle class." "[F]or it is a difficult and lofty thing to be superior to the former, but easy to be so to the latter, and a lofty bearing over the former is no mark of ill-breeding, but among humble people it is as vulgar as a display of strength against the weak." *His* moderation leads him "to be sluggish and to hold back except when great honour or a great work is at stake." His self-possession, an aspect of his moderation, prevents him from adjusting his life to another's, unless it be a friend — i.e., an equal. "Nor is he given to admiration; for nothing to him is great." Because he has no interest in blaming others or in hearing himself praised, he doesn't gossip; expressions of scorn for his enemies are recreation enough. Because he does not take small matters seriously he does not lament ordinary misfortunes or ask for little favors. The moderation of magnanimity tends toward an esthetic that favors beautiful and profitless belongings instead of useful and profitable ones. He does not hurry or shrill — he "who thinks nothing great."

All of which prompted Bertrand Russell to exclaim that, if the magnanimous man is the median between small-souled and vain men, "One shudders to think what a vain man would be like." It was, of course, neither the first nor the last time that Mr. Russell shuddered to *think* about ethical and political matters; his doctrine of ethical subjectivism precludes all but sentiment in those domains.* But Russell does have a relatively serious point: the magnanimous man's virtues "largely depend upon his having an exceptional social position," and therefore could exist in a monarchy or an aristocracy, but not in a democracy; "ordinary [democratic] citizens would be laughable if they attempted to live up to such a pattern." Laughable, presumably, to democrats: on that there can be little dispute, although one might suspect that some of the laughter would be nervous.

It is important to see that Aristotle does not deny the possibility of a magnanimous man of unexceptional social position, although he does not expect the poor to be, in general, anything other than democratic. Indeed, he explicitly describes the magnanimous man as one indifferent to the social and economic superiority of other men; it is then conceivable to Aristotle that a magnanimous man's social position might not be exceptional.

Russell's objection leads to another, more important, question. Is the magnanimous man possible in a modern republic (given its egalitarianism — best reflected by its preoccupation with economic life)?** Today, is a politics of magnanimity possible?

In the least-read and most profound of his seldom-known books, Paul Eidelberg argues that it is. To the magnanimous man, "promoting the public good is the articulation of his self," as ruling is to de Gaulle's man of character. Unlike Aristotle and de Gaulle, Eidelberg avails himself of Nietzsche's doctrine of "overflow": the abundant riches of the magnanimous man's soul don't merely 'trickle down', as in economic life; they pour into a country's everyday life, gladdening the extraordinary, ennobling the ordinary, and sweeping the weak away.*** But to make today's politics magnanimous — more precisely, to make today's political life amenable to rulers who are magnanimous — Eidelberg proposes nothing less than the revolutionizing of current fashion in epistemology, psychology, ethics, economics, education, and religion. (One example: Eidelberg links the ethical standard, magnanimity, with the epistemological standard, comprehensiveness; both require the enlargement of one's soul to encompass the world beyond what we ordinarily call the self. In this, Eidelberg synthesizes the classical Aristotle and the modern Whitehead, and the effect of such an epistemology linked with such an ethics on contemporary education alone would be striking.) Contemporary politics can become magnanimous only if it becomes less modern — less 'individualistic' in the narrow sense, less concerned with economic life. Eidelberg would redeem ancient and modern by synthesizing them.

De Gaulle is not a political philosopher, and he concerns himself with the practical problem: can the man of character achieve a position of rulership today? De Gaulle thinks so,

---

*Ethical subjectivism depends on the radical split between human nature, (usually conceived of as extremely individualistic) and the rest of nature. If modern thinkers are right about human nature and nature, subjectivism in ethics is tenable. We see this in Hume's famous argument [A Treatise of Human Nature, Book III, Part I, chapter 1], which presupposes that nature is not teleological. The 'is-ought' dilemma is especially a dilemma to those who see non-human nature as the random interaction of purposeless forces. Thus men are justified in imposing their will on that nature. Add extreme individualism to the mixture and you justify the imposition of the individual's will on others: an imposition moderated to the extent that such thinkers also partake of egalitarianism.

**We now frequently consider economic life to be a realm of elitism — as it is, in its own terms. However, removing it from that small realm, we notice that economic life satisfies not all desires, but appetites satisfied by objects or services. Even the rare eccentric who uses money to buy good books is only satisfying his appetite for objects, an appetite he may or may not subordinate to the distinctively human desire to learn the content of the books. The same is true for the commoner practice of buying the services of teachers. The appetite for objects is shared by many animals, therefore egalitarian. 'Tastes differ,' for the crow loves his tin foil ball as the man loves his stylish new suit.

***Here Eidelberg departs from Nietzsche, who would sweep away the mediocre as well. Eidelberg praises moderation as Nietzsche (usually) does not.

but the reason for his thinking so reveals the most important distinction between the man of character and the magnanimous man.

The man of character esteems honor — the admiration of worthy men — and what Eidelberg calls fame — the honor of posterity. But what allows him to rule ordinary men is prestige, something the magnanimous man ignores. Modernity, which empowers the people, or claims to, need not yield *formal* democracy, as de Gaulle saw; it can also yield dictators. But those dictators, as of 1932, depended on consent, and they tended to be *leaders,* rulers of mass-movements.* Aristotle's magnanimous man is not necessarily a ruler, and he surely is not a modern ruler. The latter could not ignore prestige. This partial democratization metamorphoses magnanimity. The question is whether it merely diminishes it, makes the great soul smaller. Eidelberg would reply that it can enlarge that soul, make it all the more comprehensive. The question's answer depends on what ordinary citizens are likely to add and what they are likely to subtract. That depends in part on the extent to which they can be elevated beyond ordinary preoccupations. Experience could settle the matter but, in the absence of it, doubt is permissible.

Despite his partial democratization of magnanimity, de Gaulle does not underestimate the difficulty of the man of character's accession to power. Aristotle's magnanimous man could exist at any moment in the life of the *polis;* at times he might rule — although, perhaps significantly, Aristotle does not present him as a ruler. The man of character, even with his democratic aspect, can become a ruler only during a time of crisis.

*Ortega y Gasset, of course, observed this two years earlier in his widely-read *The Revolt of the Masses.*

THIRD PART

CHAPTER 5

VERS L'ARMÉE DE MÉTIER (1934)

By the mid-1930's events and ideologies induced men to clarify their principles and to defend them. In a world menaced by Hitler and Stalin, polemic becomes necessary, even noble. *Vers l'armée de métier,* published in 1934, and *La France et son armée,* published in 1938, are de Gaulle's most polemical books. In them he seeks not only to persuade, but to persuade the reader to act now. In them he argues, for the first time, for a refounding of France initiated by a reformed French army. Only a refounded France can guard itself against Germany, whose vulgarized Nietzscheism, described in *La discorde chez l'ennemi,* has revived, threatening Europe with an army trained for conquest, not defense. In *Vers l'armée de métier* de Gaulle is frankly polemical, his insights aimed through the magnifying glass of contemporary circumstance, singeing opponents; in *La France et son armée,* begun in the relatively peaceful 1920's, he filters his insights through the prism of history, gaining for them in color and variety what they lose in intensity and heat.

Intensity and heat were needed in order to reforge French opinion. One year after the publication of *La discorde chez l'ennemi,* de Gaulle wrote one of the few pieces his commanders ever applauded: *"Rôle Historique des Places Françaises,"* an argument for the system of fortifications later called the 'Maginot Line.' By "examin[ing] what role permanent fortification played in the defense of French territory in the North and in the East" during the last three centuries, de Gaulle emphasizes the worth of such structures today. As one might expect, the inconsistency of de Gaulle's position, in view of his earlier and later critiques of static defense, has been noticed. But de Gaulle does mention that he will be silent on "technique" — armament and deployment — because they depend "on the means and the circumstances," whereas geography, and hence the need for fortification, is a given, a constant. To praise fortification is not to damn all mobility, as many of de Gaulle's contemporaries assumed. If de Gaulle fails to emphasize the need for a balance, it may be that the doctrine of maneuver, since Guibert, was sufficiently adored, that a swaying of opinion to the other extreme seemed unlikely. De Gaulle miscalculated, either by overestimating the worth of defensive war, or by underestimating the effect of the 'Maginot Line' on the doctrines and the perceptions of the French military. In doing so, de Gaulle forgot the Gallic temperament, as he would later describe it.

A swaying of opinion did occur, and by 1934 de Gaulle thought a strong pull in the other direction necessary. Hence *Vers l'armée de métier,* dedicated "To the French army, to serve its faith, its force, and its glory." Force is central; it upholds the others. Without force, I infer, an army can have no faith in itself, may lose the country whose ideals it supports; without force, an army loses not only battles (there can be glory in losses) but wars, an inglorious fate indeed.

Vers l'armée de métier is divided into two parts, titled "Why?" and "How?", each with three titled chapters. The chapters are divided into twenty numbered sections.

*　　　　　*

In "Why?" de Gaulle gives his reasons for proposing the institution of a professional army in France. the three chapters — *"Couverture"* (meaning "covering" or "security"), *"Technique"* and *"Politique"* (meaning both "policy" and "politics") — are divided into four, three and four sections, respectively.

*

"As the viewing of a portrait suggests to the observer the impression of a destiny, so the map of France reveals our fortune''; the first section of *"Couverture"* pertains to France's geographical weaknesses, particularly the "terrible breach, joining the German lands with the essential basins of the Seine and the Loire." The northeast frontier is vulnerable in relief, with its inviting flatness, and in outline, permitting convergent attack at Flanders, the Ardennes, Lorraine, Alsace and Burgundy. "Vanquisher at one point, [the enemy] can make the whole system of the French defense collapse" by marching on Paris; "each time in the last century that Paris was taken, the resistance of France was not prolonged an hour." "Our national defense is essentially that of Paris." In this area, too, are the bulk of French resources (farms, coal, iron) and most of the factories.

The military disadvantage of this geography is obvious. De Gaulle lists six other disadvantages (thereby hinting that this is not a purely military book). Command of the sea has been lost; expansion "mortgaged"; France has been forced into alliances "for which one pays too dearly" (this fourth, central, disadvantage refers to the war debt); extortion; the abandonment of positions; and, "in the people,, ceaselessly obsessed by the same menace, trouble, divisions, disgust." French geography exposes France to dangers from without and from within — "divisions" being the central internal danger. By contrast, German terrain guards the Germans from attack.

What geography withholds diplomats have attempted to supply. "To establish a political system that would prevent our neighbors from harming us . . . sums up the projects conceived and the treaties concluded by France in the past thousand years." Diplomacy has succeeded (France has survived), "but today, more than ever, we are destitute of guarantees." England, Spain, Switzerland and the Netherlands don't threaten France, but Italy and Germany do — Germany the more. Geography but also "the opposition of temperaments irritate this bitterness." The French are "changeable, uncertain, constradictory"; "how could the German sympathize, comprehend and trust" them? The Germans, too, are contradictory, not in their changeableness but in their permanent characteristics: artistic and savage, technicians who remain feudal, they populate a "sublime and glaucous ocean from which the net pulls back pell-mell monsters and treasures."

France had minimized the German danger "by a traditional policy that divided our neighbors," but now Germany has united. The persisting tendency toward disunity only makes Germany more dangerous; "this menace of anarchy pushes the empire to enterprises . . . expansion to the outside and great designs" — itself a traditional policy of leaders who would overcome faction.

What protects France from Germany? Belgium lies on France's most vulnerable border, a state of two rival languages and races, a "recent and suspicious state" to de Gaulle. "Let us not wait, in any case, for it to exhaust itself to defend us."

If not Belgium, perhaps "a new international order" will protect France. "The French dream, *par excellence,* is that of an organized world, where the rigor of laws, the moderation of desires, the ubiquity of the police, guarantee to all peace and to each his domain." This reflects "our love of universal systems" (in *Le fil de l'épée* de Gaulle told us what he thinks of those); in a judiciously-chosen allusion, de Gaulle writes that "a thousand practical or generous reasons make France, today, the Penelope of international work." Penelope, of course, was exemplarily chaste and loyal, but her weaving (which she had to undo every night) only gained time. Odysseus's bow was eventually needed to rescue her. As in the *Odyssey,*

> . . . time passes, and one does not see that such efforts have added greatly to French security. Without doubt, using the credit conferred on it by victory and the personal talent of our men of State aided by a certain Anglo-Saxon piety, our idealism has given, at times, an appearance of life to the statue. But in sum, and as before, nothing legal or efficacious opposes violence. In regard to certain affirmations and abstract promises, interests remain intractable and pretensions

vigilant. This liberal understanding that we are prodigal of is scarcely paid in return. Everywhere stiffens the egoism of states.

As France proclaims law, others acclaim force and the "nostalgia for danger."

From geography and diplomacy de Gaulle moves, in section III, to national character. It too gives cause for pessimism. The French are not temperamentally inclined toward preparedness; they are enthusiasts with "plenty of passion but little constancy." Moreover, "each Frenchman holds too much to his independence" and "common action [is] rendered unequal and uneasy." Finally, the French have a taste for doctrines; they aren't realistic in their actions.

That leaves the army as France's only shield. "All there is that is vexatious in the territory, absurd in *la politique*, infirm in character, she has, as compensation in the last resort, only the warlike art, the ability of troops, the sorrow of soldiers." For that reason the last section of *"Couverture"* introduces the rest of the book and summarizes de Gaulle's reasons for insisting on the need for a professional army.

France is not isolated, as Russia and America are in 1934. Circumstances compel the French to be "a military people." Germany prepares a rapid invasion; the French response must be active — mobile and enterprising — because the Germans are reverse Frenchmen: well-prepared but not adaptable, easily defeated when surprised. Fortifications alone will not suffice, as they lack depth and may not resist such modern weapons as airplanes, heavy vehicles, poison gas. Inexperienced troops (the French army is stocked with draftees) are also inadequate, as they might surrender under heavy fire. "To build our security solely on the resistance of works held by novices would be an absurdity."

An elite force would offset the illusions "that mark most of our encounters with reality," because such an elite would develop the virtue of "order, the habit of not being astonished." It would avoid "the chimeras of *la politique*" because "military honor" cedes nothing to "the strayings of opinion." (In fact it does, as de Gaulle knew first-hand; perhaps he means this as a relative statement). De Gaulle wishes to overcome the weaknesses of the French terrain with maneuverability, the chimeras of the French *politique* with military honor, the unstable and doctrinaire French character with order and realism. "No French security without a professional army."

*

"Technique" is central to "Why?"

In section I de Gaulle considers the effect of machines on warmaking. Observing that "the machine, at present, rules our destiny" (even modern art "reflects the trembling of pistons and connecting-rods"), he denies that the consequent standardization decreases human ingenuity and creativity. It excites ingenuity and creativity; technique is more complex, competition sharper. This is true in the army, as in other fields. "By being riveted so closely to the contingencies of the material, military technique, like life, is only more complex and nourished by combinations [and/or calculations: *"combinaisons"*]. Increased necessary precision brings danger, as badly-aimed machine-guns and bombs are useless. Unlike the old muskets, today's machines must be used in conjunction with other machines. Hence "the army, down to the most modest of its members, submits to the law of progress, in virtue of which every improvement which aggrandizes the power of men, in fact multiplies their labor." (Notice that de Gaulle does not claim to believe in the "law of progress" as it is usually understood: the inevitability of progress. Rather, he believes in the law of power, a 'law' so obvious as to resemble a tautology.) The condemnations of war-machines that one hears mean little because "nothing prevails against the spirit of the times" — by which de Gaulle apparently means neither a ghostly *Zeitgeist* nor a mode of economic production, but whatever is most powerful at the moment.

49

Machines need skilled men to run them. "Here come the times of elite soldiers and the selected crew."

The second section of *"Technique"* is both in the middle of the chapter and in the middle of "Why?" Its content is controversial; here de Gaulle attacks "the notion of quantity," "the foundation of the organization and the art of warriors since the end of the XVIIIth century, supported by passionate political theories, consecrated by many grandiose proofs, [a notion that] still dominates opinion and, by consequence, everything else." (Material power depends, in part, on opinion; the tension between the [quite material] Gaullist "spirit of the times" and opinion is an important theme in *Vers l'armeé de métier*.) Conscription, the mass-army, "accorded so well with the egalitarian tendencies of the old world that it took on the hard and strong character of democratic principles," and "flatter[ed] the general passion for levelling."

This did not always prevent "quality from deploying its virtue"; in the Great War, the well-trained Germans killed approximately two men for every one they lost (de Gaulle knows, and knows we know, that Germany was no hothouse of egalitarianism). Today, however, the masses find army duty irksome, especially in peacetime. "As usual, these elementary tendencies take the shape of doctrines" (de Gaulle does not claim that all doctrines are, as the psychologists assert, 'rationalizations'; he does imply that doctrines favored by the masses usually are) "and those who wish to win the masses' favor argue for less and less military service." He does not resist adding that "soon, someone will propose in principle that a nation fights better if it is less trained, as Emile acquired instruction without having studied." De Gaulle identifies egalitarianism with Rousseau — an identification of more historical than philosophic validity.

Machines will terminate the egalitarian age. The most modern technique yields ancient (to de Gaulle, that means pre-eighteenth century) methods, especially "the ancient process of maneuver." The lack of such methods compromises the prestige of the military. But "behind the *décor* of institutions, necessity accomplishes its work." Half of the Navy is professional; most of the Air Force is professional; all overseas troops and domestic police are professional. De Gaulle compares the formation of an army elite caused by "technical progress" to a chemical reaction, lending to his opinion the rhetorical weight of apparent inevitability.

Marx and others before him protested that machines atomize society. De Gaulle asserts the contrary: "To be protected, at the very least to believe it, what comfort for the individual and, by consequence, what virtue!" — namely, the virtue of "cohesion." With the tank, "maneuver was restored" and with it a "mobile protection" not enjoyed since the time of soldiers in armor. De Gaulle thus unites the theme of *"Couverture"* with that of *"Technique."*

As in "ancient" times (those of Pyrrhus's elephant-keepers, Darius's charioteers, the horsemen of the Middle Ages), the tank-corps should be an elite group; "evolution, insofar as one owes to it mechanization, gives back to quality, as opposed to number, the importance that it had once lost." De Gaulle assures worried democrats that such elitism "could be momentary." When the mass "consents to be organized, instructed with all the rigor exacted henceforth by apparatus, in brief when it ceases to be a crowd, the specialized elements will progressively lose their power." Until that day of Enlightenment, "the professionals, in their ships, their planes, their tanks, are assured of dominating."

*

Security today rests on the technical knowledge and skill of the intellectual and ethical elite. If this were sufficiently recognized there would be no need for *Vers l'armée de métier*. But this military question has political implications, as de Gaulle has noted. Accordingly, the last chapter of "Why?" is titled *"Politique"*.

All adheres. This technical necessity, which pushes the military order toward professional armies, accords with other tendencies of evolution. For there is in human affairs a sort of obscure harmony in virtue of which the most diverse forms of activity carry a like imprint.

"The material progress of the times" causes circumstances that discourage total war, especially at the beginning of a conflict. De Gaulle cites two reasons. First, the nations become more solid each year; few people believe that any nation can be annihilated. Democratic institutions, education, "the continual ethnic and social brewing" caused by "new activities and communications" give nations "a more profound consciousness of themselves." The dissolution of "certain material and moral subjections" — e.g., the Roman Catholic Church, the belief in the divine right of kings — has aided this process. "After intense ebullition, the world is crystallized . . . . The era of great conquests is closed."* Second, the imperialist's dream of vast benefits from military victory has proved false. As political independence heightens, economic interdependence grows.

Of course, this does not mean that nations no longer want to expand. They do; but their leaders are careful to restrain their aspirations. Two years before Hitler's invasion of the Rhineland, de Gaulle sees that the new tactic will be the rapid seizure of limited areas. Total war will come only when a partly defeated nation resists. Therefore, a professional army, capable of matching the speed of an attacker's troops, "responds to the new political conditions."

De Gaulle next moves to the French political situation. The French, he writes in section II, do not intend to expand.

> Contrary to appearance, this conception of her destiny entails . . . certain dangers. It will be necessary to think, in fact, if some great national dream is not necessary to a people for sustaining its activity and conserving its cohesion. The collision of ideas and of passions, the opposition of interests, in which consist the existence of a State, risk becoming intolerable, if the citizens lack a common hope that lessons the divergences and gathers together devotions.

What de Gaulle names "the sentiment of the general interest" seems to depend on "a common hope," "a great national dream"; Germany's foreign "enterprises," mentioned in the first chapter, are not, apparently, unique.

Whether or not they intend to expand, the French cannot isolate themselves. They "form part of a certain established order, all of whose elements prove interdependent." The union of nations that France now seeks (the current "national dream," which de Gaulle may not share) must be supported by force if it comes into existence at all, because justice unsupported by force invites ridicule. "So, the professional soldier becomes the necessary guarantee of great human hopes." And, making what I suspect he takes to be a more realistic point, de Gaulle writes that he prefers an army of professionals to an army of natives as defenders of the French colonies. Nationalism, he has noted, increases.

Equally real and more immediate is German rearmament. To the objection that a professional army would be likely to ease a government's way into a war with Germany, de Gaulle replies, in section III, that unskilled armies can also be sent to the attack, with bloodier results. He does not attempt to tell us that professional armies are not aggressive, or that they are more aggressive than mass armies — only that their battles are less destructive. He thus appeals to humanitarian pacifism while undercutting its policies.

The fourth section of "*Politique*" is a comparison of France's military capacity with Germany's. When France invented the mass army at the end of the eighteenth century, her

---

*Alexander Werth criticizes de Gaulle for not foreseeing Hitler's "boundless ambitions" [*De Gaulle: A Political Biography,* Penguin Books, Baltimore, 1969, p. 82]. But, on the other hand, Hitler's failure shows that de Gaulle was right.

population exceeded that of the other major European powers combined. France was wealthier and more centralized than any of those powers. Today, France is the least populated of the great powers, less powerful industrially than Germany, with no advantage in organization. Many of the French subscribe to pacifistic notions unshared by most Germans and Italians.

France's one advantage is "in the domain of quality," where "our gifts of initiative, adaptation, *amour-propre*" become useful, not bothersome. A force of well-trained professionals is the only thing that can maintain France.

*   *

After "Why?", "How?" Its three chapters each have three sections. The chapters are arranged in ascending order: "*Composition*," the makeup of the troops and equipment; "*Emploi*," how they shall be used; "*Commandement*," how the troops shall be led.

*

In "*Composition*" de Gaulle treats equipment, recruitment and training, in that order. A force that can deliver a first blow of "extreme power" and "hold the adversary in a state of chronic surprise" must move rapidly and know where it's going; de Gaulle would move whole armies on caterpillar wheels (not foreseeing the use of airplanes for transport) and employ aerial units to "give eyes to the great unit." For defense he recommends anti-aircraft guns and camouflage.

The recruits should be young men who lack habits, interests, family ties. One hundred thousand soldiers should not be hard to find, de Gaulle argues. People are now more group-oriented; "no one today is his own master," and military life seems less unusual to outsiders. In the machine age, "choice machinery" confers prestige on those who use it. Modern war brings specialization and specialization brings diversity; the soldier has to cooperate with other specialists and know something about their specialties. Instructors of troops should make use of "the flame of the spirit of sports": competition, the desire to excel, love of fame. Routine promotion, therefore, should be abolished. Finally, there is the desire to leave home, to escape the boredom of familiar things (one motive that isn't new).

De Gaulle next treats ethical training. "One gives *valeur* [value and/or valor] to troops as savor to fruits only in contradicting nature." This is a post-classical dichotomy: nature, which tends toward the path of least resistance, versus ethics. (In *Le fil de l'épée* de Gaulle rejects this duality, but *Vers l'armée de métier* is intended for a larger, more vulgar, audience, and must therefore reflect that audience's beliefs concerning human nature). Hardship, privations and boredom yield "collective energy": the power and ennoblement that comes of serving the whole. "There is in that a moral capital that no people can repudiate without renouncing itself," and in times of decadence states cultivate the military spirit, along with family, work and thrift, in order to right themselves. Evidently, de Gaulle wants something more than the mere survival of France.

To this end he argues for the stabilization of each regiment. The army is too large for the ordinary soldier to comprehend. His regiment, however, is tangible, peopled by men he knows, and hence wins his loyalty. Earlier de Gaulle wrote mechanization unifies by protection; the specialization it entails causes dependence on others, "exacts therefore, more than ever, military solidarity." De Gaulle adds that if the public watches competitions — athletic events and so forth — between local regiments, some of the military's *esprit de corps* may extend to civilians.

The subject of "*Composition*" was matter: machines and soldiers (the latter animated by the non-material "*valeur*"). The subject of "Emploi" is movement. Today's army constructs "its doctrines, themes and regulations after the vagaries of the last conflict." This should not become a "servile imitation," de Gaulle warns, because the armies of the 'Great War' were slow and rigid. A professional army moves rapidly, making the transition from peace to war without the agony suffered by the first troops in 1914. Indeed, it is possible that not only de

52

Gaulle's experience in those early battles but his study of the demoralization of the German populace, as described in La discorde chez l'ennemi, led him to recommend that wars be fought by professionals.

Section II, central to "Emploi" and to "How?", begins with the observation that the surprise attack was abandoned in the Great War. A motorized professional army, needing little preparation, would return to that ancient tactic. Two themes of the central section of "Why?" were the inadequacy of the mass army and the revival of "ancient" modes of war with modern equipment; these themes recur here.

Surprise attacks, obviously, depend on secrecy. Today, when "a thousand trouble-makers" involve themselves in military affairs, when "honor persuades less than money," when there is a ubiquitous press and electronic means of communication, it is impossible to stop the enemy from getting information. Still, one can confuse that enemy by misleading one's own camp, by "hid[ing] the truth behind falsehood." Professional troops can tolerate such deception; the masses cannot.* There follows a description of the sort of surprise attack de Gaulle visualizes: tanks, followed by infantry and mobile artillery. "In place of fixity, map-firing, centralization, there are mobility, direct views, initiative, which form [surprise attacks] philosophy." Airplanes will be used for reconnaissance and for making smoke-screens; it is here that de Gaulle added, in the second edition published in the 1940's, a passage on airplanes as instruments of attack, an addition that changes the emphasis of his scheme.**

From matter and motion de Gaulle proceeds to results. After a victory, "one must hasten to gather the fruits," as one could not do in the Great War. Attacking the enemy's system of communications—an "ancient percept, but rejuvenated by a regime of war," which necessitates "enormous material"—again becomes possible and important. And not only the enemy's system of communications:

> In the conflict of the future, at each rupture of a front, one will see rapid troops hasten far behind the enemy, attacking the sensitive points, upsetting his entire system. Thus will be restored that strategic extension of the results of a tactical order that could never be obtained by Joffre, or Falkenhayn, or Hinden-burg or Foch, who lacked of appropriate means, and which constituted, former-ly, the supreme end and almost the nobility of the art. For, if war is, in essence, destruction, the ideal of those who wage it remains, nonetheless, economy, the least massacre for the greatest result, the combination to obtain advantage of death, of suffering and of terror for reaching the purpose most quickly and stopping all three.

Again, modern means restore "ancient" ends. It is worth noting that if "economy" — victory with minimal sacrifice — is the end of war, it is not the end of political life. De Gaulle has yet to elaborate on the political end; the earlier, vague passage on the "national dream" is all we have so far in Vers l'armée de métier.

De Gaulle is an army man; that may partly explain his minimizing the role of aircraft. A few pages before this, he visualized their use for reconnaissance and for camouflage, knowing that in the Great War they became glamorous, if not very effective, offensive weapons. Now he

---

*In La corde et les souris [Gallimard, Paris, 1976] André Malraux writes: "He said to me one day, with a manifest sincerity, 'I acknowledge that you have convinced me'; the next day he did what he had decided before our conversation." Malraux regards this as an example of de Gaulle's "determination" [p. 190, p. 48 in the Kilmartin translation, Felled Oaks]. It is possible that de Gaulle may have regarded Malraux as professional troops.

**And only the emphasis, inasmuch as he explicitly writes of the use of aerial bombardment several pages later. De Gaulle's interpolation is not, therefore, quite the deceptive bit of after-the-fact prophecy his critics say it is. See pp. 133-134, 151-152. The Livre de Poche edition does not contain this interpolation, by the way; the 1941 American translation does.

does mention bombardment, writing that aircraft can bomb but cannot occupy; complementary ground forces must do that, and with mobility they can. (Again, de Gaulle overlooks the possibility of using airplanes for troop movement). Coordination between air and land forces, nonexistent during the last war, will be seen in the next war. As in "ancient" times, coordinated attacks are now practicable.

*

The theme of leadership never stays in the back of de Gaulle's head for long. He intends *Vers l' armée de métier* for army commanders and politicians, among others. The last chapter's title is "*Commandement.*"

The training of commanders must change. Not the principles of command:

> There is, whatever the times and places, a sort of philosophy of command, immutable as human nature and which is the true lesson of military History . . . .
> To rise above oneself in order to dominate the others and, thereby, events, is an effort that does not vary in its essence. But the procedures change radically.

This "philosophy of command" resembles Machiavelli's, but we know from reading *Le fil de l'épée* that it is not truly Machiavellian. Unless de Gaulle changed his mind between 1932 and 1934, only to return to his earlier "philosophy" during the 1940's, we must conclude that *Vers l'armée de métier* is not a full statement of Gaullist "philosophy."

De Gaulle traces the changes in these "procedures" of leadership. In "ancient" times the leader saw the whole battlefield, was present to instill enthusiasm in his troops. Observation plus example was the tactical and ethical equation. When firearms became common, direct observation of the entire battle was impossible; leaders needed to conceal themselves, as did the soldiers. Leaders enthused their troops with occasional appearances at critical times and places; Napoleon mastered that. The 'Great War' "brought to the summit the predominance of material elements." Courage has no place against barrages, so calculation prevailed, with the necessary "bureaucracy of combat." It "drove into the shade genius and sentiment."

Contemporary leaders need technical knowledge of the equipment. This is the least difference between themselves and their predecessors. For machines will "make reappear in the exercise of command certain conditions of speed and audacity that will restore to personality all its luster." The rarity of carefully-planned battles — due to the speed of machines — will result in a greater need for intuition: a basis of knowledge, according to de Gaulle in *Le fil de l'épée*. The ethical effect will be that "initiative . . . will again become sovereign," and "character, venerated at the bottom [of the army] but dreaded at the top, will reascend in all its glory on the shield of battles." Moreover, leaders and troops will know one another again, resurrecting "the familiar *rapports* which pulsated in the ancient armies," "that comradeship of arms, which, more than stars and braids, remains the most noble jewel of the military crown." Like his future political friend, André Malraux, de Gaulle praises comradeship or fraternity, although Gaullist fraternity, we may trust, would have rather more hierarchy to it.

Section II is a discussion of the new military education. Because wars now occur less frequently than in the past, contemporary leaders have less experience than their predecessors; indeed, technological progress makes what experience they've had partly obsolete. Theory takes the place of experience, and "it is here that the peril begins," for theory derives from the same none-too-adequate experience — specifically, the experience of the 'Great War.' Further, those periods "wherein command made proof, on the whole, of the highest qualities" were peopled by untheoretical men. Xenophon and Caesar never refer to principles; they refer to circumstances and decisions. In the 'Great War' itself, the best leaders established a "notorious independence" from "official doctrines"; their success originated in their own "creative spark," the intuition and character praised in *Le fil de l'épée*.

Accordingly, de Gaulle proposes to teach would-be leaders less doctrine, and insists on "the development of personalities": the faculties of imagination ("a discipline of the mind exclusive of fantasy"), judgment (respect for usable means) and decision (which includes loyalty to the assigned mission). Young officers should "exercise" these faculties with a view toward "rendering them strong and free." Military problems are not the only means of "exercise," as "the true school of command is general culture." In that school, the would-be leader develops a sense of order, the capacity to distinguish the essential from the secondary, thereby "elevat[ing] [his mind] to that degree where the whole appears without prejudice to the nuances." Cultural studies generate comprehensiveness.

> There was not an illustrious captain who had not the taste and the sentiment
> for the patrinomy of the human mind. Behind Alexander, one always finds
> Aristotle.

Gaullist educational reform would be for nothing if Gaullist structural reform were neglected. The army, de Gaulle argues, is too centralized, with little space for individual action. The ethical and intellectual education de Gaulle proposes would yield large men suffocated by small rules. Authority loses prestige when over-extended; paradoxically, decentralization may enhance it. (In 1969 de Gaulle will argue for the same thing in the political domain, with his referendum on "participation.")

De Gaulle knows that educational and structural change work limitedly. Environment does not explain greatness. In a crisis, the state depends on those who have educated themselves. Ambition — "the hope of playing a great role in great events" — saves such men from enervation or corruption. De Gaulle, to whom advancement in the peacetime army seemed inordinately slow, refers to himself, of course. Unlike most people, he continued serious reading in military affairs, philosophy and history long after his formal education ended; he was indeed self-educated to that extent. The hope for greatness sustained him during those periods in his life when he had almost nothing to do.

For the individual, so for the collective (in this instance): the state would be "supremely impolitic not to feed in the army the thought of a great task and the taste for great designs." The army would otherwise rot before the next war comes, "for glory is given only to those who have always dreamed of it."* The ambition to recover Alsace-Lorraine after the defeat in 1871 is an example of what de Gaulle means. What could so animate the French army today?

The army resists change, especially in peacetime. Departmental jealousies, hierarchy, traditionalism and political difficulties contribute to its ossification.

> . . . it is necessary that a master appear, independent in his judgements,
> irrecusable, in his orders, credited by opinion. Servant of the State alone, divest-
> ed of prejudices, disdainful of connection; committed firmly to his task, imbued
> with long-range designs, incidentally of the people and the things *du ressort* ["to
> be dealt with," in the American edition, is a close paraphrase]; leader at one with
> the army, devoted to those he commands, avid to be responsible; man strong
> enough to impose himself, skillful enough to seduce, great enough for a great
> work, such would be the minister, soldier or politician to whom *la patrie* owe
> the next economy of its force.

The soldier is central on that list; de Gaulle does not expect a civilian to undertake this enterprise, and he may well be thinking of himself (he is not yet "credited by opinion," but *Vers l'armée de métier* may remedy that). It is 1934; de Gaulle still might reasonably hope for the appearance of a "master" other than himself.

*"*Car la gloire se donne seulement à ceux qui l'ont toujours revée*" — the alternative translation is, "For glory gives herself only to those who have always dreamed of her." 'Psycho-
historians' and other sentimentalists will prefer the latter, as it allows them to speculate
learnedly on 'transference.'

A "master" needs the right circumstances, and "the conditions in which the State functions today allow no one the authority or the time to carry out such an enterprise." Impatience with conditions provides the chance for their abolition, however. De Gaulle thinks that this generation is eager for clarity and for results, that this century loves displays of force. For the first time he calls for a refounding, not merely reform.

> If this national refounding must be commenced by the army, it is only conforming to the natural order of things. Not only because force remains more necessary than ever to nations that want to live, but also for the reason that the military is the most complete expression of the spirit of a society. It is by the history of its legions that one can best comprehend Rome. The royal troops were the mirror of our old Monarchy. Who thinks of the Revolution without evoking the Volunteers? In the hard work which goes to rejuvenate France, the new army shall serve as *recourse* ["resource" or "remedy"] and leaven. For the sword is the axis of the world and greatness is not divided.

Greatness is not divided from without — shared with other countries — or from within. This does not mean that de Gaulle would eliminate diversity; he alluded to the *concordia discors* in other passages. Rather, the "great design" that will save the army from decadence is this "national refounding." There is no reason to suspect that de Gaulle plans a military coup; he nowhere repudiates the lesson of *La discorde chez l'ennemi*. The army will be a "resource and leaven," not a new ruling class.

De Gaulle does assert that "the military is the most complete expression of the spirit of a society." By "most complete" does he mean that it comprehends all of the society's characteristics, or only that, it is nearer to such comprehension than all other social phenomena? The final paragraph of *Vers l'armée de métier* directs us to *La France et son armée*.

CHAPTER 6

THE FORCE OF WAR: REFLECTIONS ON *VERS L'ARMÉE DE MÉTIER*

Extreme modernity yields ancient military practices. The ancient tactic of surprise ("hiding the truth behind falsehood"); the "ancient precept" of attacking the enemy's system of communications; rapid maneuver; the need for a military elite; the possibility of coordinated attacks by different kinds of soldiers; the possibility of continuing the attack and occupying enemy territory: these characterize war as foreseen in 1934, distinguishing it from war as fought in 1914. From Bacon to Marx, thinkers believed that technology serves egalitarianism; de Gaulle recognizes that it need not, that quality's force exceeds quantity's force because it concentrates force more efficiently — moving rapidly and knowing where to move. The machine "rules our destiny" today because "destiny" is only the reflection of force. The nature of war (force is an aspect of that nature) limits war's history.

Thus, in antiquity, Surenas defeated the Roman general, Crassus, in a battle at Carrhae. He used a well-trained professional army of 10,000 archers, mounted on horses, and supplied them with innumerable arrows carried by 1,000 swift Arabian camels: mobility, professionalism, force, and (modest) technology.

Max Weber argues that military technology "presupposes discipline" — an aspect of Gaullist professionalism. Discipline interested Machiavelli, whose *Art of War* presents itself as a resuscitation of ancient military practices in modernity.*

The book is a species of dialogue. Its central figure, a mercenary commander named Fabrizio, converses with four young men, among whom is the late Cosimo Rucellai — described as a virtuous youth but now, as this dialogue is recorded, also a dead one, victimized by Fortuna. (Machiavelli would surely agree with the humble truism that the good die young.) They speak in private, in "the most retired and shady place in the garden." The trees are old, and such groves are "in the ancient manner"; one recalls Plato's Academy. But Fabrizio disapproves of this ancient custom, wishing that Cosimo's ancestors and other such princes

> . . . had endeavored to imitate the ancients in bearing hardships and in-
> conveniences, instead of giving themselves up to ease and indolence, in perform-
> ing such exploits as were done in the sunshine and not in the shade, in following
> their example while they continued honest and wholesome, and not when they
> had become dishonest and corrupt. For once these pleasures had distracted my
> fellow Romans, our country soon fell into ruin.

Inasmuch as the five interlocutors may be such as are "desirous of gratifying the rational appetite," Fabrizio's statement seems paradoxical. Leisure, philosophy's prerequisite, seems politically ruinous.** Yet to restore the ancient virtues — the active, public virtues, not the contemplative, private virtues — one must philosophize in a shady place. The method appears Socratic: ". . . it often happens that a pertinent question sets a man to considering many

---

*A serious interpretation of this book, the only one the circumspect Machiavelli allowed to be published in his lifetime, would involve (among other things) a careful treatment of Vegetius' *De re militari,* from which Machiavelli deviates significantly at times. What follows here, then, is merely impressionistic.

**One reason it can be ruinous appears several pages later. Rome, "as long as [it] remained uncorrupt," [*Art of War,* Wood translation, p. 17], allowed no full-time, professional soldiers, and hence no tyrants. The division of military labor — a military class and a 'leisure class' — invites disorder. Machiavelli, in an odd prefiguration of Marx and metamorphosis of Plato, evidently advocate the rule of philosopher-militants. "I study the arts both of peace and war," says Fabrizio [p. 23].

things, and gives him light into many others which he would otherwise never have thought of or known." But the dialogue that follows is not Socratic; Fabrizio answers questions and objections with the loquacity associated more with rhetoricians and sophists than with Socrates. It may be significant that Fabrizio's name reminds one of the verb "to fabricate": an appropriate speaker on the *art* of war.

Fabrizio would introduce several innovations in imitation of the ancients. The central innovation would be "good order and discipline in their armies." "He that takes this course plants trees under the shade of which he may enjoy himself with greater pleasure, and more security, than we do here." The peculiarity of Machiavelli's teaching, which is the paradox of modern political thought, inheres in those lines: one acts with *virtù* (as opposed to virtue), one imposes good order and discipline, in order to enjoy oneself with greater pleasure and more security.* Means alien to the democratic soul serve an end consonant with the democratic soul.** Machiavelli may or may not know this; he blames the democratizing Gracchi for ruining Rome. Perhaps he recognizes that the ends of democratic souls (he might come close to saying: all souls) can be achieved only by the few.

Although Fabrizio professes admiration for the ancients, at the center of Book One he criticizes "those . . . who have prescribed the rules of war" — specifically, the unnamed ancient, Vegetius***: " . . . I say that every prince or republic should select his men from his own dominions, whether hot, cold, or temperate; for we see by ancient examples [which remain uncited] that good discipline and exercise will make good soldiers in any country, and that the defects of nature may be supplied by art and industry — which in this case is more effective than nature itself." Fabrizio lauds the ancients in order to refute them; nature is not a standard for him, but something to overcome by art and industry. More precisely, he carefully chooses specific ancient practices and uses them as examples with which to refute many writers, ancient and modern. Thus, in the Second Book, whose announced subject is armament, he repeats his comments on the inadequacy of nature ("For it is not the natural courage of men that makes an army bold, but order and good discipline" — this, in the center of the Book), and goes on to suggest that the Roman Empire declined because it succeeded in reducing the number of independent nations, thereby reducing the strife that encourages *virtu*.**** "And although that Empire was afterwards dismembered by the barbarians, yet the several parts into which it was divided never recovered their original *virtù*"; he then mentions Christianity.

Cosimo resigns as interrogator; with the refutation, as it were, of Christianity, the heir to respectable princeliness withdraws. It was obvious that he is no more intelligent than, for example, Plato's Cephalus. Luigi, a somewhat less doltish younger man, is designated by Fabrizio as Fabrizio's next interlocutor. He listens to a lecture on battle-order and armament; at the center of this Third Book Fabrizio replies to the 'modern' objection that heavy artillery

---

*This peculiarity exists in both Locke and Marx — recall the latter's famous sketch of the idyllic life at the end of History in *The German Ideology.* 'Virtuous' acts are rewarded, after a while; the period of time between today's austerity and tomorrow's reward lengthens as modernity advances, and one begins to wonder if tomorrow shall come. The modern disjunction between present and future contrasts with ancient understanding, whereby virtue, if not 'it's own reward,' yields the reward of happiness rather more quickly.

**If one replies that the glory of the conqueror — the conqueror in action or the conqueror of minds — is a non-democratic goal, one has glimpsed something important. It is then illuminating to reflect on the nature of glory, recalling that to desire glory is to care very much for the opinions of lesser men; that is, *eros* aimed at glory has a democratic potential.

***Professor Neal Wood, in his introduction to the Bobbs-Merrill edition of *Art of War,* locates the source: *De re militari,* I, 2.

****This is the third explanation of Rome's decline. A careful reader would examine these passages with discernment. He would also consider the significance of numbers in Machiavelli's book — specifically, 3 and 7. Unfortunately, there is no space for such considerations here.

makes the arms, armor and military discipline of the ancients laughable. He says that a rapid infantry attack can defeat heavy artillery, whose gunsmoke obscures vision and whose aim is inaccurate. Fabrizio sees de Gaulle's argument in favor of maneuver, mobility, although he does not see the importance of technological progress.

In the central Book, Book Four, Luigi gives way to Zanobi, the most learned interlocutor Fabrizio encounters. While Luigi asked exclusively military questions, Zanobi has some knowledge of military history. Accordingly, Fabrizio shifts what one might call his tactics — citing numerous ancient battles, and some modern ones, in a striking display of historical erudition.* Fabrizio's central advice in this central Book concerns preventing an army from running away: one positions soldiers behind the main army with orders to kill. Machiavelli thus reintroduces the subject of nature — more precisely, human nature — anticipating Bacon's advice on using nature's laws to conquer nature. The use of fear to conquer fear may constitute Fabrizio's answer to the question Zanobi asks at the center of Book Five: how can troops be forced to reconnoiter ahead of the main army? Fabrizio promises to return to this question but fails to do so; a pertinent question sets a man to considering many things, and gives him light into many others which he would otherwise never thought of or known.

For Machiavelli, then, discipline is the soul of force. Effective discipline is based on human nature, that is, on fear. It is more important than quantity of troops. Toward the end of *Art of War,* Machiavelli compares the military/political artist disciplining his people to the sculptor shaping his material: "Just as no good sculptor can hope to make a beautiful statue out of a block of marble that has been previously mangled and spoiled by some bungler, so he will be sure to succeed if he has a fresh block to work." Hence the Machiavellian need for youthful colleagues; hence also the characteristically Machiavellian recommendations of Book Six concerning security, justice and religion. Hence, finally, the central anecdote of the seventh and final Book is on the art of conveying secret messages, and concerns an unnamed modern who used invisible ink to write between the lines of a traditional and pious document. The Machiavellian art of writing curiously resembles aspects of the Machiavellian art of war.

*

In Clausewitz, by contrast, we find a soldierly directness. Clausewitz also recognizes that force is a principal aspect of war's nature and that war serves political ends. But Clausewitz regards politics as a realm of moderation, whereas Machiavelli moderates his extremism, in ethics, politics and war, only with cunning. In tactics, this allows Clausewitz to praise defense, while Machiavelli insists on attack. "Defense," Clausewitz writes, "appears to fall into disrepute whenever a particular style of it has become obsolescent"; it is easier than attack because "time which is allowed to pass unused accumulates to the credit of the defender," who prepares a counter-attack. Machiavelli, who would conquer Fortuna, minimizes the importance of time in battle.

Beyond tactics, Clausewitz moderately refuses to regard war as an art; "strictly speaking, war is neither an art nor a science" but "part of man's social existence." He insists on a point Machiavelli obscures: "In war," unlike art, "the will is directed at an animate object that *reacts.*" Without ignoring discipline, Clausewitz does not regard it as war's decisive aspect. Such a mundane thing as superiority in numbers brings victory more often than not. While entirely modern in his view of nature, he respects nature, including human nature, significantly more than Machiavelli does; most important, he does not recommend the use of fear to overcome fear but recommends battlefield experience. And in writing, Clausewitz dislikes those who "would construct all history of individual cases" that are the most striking; such

---

*As always with Machiavelli, the erudition deserves careful investigation and consideration.

writers "consider a philosophy that encompasses the general run of cases as a mere dream." In method he resembles Aristotle more than Machiavelli.*

Writings on war are more dated than writings on politics because war is almost entirely instrumental and instruments change. Clausewitz, in the early nineteenth century, could write that "an impartial student of modern war must admit that superior numbers are becoming more decisive with each passing day." Part of his disagreement with Machiavellian practice merely reveals the assimilation of Machiavelli's discipline during the three centuries that had passed since the publication of *Art of War*; if everyone disciplines his troops equally well, or badly, other things become more important. He also writes (here agreeing with Machiavelli) that artillery, while destructive, lacks flexibility. That changed a century later.

*

As we know, eleven years after *Vers l'armée de métier* things changed again. The force of war was no longer found so much in land armies as in a species of bomb and, soon, in a species of missile. The guided nuclear missile does not, however, refute the Gaullist doctrine of mobile firepower; it confirms it. Indeed, it confirms the principles behind the military practice of Surenas, permanent beneath the impermanence of strategies and tactic. The maximization of technology in war results in machines replacing soldiers.** *Vis-à-vis* the principal force of contemporary war, everyone is a civilian (or, in another way, a soldier — vulnerable to military attack).

That much is obvious. What seems obvious but, apparently, is not, is that the force of war then becomes limited primarily by technological development itself, and that the limitations of technological advance, in practice, are as yet unknown. The 'nuclear age' hasn't featured a Machiavelli or a Clausewitz, so on this we must make do with Henry Kissinger. Kissinger remarks two effects of nuclear force: that it "makes possible, for the first time in history, to shift the balance of power solely through developments *within* the territory of another sovereign state" and that it "obliterate[s] the traditional distinctions between ground, sea and air warfare." He is less sure about the nature of force-of-war superiority when nuclear weapons are its basis. In 1957 he wrote:

> It is . . . no longer possible to speak of military superiority in the abstract. What does 'being ahead' in the nuclear race mean if each side can already destroy the other's national substance? What is the strategic significance of adding to the destructiveness of the nuclear arsenal when the enormity of present weapons systems already tends to paralyze the will?

But when, in the early 1960's, the Soviets appeared to have achieved such nuclear superiority, Kissinger's will became unparalyzed:

> . . . the outlines of what may be ahead are not difficult to discern. Tempted by the growing disparity in power the Soviet Union will bring pressure on all surrounding areas. The loss in ideological dynanism [of Marxism-Leninism] will be more than compensated by our [the United States'] weakness. Communist

---

*Reginald Bretnor, the clear-sighted military critic, writes that "in principle, there is no difference between the 'mobility' of weapons and that of men, munitions and material." [*Decisive Warfare — A Study in Military Theory*, Stackpole Books, Harrisburg, Pennsylvania, 1969, p. 116].

**Of course, the principal difference between Machiavelli's writing and Clausewitz's has to do with what one discerning reader calls logographic necessity. Machiavelli must be artful; he must conceal his radicalism from the powers of his day. Clauswitz writes under no such constraint. And Machiavelli's intellect is far greater than Clausewitz's — a fact that has little to do with the accuracy of their thoughts.

policy will alternate between protestations of peaceful intentions and spasms of intransigence designed to demoralize the West. Negotiations will turn into a kind of psychological warfare. If the West can be humiliated over a period of time, the new nations, whatever their moral preference, will consider Communism the wave of the future . . . . No amount of economic assistance will avail against the conviction that the West is doomed.

A non-overwhelming nuclear superiority, indecisive in itself, may be used for purposes other than nuclear war. The postwar ascendency of the United States, even after the mid-1950's when its nuclear superiority was no longer overwhelming, confirms this.

Kissinger added that the United States could "still reverse these trends" and, given the non-existence of the Soviets' advantage at the time, his hope was justified.* A polemicist might note that when Kissinger wrote of United States superiority he described a paralysis of will, but when he wrote of Soviet superiority he described victory — a reflection on Kissinger or a reflection on the countries he describes? But in military terms, Kissinger ignored the fact that the country that enjoys some nuclear superiority knows that only the most remarkable technological innovation by the enemy could shift the correlation of force quickly; nuclear inferiority reduces one's 'margin of error' when calculating future probabilities.

Also, Kissinger did not seriously discuss the possibility of radically new weapons that might exceed the guided missile in mobility and/or force. While seeing the likelihood of improving existing weapons, he ignored the possibility of weapons that would be to nuclear weapons what nuclear weapons are to those now called 'conventional.' (Example: a laser-weapon, whose 'ammunition' travels (by definition) at the speed of light, or some other beam-weapon, would destroy a missile with ease — again, the Gaullist principle of mobile, well-directed firepower. It would be ridiculous to fault Kissinger for failing to think of the laser in the late 1950's and early 1960's, but to fault him for missing the conceptual point is fair, and the conceptual point is more important than any specific weapon, which may or may not prove feasible.) Machiavelli criticizes artillery without considering the possibility of improving it; Clausewitz evidently believes that numbers of soldiers would continue to be decisive. Kissinger, less confident that the war-instruments of his own time were near-constants, nonetheless assumed that the species of weapons he knew (if not its varieties) was the ultimate weapon.

*

Nuclear weapons, consistent with the Gaullist principle of mobile, well-directed firepower, minimize Gaullist military leadership. 'Discipline' in nuclear war nearly becomes the missile's guidance system, and to speak of 'training' a missile is to use a grim sort of pun. An effective nuclear army must be more centralized than earlier armies were. During a nuclear war, the character of a general means little in terms of his ability or inability to lead men; he orders men to shoot missiles. (Leadeship comes not so much during a nuclear war but before and after it; the importance of day-to-day political leadership increases.) Finally, because no

---

*The Kissingerian prescription for political health: "move boldly and with conviction . . . overcom[ing] our penchant for choosing the interpretation of current trends that implies least effort" [*The Necessity for Choice,* p. 6]. "As the free world gains in purpose, cohesion and safety, the Communist approach to negotiations may alter. Instead of using arms control negotiations to tempt or blackmail the West into unilateral disarmament, the Communist leaders may address themselves seriously to the problem of how to reduce the tensions inherent in an unchecked arms race. Then coexistence may become something other than a slogan. But whatever Communist purposes may be, our task is essentially the same: to define for ourselves the nature of a peace consistent with our values and adequate for our security." [*ibid.,* p. 7]. Kissinger's policy of detente, undertaken in the early 1970's, failed because he attempted serious arms negotiations with the Soviets when the West was less purposeful, cohesive and safe than it was in 1960. Too, the rift between the Soviets and the communist Chinese was then more than compensated for by the advances in Soviet military force.

general has experienced a full-scale nuclear war, theory and speculation necessarily guide action; some of the doctrinalism that de Gaulle criticizes becomes unavoidable.

Nonetheless, more than ever machines increase human dependence on each other and on machines while apparently decreasing human dependence on fortune and on the surface of nature. De Gaulle sees that, and leads us to consider the relation of ethics and nature.

FOURTH PART

CHAPTER 7

LA FRANCE ET SON ARMÉE (1938)

In 1928, Pétain encouraged de Gaulle to write a history of the French army. Some biographers report that it was to have appeared under Pétain's name, that the project was abandoned when the Marshall saw that no one would be fooled. For ten years, de Gaulle kept the manuscript, completing it and publishing it in 1938, with a dedication to his protesting ex-mentor.

La France et son armée contains seven chapters: five of these have three numbered sections; chapters Two and Four have two numbered sections. De Gaulle presents his subject chronologically, beginning with *"Origines."*

*   *

In *Le fil de l'épée* de Gaulle asserts that the sword made the world what it is. As with the world in general, so with France in particular:

> France has been made by sword-blows. Our fathers entered into history with the glaive of Brennus. It was the Roman armies that brought civilization. By the grace [!] of the hatchet of Clovis, *la patrie* recaptured consciousness after the fall of the Empire. The *fleur de lys,* symbol of national unity, is only the image of a javelin with three lances.

But force, which dictates history, is instrinsically purposeless. "[I]f building a state necessitates force, reciprocally the war effort has value only in virtue of a *politique":* force *for* some end. As de Gaulle implies in earlier books, thinking about military affairs leads to thinking about politics. An army needs a strong state to maintain it, and vice-versa. *La France et son armée* is a study of this reciprocity. Political "maintenance" of an army involves the elaboration of a "grand design" — as de Gaulle wrote in *Vers l'armée de métier.* The army expresses the "spirit" of a *patrie,* not completely, but more completely than any other institution; it reflects the state and the nation — that is, the polity. Its harmonies and its tensions are those of the "society," to use de Gaulle's word, or of the "polity," to use mine.

He passes over the Gauls quickly, mentioning Vercingetorix, then identifies Rome's contribution:

> . . . during five hundred years, Rome imprinted on our laws, our *moeurs* [customs/morals], our language, as on our monuments, roads and works of art, the mark of rule and of authority; she revealed to twenty generations the spirit of military power. From there [came] the ideal — or the nostalgia — of a centralized State and a regular army . . . .

As in *Vers l'armée de métier,* military power leads to politics; politics is the end of military activity and military "spirit."

The Merovingians "essayed to use the debris of the Roman organization"; the Carolingians essayed to restore the Empire and the army. They failed. "In the chaos of races, of passions, of interests, the central power was only a fiction, the military art only a memory." Slowly, feudality "imposed itself as antidote to anarchy." With it "a chronic struggle" between fiefs began, "but the feudal principle is a sort of advance," a tenuous order preferable to no order.

The army itself was not unified. Each fief had his men, allied with those ruled by other fiefs when circumstances required collaboration. At such times intra-army debates over prerogative, order in battle and the like revealed "the desire for privilege and the taste for

65

equality, dominant and contradictory passions of the French in every epoch."

After describing the armor and the weapons of the period, de Gaulle writes of the troops' discipline and training. There was much insubordination, mitigated partially by the 'point of honor.' Reputations, titles and fortune were acquired in combat, hence training consisted of "developing [the troops'] valor and vigor." "Individual audacity and address, good if badly combined, often untimely, frequently absurd, gave to the military enterprises of the time a strain of heroism which adorned their confusion."

In the nation, only "a great peril" brought consciousness of France-ness — more accurately, a series of great perils, including the Norman invasion. (A prefiguration of 1940? De Gaulle has been warning his people since the 1920's.) Expeditions of conquest had the same effect. "Finally, religious ardor hastened the masses to arms." "These wars of national defense, of conquest or of proselytism, took a very different character than the habitual escapades"; they were larger. But the techniques were the same; "the maneuvering of the armies of this time could only be rudimentary." De Gaulle writes of the preparations for, fighting and aftermath of, a typical battle, concluding that "feudal *moeurs* and institutions blurred the art of calculation in war, formerly taken to the most high degree by certain antique peoples." There was little of the cohesion that results from living, acting and suffering in common (recall that comradeship is "the most noble jewel of the military crown"). Nonetheless, "the bellicose order of the Middle Ages had produced, in the moral order, certain good effects" — namely courage and honor, constituents of "the chivalric spirit."

At the same time, on the 'level' of the state, "the royalty worked for unity" and "personified national consciousness." Having observed this at the beginning of section II, de Gaulle considers the decline of the "feudal regime" which, by the thirteenth century, "showed signs of wear." Many of the knights who survived the Crusades were corrupted by their encounter with Oriental luxury. The long absences of the fiefs disaffected the vassals. New powers arose: industry, the universities, commerce; "in many regions, some Parliaments wanted to substitute the justice of the king for that of the seigneurs." The taste for collective enterprise began to override the taste for individual enterprises.

In the military there was "a parallel evolution." With the use of firearms, cannons, and crossbows knights became anachronisms. "The permanent army became a necessity." The kings attempted to form one, but it took several defeats in battle (notably, those at Crécy, Poitiers and Agincourt) to convince the feudal lords — and not before factionalism nearly destroyed the country. "The defeat at Agincourt literally broke up France," ruined the monarchy early in the fifteenth century; only Joan of Arc could renew popular enthusiasm for unity. Not until 1439 did Charles VII institute a permanent army. "In place of the episodic heroism of paladins, the avid guile of the mercenaries, the short-lived *élan* of the militia, the constancy of professional troops would be, during three and one-half centuries, the rampart of France." Faction and defeat cured by unity and the institution of a professional army: too, is a polemic, but indirectly.

Section III concerns the Renaissance — the last half of the fifteenth century and the sixteenth. With national unity established, France "turned toward the outside ambitions that, just before, consumed her in internecine quarrels."

The masses took part in these conquests because the musket reduced the cavalry's effectiveness. De Gaulle thinks that "misery, ignorance and servility" were "pulled back" as more men participated in combat, which heightened their "*valeur*" and, "by consequence, their military virtues": once more, the mutual intensification of very different virtues.

The conjunction of "the old spirit of chivalry with the new discipline suscitated a brilliant efflorescence of leaders." In battles, "the energy of the captains played the preponderant role"; we recall the Gaullist idea of excellent troops led by great men. "In the martial order, as in the others, the Renaissance prepared the classic epoch." For de Gaulle, "classic" means the *ethos* of seventeenth-century France, the era of the French landscape garden — itself embodying a Gaullist ideal. French neo-classicism, as the name implies, synthesized ancient and modern, as did the Renaissance army, while it prepared the material circumstances necessary for such a cultural eminence.

*

Chapter Two, *"Ancien Regime,"* begins with de Gaulle's summary of the prevailing epistemology: "The *politique* of the Old Regime is that of circumstances; forbearing abstractions but delighting in realities, preferring the useful to the sublime, the opportune to the resounding, searching, in each particular problem, not the ideal but the practical solution, little scrupulous as to the means, great, nevertheless, by the proportion between the end pursued and the forces of the State." The fulfillment of any hope depends on one's seeing this "just proportion"; the problem of ends and means proceeds from hope. De Gaulle's analysis is in keeping with the nature of a history: concrete, not theoretical.

The French army of the Old Regime stressed empiricism and facts instead of laws and theories; "good sense, experience, the seeking for the occasion, guided, without care for formulas, strategy and tactics." De Gaulle admits that "the wars of this time rarely excited . . . the surge of national passions . . . . The majority of the French lived their life in peace." Good sense is more likely to rule, he seems to imply, if national passions are excluded. It would seem that his praise for national passions, in this book and in others, is a praise of the second-best possibility.

Colonels recruited their own regiments, using enlisted men (who signed, de Gaulle tells us, only when persuaded, inebriated or intimidated) and foreign mercenaries (it was not "'the French army' but: 'the army of France'"). Efforts were made to correct the excessive vices. Locally-based militias also existed, but were not especially important.

"The same empiricism guided the royal power in the choice of officers." Like the colonels, the king took men as he found them. He found a titled nobility that had "the taste and the tradition of war," "the habit of command" produced by "social conditions." They were ambitious, threatening "the authority of the king and national unity." And they had money that could be used to strengthen the army. In all, "the government had the best reasons for pushing this class into combat against the enemies of France." Empiricism, indeed.

Discipline, understandably, was necessary. The not-always-voluntarily enlisted men deserted frequently; the officers were fractious nobles; the great generals bristled with pride. Indiscipline would have ruined the Old Regime's army had it not been for Louvois.

Louvois is literally and thematically the central figure in this section. He was a minister; this is the first time de Gaulle accords such importance and worth to a civilian — an indication of the increasingly political nature of his thought.* In his thirty-year tenure Louvois "realized all the possible in taking his part in the inevitable." De Gaulle bestows no higher compliment. That is what a soldier or statesman can do, at best: select from givens — human nature, political circumstances, fortune. It takes "will and discernment," which Louvois had, and a man "disdainful of theories . . . amorous of the real," as Louvois was. "Severe with men without holding them in contempt, lucid but not skeptical, without illusions but not without faith, he is hard toward the incapable, unpitying toward the pretentious, but generous in recognizing the aptitudes that he upholds and encourages." He "call[s] forth counsel but [is] jealous of decision"; "he has some adversaries, some partisans, and no friends." He is, one might conclude, a man of character, worthy of de Gaulle's emulation.

---

*The only minister he had described previously was the German Bethmann Hollweg, and that was a mixed portrait, although predominantly favorable.

Louvois made the troops "live in conditions that favored subordination." Each man wore "the uniform of the king"; the armament of each unit had to conform to ordinance; the first barracks were constructed — on the peripheries of the towns; men changed garrisons frequently, according to a preordained schedule; the men were instructed; inspectors visited each unit; regular payment of salaries was instituted.

Louvois disciplined the officers. In wartime they had to present themselves to the king at the beginning or the end of each campaign. In peacetime they were responsible to the inspectors. More ranks were instituted, and an officer advanced by displaying merit.

In managing "the great leaders" — the likes of Conde and Turenne — Louvois gauged individual personalities and accorded different treatment to each. There was resistance, of course, because these were men of character. But Louvois preferred strong personalities to weak ones. In this, as in other things, Louvois conforms to de Gaulle's criteria of leadership as set down in *Le fil de l'épée*.

> Discipline, thus reinforced by Louvois, remains nonetheless rough. But military honor is for the army of the Old Regime a powerful moral link. Self-love and comradery joined with devotion toward the King, in what is called patriotism, and in the still-living spirit of chivalry.

The French army had elite corps with a special tactical role: they were given the newest weapons and had important places in battle-formations. De Gaulle tempts one to think that Louvois, were he alive in 1938, might look favorably upon a professional army skilled in tank-warfare.

As a result of these efforts, "at no other period in History was war, in fact, more closely obedient to *la politique*." This may be de Gaulle's answer to those who fear that a strong professional army would inevitably dominate the government and lead to inordinate militarism, the ambition to conquer. The governments of the Old Regime limited the results they pursued, avoided the excitation of popular fury. Territories were acquired and defended, allies supported, enemies punished; there were no wars of annihilation or other mass-movements.

De Gaulle ends section I with portraits of Condé — a man of audacity and discernment — and of Turenne — characterized by his careful preparation and economy of means.

"French society, after the Wars of Religion and to the day after the Fronde, put to the proof the need of rule." The eighteenth century, discussed in section II, saw France ignore this need. Skepticism and corruption "dissolved loyalism and paralyzed authority." The army was injured; in the War of the Austrian Succession "signs of disorganization" appeared. By the time of the Seven Years War traitorousness and bad administration were sufficiently ingrained to yield defeat; "good sense ceded its place to dogmatism, discipline became formalism, systems were seen preferred to personalities."

In the middle of this section de Gaulle has Frederick the Great appear. The Prussian king applied "to its perfection the martial art of the Old Regime . . . . Opportunistic *politique*, reduced means: the strategy of Frederick remained the classic strategy," involving "a skillful adaptation of the means to the circumstances," professional soldiers and experienced officers.* Frederick was "at the same time sovereign and army leader," a role de Gaulle took in 1940 and in 1958.

"In total . . . the work of our Old regime remains efficacious and durable." De Gaulle

---

*The Germans of the 1930's were practicing some Gaullist military principles: preparing a flexible and aggressive strategy. German imitation of France may have seemed ordinary to de Gaulle.

lists the stabilization of frontiers, the increase of territory and the successful alliances and wars as the Old Regime's best achievements.

*

The Revolution of 1789 "alarmed the consciousness of the masses and the prudence of governments." It wasn't merely a disturbance, however violent, but "a new order which pretended to impose ideas, *moeurs* and laws." The Revolution and its effect on the French army are the subjects of the third chapter.

1792 was the year of a different species of war; "not only, this time, [a] war of interests where one fights for a province, a local right, a succession, but a war of principles, national war, fierce by consequence." Ideology and mass, national passions combined to yield a war that was "gigantic and without precedent."

The Revolution's "grandeur and confusion" were imprinted on "the military effort." France raised a mass army bound, ostensibly, by shared principles. "The declaration of [The] Rights [of Man and the Citizen] had proclaimed the French free; the good will of individuals was therefore sufficient to provide France with defenders." But not with steady defenders: these soldiers were possessed of a "generous ardor" that did not last during the hard winter of 1792-1793. Desertion and sickness weakened the army.

> The principle of liberty could not, alone, assure recruitment. Constraint is necessary and the Revolution goes to arm itself.

Organizing the impassioned mass was problematic. The necessity of treating older soldiers differently from new recruits "excited between the one and the other a vexatious acrimony" — not surprising, one might think, among a people animated by the egalitarianism of the *philosophes*. When old and new soldiers were mixed, organization improved. By 1794, nearly two years after the war began, the Republic "had comprehended that order and discipline are necessary conditions of force."

Having learned that, the Republic's difficulties didn't end. Several of the older generals adapted to the new circumstances; of them Dumouriez shone. With his "largeness of views, firmness in design, vigor and appropriateness in execution," he "understood that enthusiasm [was] the true force of his improvised troops" and sought to turn it to France's advantage. The insistence that new circumstances require a new approach should be familiar to de Gaulle's readers by now, although de Gaulle's superiors remained impervious to it.

Despite good generals, "unchained passions" "destroyed their advantages"; "political frenzy took away prestige, often life, sometimes honor." The Jacobins criticized Dumouriez, and the controversy emasculated "his liberty of spirit and the confidence of his troops." He soon defected to Austria.

The midpoint of section II is an interlude between the portrait of Dumouriez and the portrait of his like-minded successor, Carnot. The Assembly, de Gaulle reports, put commissioners with "unlimited powers" on all fronts as "representatives of the nation." These men "contributed to forcing to energy the leaders who had abandoned it," but some of them abused their powers. Failures ensued their meddling.

Again de Gaulle writes of amateurs bungling and professionals rescuing them, hoping that his contempories will notice. In August of 1793 Carnot became the leader of military affairs. This professional soldier taught another Gaullist lesson by allowing the army divisions to play "an autonomous role." More reorganization followed, and the army endured the winter of 1794-1795.

De Gaulle begins section III by observing that Carnot's strategy had to be commensurate with mass-warfare (as Dumouriez had seen). He had his republican enthusiasts attack with

69

"ardent and precipitous blows . . . permitting us to exploit our advantages of number and of *élan.*" The French position improved as Carnot worked to consolidate his troops on one front at a time.

Several young generals distinguished themselves in the 1790's, — none so much as Hoche, who occupies the center of this section. Hoche shared the precocity and inclination to precipitous action "that marked his epoch." Like Dumouriez, he suffered from partisan hostility; Saint-Just had him jailed. Released, Hoche was named commander-in-chief of *L'Armée de Sambre-et-Meuse* in 1797 and defeated the Austrians outside Frankfort. He died after reaching the banks of the Rhine; he was twenty-nine years old. De Gaulle thinks that Hoche's death marked the end of this period. wherein a mass army, a revolutionary army, learned "the eternal laws of action" — the necessity of hierarchy and discipline. "France saved, the army turned its eyes toward the interior," seeing weakness, license and vices, "the anarchy of the State." The circumstances favored "a young ambition" that would "raise itself."

*

"*Napoléon*": it is the central chapter of *La France et son armée,* the only chapter whose title is the name of a person. Previously, de Gaulle used the centers of a number of sections to praise excellent leaders; after this chapter, favorable portraits will not be placed in the centers. Napoleon, it would seem, is central and, somehow, pivotal in French history — after him, things are not the same. De Gaulle's ambivalence toward him manifests itself in the opening paragraphs.

In a "natural reaction against disorder and the abuse of liberty," France "abandoned herself to the master and shortly to obeisance." Because imperial power "only exists in virtue of glory" it "pushe[d] France into the infernal cycle of battles." Napoleon found a good, experienced army when he ascended to power, an army he exhausted in numerous campaigns. Napoleon also found Europe divided, therefore conquerable.

> At the same time, each victory excited even more the ambition of Napoleon, exaggerating his projects, pushing them beyond the boundary of the possible. There comes a day when the proportion between the end and the means breaks, and the contrivances of genius are vain.

We recall Chapter Two, "*Ancien Regime,*" the only other chapter divided into two sections. Napoleon, I observe, restored some of the institutions of the Old Regime, but he forgot the most important thing: *mesure.*

Napoleon's reforms were numerous. He instituted conscription and "did much to elevate the intellectual and social standard of the cadres" — founding schools, encouraging the sons of 'good' families to join the army, and so forth. He "imprinted the mark of grandeur" on a generation, fortifying its "taste for high actions" by forming elites (including "The Guard," his personal escort), by enhancing the army's prestige (the "magnificence" of parades and other ceremonies awed the masses) and by attempting to "ennoble" even the misery of troops in the field with the revival of Les Invalides and with a pension for the families of dead soldiers.

Nor were the changes solely or even mainly institutional. Napoleon used his personality to "influence the moral force of his soldiers":

> Honor, discipline, recompenses, and even justice, all proceeded from him, amounted to him, shone brightly in his glory. Duty like ambition, effort like merit, submit to his sole arbitrage, no longer having any other object than satisfying him.

His high subordinates were competent, but he tolerated no independence; to that extent he was un-Gaullist, although de Gaulle does not mention it.

"He formed a new nobility," giving titles to many of his soldiers. One might say it is the Old Regime again, but always with one difference: Napoleon.

"His contrivances" worked because his enemies were "discordant and badly prepared." Napoleon's typical battle-plan had little plan to it, consisting of a series of "incessant attacks and counter-attacks"; his genius "discern[ed] . . . the opportune moment [for] and the suitable form" of the attack. He would sometimes appear at a critical time and place, exalting the courage of his troops and thereby "animating the general offensive." In *Vers l'armée de métier* de Gaulle praised these tactics, well-adapted to the sort of rapidly-maneuvering mass-army Napoleon had.

From Napoleonic military opinions and actions de Gaulle moves to Napoleonic *politique*. In the early campaigns it had "a relative moderation" to it, but after Tilsit "the political projects of the Emperor surpassed all *mesure*." The other countries united, became more nationalistic. The French nation,

> . . . stupefied by so many sacrifices, of which it did not see the necessity, supported them, however, because the imperial authority constrained and dazzled them. But, every day, trouble gained on confidence, inertia on good will, secret revolt on resignation.

Napoleon foresaw disaster in Russia. "For, if his political projects surpassed all *mesure*, he never lost, in military execution, the sentiment of the real." He had difficulty replacing the troops lost there because conscription began to provoke resistance.

In 1814 "a mournful stupor seized France"; the French will broke, and France "abandoned herself to destiny, vanquished in her heart." Napoleon's troops declined physically and in morale because he had promised, after each "great effort," that peace had come — and then disappointed the hope he had roused. The Napoleonic abuse of hope is the reverse of what de Gaulle attempts with *Vers l'armée de métier* and with *La France et son armée;* Napoleon's evocation of hope excited the sentiment of peace-loving, the easy life, whereas de Gaulle's evocation of hope excites the sentiment of — if not war-loving — combativeness, the hard life. Napoleon's evocation of hope led the French to defeat, whereas de Gaulle's evocation of hope was the first thing needed to save the French from defeat. "Souls, like matter, have their limits," and Napoleon exhausted the French.

De Gaulle writes a conclusion, a judgment:

> His fall was gigantic, in proportion to his glory. The latter and the former confound thought. In the presence of so prodigious a career, the judgment remains split between blame and admiration. Napoleon left France crushed, overrun, empty of blood and of courage, smaller than he had found her, condemned to bad borders, of which fault she was never redressed, exposed to the mistrust of Europe, which, after more than a century, she still carries the weight of; but is it necessary to count as nothing the incredible prestige with which she surrounded our arms, the consciousness given, one time for all, to the nation of these incredible martial aptitudes, the renown of power that *la patrie* acquired and whose echo still resounds? . . . Napoleon exhausted the good will of the French, abused their sacrifices, covered Europe with tombs, ashes and tears; however, those same whom he made suffer so much, the soldiers, were the most faithful . . . .

Today people "render homage to his memory and abandon themselves, in front of his tomb, to the shiver of *grandeur.*" De Gaulle preserves his sense of balance as Napoleon did not: "Tragic revenge of *la mesure,* just wrath of reason; but superhuman prestige of genius and marvelous virtue of arms!" Perhaps that explanation point tips the scale toward admiration, against de Gaulle's better judgment.

71

One remembers de Gaulle's criticism of the Germans' "Nietzscheism," although in that case his admiration was overbalanced by disapproval. De Gaulle remains a soldier, esteeming military skill more than political skill in his heart if not in his head. If he hopes for a political career, he is determined to retain the sense of *mesure* that politics (perhaps even more than warfare?) requires. His individualism will be controlled. His ambivalence toward Napoleon may also relate to the Emperor's combination of classical efficiency and organization with modern, passionate individualism and the modern, passionate mass-army.

There could be more. After Napoleon, France changed. France "was *never* redressed" of her "bad borders"; "she *still* carries the weight of" "the mistrust of Europe." At the same time, Napoleon gave the "consciousness . . . *one time for all*" of "these incredible martial aptitudes," a "renown of power" — if not power itself — "whose echo resounds *still*." De Gaulle's ambivalence toward Napoleon, the central figure in French history, may reveal an ambivalence toward France. If so, did 'the man who is France' feel such an ambivalence toward himself? Malraux's portrait in *Le miroir des limbes* suggests as much.

*

In Chapter Five de Gaulle writes of the period between Napoleon's defeat and France's defeat in the war with Prussia; hence the title, *D'Un Désastre à L'Autre*. In 1815 France was "without army." "It was necessary to find, between the ancient traditions and the recent principles, painful compromise." For example, the reinstated Bourbon family wanted an army based on quality, but many of "the liberal and doctrinaire parties" demanded recruitment of the masses — the quantitative principle. So the 1818 law "had the mean of these opposed tendencies": voluntary recruits and conscription. The bourgeoisie, now the ruling class, could avoid conscription, and "the poor classes" formed the army. Peasants comprised seventy-five percent of the population, so there was no military disadvantage in that. Characterized by "vigor and docility," an "obscure desire for adventures" and "the faculty of adaptation to circumstances," the peasants were, in de Gaulle's view, exemplary in their virtues. (During the years he ruled France, de Gaulle had the electoral support of peasants; so the esteem was mutual.)

Selection of officers was equally discriminatory. In previous years courage and the opportunity to show it made an officer; it was wartime. Now education formed an officer, and the bourgeoisie and the nobility were the educated classes. These men, "strongly attached to order, to discipline, to military stability," reacted against the "agitation of the parties." Unfortunately, they also disliked "discussion, originality, even initiative," and lacked "general ideas." The "minute and imperative" regulations they devised and upheld conformed to "the general tendencies" of the period.

The high commanders, however, were good. Marmont, Gérard, Bugeaud, Pelissier and others had experience during the Empire. Their ardor exceeded their methods; often negligent in preparation, they too often intervened personally during battles and got killed for their trouble.

It was "a solid and routine army." Adequate for limited uses, it had no place in a major war — and one was coming.

In section II de Gaulle shows how the French blundered into the war with Prussia. The Restoration followed a *politique* of moderation in its enterprises. By 1830, unfortunately, "a current, whose force grew ceaselessly, pushed opinion to great adventures." *La mesure*, "the renewed wisdom of the Old Regime," seemed anachronistic to many patriots, and the 1815 treaties "appeared as the consecration of an abasement."

Napoleon III "prepared all the conditions of a conflict where France would have to defend, be its means only, its soil and its future." In the late 1860's he was building an army, poorly; in 1870 "France threw herself into a war of peoples, armed for a local war" against a good Prussian army. Moreover, the French strategy was too passive. France's military leaders had experience and courage, did not have "largeness of views" or "amplitude of judgment."

The troops were good. De Gaulle ends the section with a panegyric to their valor, consciousness of their own worth, solidity, skill with arms, and faithfulness. These virtues were not sufficient for victory.

In the last months of the war, section III begins, France's material disadvantage made "all effective resistance impossible." A change in regime occurred; the republicans took power, with all "the deplorable inconvenience of a revolution accomplished in the presence of the enemy." Gambetta, the new Minister of the Interior, "personifie[d] before History the start of *la patrie.*" He "pretended to make up for his superficial understanding of affairs with eloquence, ardor, will," was "passionate more than clear, active more than laborious"; for a dispirited nation this "powerful personality" was a tonic.

But it was a general, Chanzy,* who saved France. He "mingled with war-instinct the general intelligence of events"; he was a strong-souled man. "If it were possible that one man could have changed the destiny of France, that man was Chanzy." The war was lost, but Chanzy gained time during the winter of 1870-1871. He reinforced Paris — which, de Gaulle has written, is essential to the defense of France. Consequently, the Prussians forced an armistice upon France, but Paris wasn't lost.

A defeat is bad enough. "Ideology, insouciance, brought their bitter and bloody fruit."

*

"*Revanche*" means "return-match" or "revenge." In the title of the sixth chapter, *"Vers la Revanche,"* de Gaulle could mean either or both. France prepared for the 'Great War,' a salutary departure from her normal way of behaving.

After the 1871 armistice three laws passed the French parliament without opposition. In 1872, recruitment concerned the legislators; obligation to serve in the military was imposed on all citizens. The next year the project was organization; the legislators instituted a permanent army and a large school of instruction, proclaimed that "the defense of the country [is] assured by the nation itself." And in 1875 the "cadres" were formed: groups of reservists to be mobilized when the country was endangered. In making these reforms, the French imitated the Prussian system; "in the military order as in others, the French *esprit* submitted for a long time to the influence of German thought."

Republicanism had won, but "democracy had not yet penetrated the *moeurs* enough so that the law could realize a veritable equity of burdens." The bourgeoisie kept its advantages of wealth, education, local influence; those with diplomas served only one year in the army (five years was normal until 1889, three years thereafter), and clergymen and teachers did not serve.

De Gaulle entered the army before the Great War; understandably, we begin to hear a more personal tone. He describes the life of the draftees and the officers with sympathy and occasional light irony — an interlude between controversial paragraphs.

'Lessons of history' concern him more than vignettes, however. "The lessons of 1870 showed that modern war exacts of command a science and a method without which one saves nothing, not even honor." The *École de Guerre,* whatever its faults, did teach some of that. But "nothing comes only from mind," and the French army improved its armaments as well as its instruction during this period.

---

*Neither the portrait of Gambetta nor that of Chanzy is placed in the center of the section; they are not equidistant from the center. The sections after the chapter on Napoleon are not structured as those before the chapter on Napoleon.

It was also during this period that, "for better or worse," France "took the first rank in the race to new lands." The colonies were "an excellent school of initiative and energy," providing the army with varied terrains and dangers. But they misdirected that initiative and energy:

> Above all, France always looked toward the Vosges. In distracting some troops, would it not commit an infidelity?

The nation, "which desired peace, caressed, at the same time hopes of revenge." Again the theme of hope, this time directed at the recovery of Alsace and Lorraine: colonialism diluted it.

By the 1890's, the desire for revenge faded. Between 1871 and 1891 the population of France declined from equality with that of Germany to sixty-five percent of that of Germany. And "political struggles divided the citizens": "To establish the Republic, to put in place the republicans, in a country in which one great party remained attached to the past, this did not happen without battles that absorbed the best of ardors and ambitions." De Gaulle, who called for a "national refounding" in *Vers l'armée de métier,* knows what such an effort can provoke. In the 1890's, too,

> A sort of doubt of itself invaded a people humiliated by defeat and ener-vated by polemic. What was most elevated in French thought turned away from national sources.

Kant, Fichte, Hegel and Nietzsche were studied in the Sorbonne; Fourier, Proudhon, Le Play and Blanqui were "disdained," Marx respected.

Anti-militarism grew, especially as the Dreyfus Affair continued. There were fewer active and effective soldiers. Technological progress might have recovered for France "the superiority she lost in the domain of mass," but the army, intimidated by the hostility of the Chamber of Deputies, did not reform itself. More important, "the army itself manifested none of the ardor to renew itself that commands the spirit of the times." Believing the "will to vanquish" sufficient, the leaders neglected material. De Gaulle need not make the contemporary parallels explicit, and he does not.

Finally, also resulting from the Dreyfus Affair, numerous arbitrary decisions were made regarding punishment and favors, "under the pretext of assuring the loyalty of the army." Informants, dismissals and duels proliferated; discipline suffered.

At the end of the nineteenth century, German leaders were satisfied with the *status quo*. But with the Germans "moderation does not endure"; they began to acquire colonies, gratifying a new taste for expansion. De Gaulle's observation in the third section is meant as an obvious warning: "the inclination of History always brings the Germans back to the struggle against the Gauls." He explains this not here but in *Vers l'armée de métier;* what he calls "History" combines geography and national temperament. After 1905 (the year of the first Moroccan crisis), events "brought to conscious opinion that conjunction of obscure forces that the Ancients named Destiny, Bossuet, divine judgment, Darwin, law of species, which pushed Europe to the catastrophe." This "change of the public *esprit*" affected the army; "solicitude replaced the indifference, if not the disaffection, which the State evinced toward the military element." A regeneration of the army began, insufficient in view of the Germans' advantage. De Gaulle takes the opportunity to regret France's lack of a professional army at that time and, by implication, now.

*

"The Great War is a revolution," a true mass-war, with millions fighting.

> . . . the regime on which the world lived was turned over in its foundations. Farewell, liberty, in production, distribution, exchange; finished, the stability of classes and of fortunes; suspended, elections; supervised, opinions; censored,

74

the press. Thoughts, passions, interests were concentrated on the same terrible and obsessing drama.

"Like other revolutions this one was only the issue, by means of a cataclysm, of changes begun long ago": universal suffrage, equality of rights and burdens, obligatory instruction, the effacement of local character by industry and urban life, standardization of objects and subjects (by machines and journalists, respectively), "the ubiquity of interests" resulting from moveable property, the exaltation of "the sentiment of the collective" by parties, syndicates, athletics, "a thousand common constraints imposed by transportation, circulation and hygiene." "In brief, this uniform, agglomerated, precipitated life, to which the mechanics of the century submitted contemporaries, determined them in advance to submit to gatherings in mass, gigantic shocks without gradation, which marked the war of peoples."

August 20-23, 1914 was the time of the "first shock" of modern war, "an immense surprise" to men whose strategy, tactics and illusions were formed in the previous century. Marching in columns and trained to attack, infantrymen were exploded by artillery shells. (De Gaulle fought in the early months of the war, and his description feels like a memory of something lived, not read.)

> . . . reports, histories, journals, would be able to give a logical appearance to a thousand confused events. But the actors, at the moment, only had one thought: "It is absurd!"

A "precipitous retreat" followed that shock, and soon the German Emperor was in Paris: "Such is the infirmity of our Northern frontier, that one reverse suffices to put France in peril of dying." General Joffre, a believer of "the doctrines of the school," now "discern[ed] that the only recourse was in himself . . . [and] freed himself from the theories and raised against the event his powerful personality." That personality included such virtues as good sense, obstinateness and insensibility to physical hardships.

Joffre counter-attacked. Although materially inferior, the French army won because it surprised the Germans (confirming de Gaulle's statement in *Vers l'armée de métier,* that the French are bad at preparing and good at improvising, whereas the Germans are good at preparing and bad at improvising). "For the first time, in more than one hundred years, France had defeated Germany in a general battle." The "poison of doubt" entered the Germans' blood; an "assurance in the national force" bolstered the French, "a people long dispersed in humiliation." This is, I think, the first Biblical allusion in de Gaulle's writings.

The next section contains de Gaulle's account of the middle three years of the war, in which the adversaries, equal in number, material and valor, were stalemated. He describes the complicated preparation necessary for starting an attack, and tells of soldiers calculating their chances of survival by watching the enemy's artillery. He describes the monotonous rhythm of the battle, the night after it, the officers' calculations for the next day, the enemy counter-offensive. And he concludes:

> Implacable, gloomy, ruinous for the defense as well as for the attack, such was the war of wear [*la guerre d'usure*]: of immense and valiant armies devoured on the spot; of prodigies of courage, activity, skill, accomplished on two sides; of gigantic labors, undertaken, destroyed, begun again; of battles of many months, fought on confined terrains, with an unheard-of expenditure of human lives and means; ten million soldiers disabled on the French front, a billion shells fired; and, in spite of everything, an obstinately immobile front, starts without victory, a task always obstinate and of which the end was deferred in proportion to the efforts; *espérance* [hope, trust, expectation] that lived on credit.

If there is a central theme to de Gaulle's rapport with the French it is the attempt to find a basis for French *espérance* during a time when such bases seemed rotted.

In the chapter's, and the book's, final section de Gaulle brings his readers to the end of the 'Great War.' Errors and delays caused the death of 3.5% of the French population — a much higher percentage than in any other country. As the war continued discontent increased, which "turned into indiscipline." Fatigue caused many desertions. Pétain saw that and counterracted it by allowing lengthier furloughs, more honors. He had armaments improved. "Passing through the winter of such a war [in 1917-1918], the army retrieved its equilibrium" because "in a struggle of material, morale is only a consequence of the value of the apparatus."

To sustain morale and employ material, leaders are necessary, but France had too many of them. "Assuredly, the political game gives the exercise of power a deplorable character of instability, of tumult." In four years France had five presidents, seven cabinets and seven war ministers; de Gaulle is contemptuous of "politics" and "politicians" insofar as they fail to serve France, particularly insofar as they fail to defend France, in war and in peace. What is now called 'interest-group liberalism' opposes every Gaullist inclination.

Good leaders did exist. Poincaré, "the reason of France," and Clemençeau, France's "rage," earned de Gaulle's approval. Among the generals, Pétain "inculcated in the army the art of the real and of the possible." By the tactic of "alternating methodical attack and well-calculated defense" and of concentrating "all efforts in one, that wilfullness to constantly double the stake, that passion for risk, which are the essence of strategy," Pétain revivified the French troops.

La France et son armée ends with a panegyric to the French nation. It is not an ordinary panegyric because de Gaulle balances virtues with vices: the French people is by turns "tyrant, victim or champion," a people of sorrows and vices that "experience has not uprooted," and of illusions, but also a people of hope, strength, enterprise and combat, "always in the limelight of History . . . faithfully reflecting itself in the mirror of its army." De Gaulle's ambivalence corresponds to contradictory elements: his panegyric, more realistic than most, seems to be an attempt to inspire *espérance* or *espoir* among the French, without the flattery that yields complacency. The French weren't listening.

La France et son armeé ends with a specific expression of the generality that ends *Vers l'armée de métier*. Its narrative ends with the end of the 'Great War,' whose aftermath *Vers l' armée de métier* describes. In both theme and narrative it points to *Vers l'armée de métier,* completing the circle.

CHAPTER 8

WAR AND POLITICS: REFLECTIONS ON *LA FRANCE ET SON ARMÉE*

Military force helps to build a state, and de Gaulle observes that wars fought by states have "value only in virtue of a *politique*." A strong country needs a "grand design," and a grand design requires a "just proportion" between the end and the means, without uncontrollable personal or national passions. For that reason the 'nobility' of France's neoclassical period were encouraged to fight in the army (deferring or extinguishing political ambitions) and the mass of Frenchmen did not participate in military affairs. "[A]t no other period in History was war, in fact, more closely obedient to *la politique*."

The French Revolution, following the corruption of the neo-classical order,* yielded first the ascendency of the mass-army (following the ascendence of the mass, or much of it, to political power). After a brief period of renewed order and discipline, Napoleon emerged, and his vast personal ambition caused him to ignore that "souls, like matter, have their limits." After Napoleon, France did not recover its balance — a fact de Gaulle criticizes and laments.

Much of de Gaulle's outline of the proper relation between war and politics evidently derives from Clausewitz. War, "a part of man's social existence," "is nothing but the continuation of policy with other means," added to specifically political means. The means should be commensurate with the end, for "once the expenditure of effort exceeds the value of the political object, the object must be renounced and peace must follow." A modest political end requires modest military force; an extreme end may require extreme force.** With de Gaulle, Clausewitz cites the military effect of that most famous political revolution: "the transformation of war [in 1792 and after] resulted from the transformation of politics [in 1789 and after]."

Clausewitz, however, goes on to contend that war and politics share a fundamental identity. "Politics . . . is the womb in which war develops — where its outlines already exist in their hidden rudimentary form . . . ." In a sense this must be true, or else political orders could not generate wars without some intervention, divine or infernal. But Clausewitz apparently means something more complex than a reference to human nature or to the 'inevitable' conflicts between differing countries.

> Is war not just another expression of [governments'] thoughts, another form of speech or writing? Its grammar, indeed, may be its own, but not its logic.

This suggestion pleases Marx and Lenin, who believe that political life consists of a 'mass of contradictions' or power-clashes. What Clausewitz may intend as a more or less precise metaphor — the "grammar" and "logic" of force — Marx and Lenin took literally, insisting that material force, not *logos,* rules political life without qualification, and that *logos* is epiphenomenal.***

---

*De Gaulle might have studied this corruption with more care; for if neoclassicism was sound, why did it decline?

**Bismarck's corollary: " . . . it is a political maxim after a victory not to inquire how much you can squeeze out of your opponent, but only to consider what is politically necessary." [Bismarck: *Reflections and Reminiscences,* edited by Theodore S. Hamerow, Harper and Row, New York and Evanston, 1968, p. 142.]

***Obviously, Clausewitz does not share the Marxian belief that 'contradictions' must be resolved by 'History,' that political and military life disappear when the 'contradictions' are resolved.

By obscuring the difference between the logic of words and thoughts and the 'logic' of force, Clausewitz tends to overlook that real logic proves statements whereas force's 'logic' proves capabilities. Thus Hitler proved that he could overrun France without proving Nazism politically superior to parliamentarism. Precisely because politics is a realm of purpose, whereas war is an instrument for a purpose, the former should determine the latter — as Clausewitz himself insists.

Nonetheless, everyone knows that politics involves force, although it does not always involve military force. And certain kinds of politics (French parliamentarism, for example) seem vulnerable to conquest. Montesquieu considers these problems.

*

Montesquieu's Rome saw a republic whose *ethos* was military. "[A]n endless and violent war" was "the very principle of its government." Hence the Romans feared idleness more than enemies; hence "constancy and valor became necessary to them." Courage, however, is "the virtue which is the consciousness of one's own strength"; strength of power underlies Montesquieu's conception of (at least this) "virtue," or, as another might spell it, *"virtù"*. Successful war meant conquest; conquest yielded pillage (the basis of Rome's non-commercial economics); pillage yielded wealth; wealth yielded more power. But the propertied class that arose yielded arts, luxury, decline, for not only do the rich become decadent, but the poor who are artisans have "no country in the proper sense of the term," as they can pursue their trade anywhere; with "little to lose or preserve," artisans make poor citizens. Montesquieu writes that occasions only "produce" change, whereas human passions are the "causes" of "great changes" in politics, both for greatness and for decline. A republic —to Montesquieu, a regime ruled by the people — became military because pillage satisfied a distinctly popular appetite or passion: greed. That same appetite caused the republic's decline. The apparently non-economic *ethos* in fact existed by 'virtue' of an economic phenomenon.

Montesquieu's importance comes from his status as a mediator after Machiavelli's spirited and martial form of modernity confronts the appetitive and economic form of modernity propounded by Hobbes and Locke. To speak more strikingly and less precisely, France, located between Italy and England, contained a struggle between them. However, Montesquieu predetermines the outcome of this confrontation by metamorphosing the Rome presented in Machiavelli's *Discourses* — making it based fundamentally on both an appetite of the people (not the spiritedness of the leaders) and on the popular fear that rationally unrestrained spiritedness yielded.

Montesquieu nonetheless recognizes the advantage of Rome's apparent militarism. He contrasts the military republic of Rome with its rival, the commercial republic of Carthage. In Rome, men obtained public office by means of virtue, thereby gaining honor; in Carthage men obtained public office by means of purchase, thereby gaining a salary. In Rome before its decadence there was no individual wealth; in Carthage there was. In Rome, war united all interests or factions; in Carthage, which had a war faction and a peace faction, war antagonized the interests or factions. Rome was governed by laws, and the people allowed the senate to direct public affairs; Carthage was governed by abuses, and therefore the people, distrustful of politicians, wanted to direct public affairs. Rome made war with virtue, constancy, strength, poverty; Carthage made war with opulence. The Romans, ambitious from pride, wanted to command, whereas the Carthaginians, ambitious from avarice, wanted to acquire; hence the Romans, guided by the passion for glory, obeyed the laws passionately, not be fear or by what Montesquieu calls reason, whereas the avaricious Carthaginians "always

78

made war without loving it," and often "accept[ed] the most severe conditions of peace."* The central contrast — Rome used its own troops; Carthage used foreign troops — derives from Machiavellian advice. The Romans used greater forces for defense; the Carthaginians used greater forces to attack (this is not Machiavellian, but anticipates Clausewitz). Rome had secure 'geopolitical' surroundings; Carthage did not. Roman citizens and soldiers were fed well; Carthaginian soldiers and civilians were occasionally starved. Roman troops that fled a battle were decimated and sent back; defeated Carthaginian troops insolently punished the generals. The Romans were stern to conquered peoples; the Carthaginians were very harsh to conquered peoples. Montesquieu adds that Alexandria weakened Carthage by rivaling it as a trading center; he also remarks that the Carthaginian cavalry and navy excelled Rome's, but in later chapters he questions the military importance of cavalry and of navies.

Still, a great leader can temporarily reverse a great advantage. Hannibal won several battles. "Rome was saved by the strength of its institutions," which were not yet corrupted; for the consternation of a warlike people becomes courage, whereas the consternation of "a vile populace" becomes consciousness of weakness, that is, cowardice. Rome's eventual victory came because the great leader finally lost the support of his corrupt people. War, although based on economic appetite, necessitated the cultivation of spiritedness for some time, and spirit-strengthening institutions saved Rome from conquest, yielded eventual victory.

The success of the Roman *ethos* brought its decline. "Nature has given states certain limits to mortify the ambition of men"; Montesquieu intends nothing teleological, however, for he explains that while one may conquer with all of one's forces, one defends one's conquests with only part of them. Nonetheless, one can preserve conquests by dividing a people after conquering it and by abstaining from changing its laws and customs. What Rome could not bear was rapid expansion and quickly-acquired revenue that Pompey's successes brought. Things became too easy to do. If poverty is virtue and riches are scorned, the few who are rich must yield to the many who are poor. But after democratizing, riches become powerful because the many are avaricious, and that in turn ruins the martial republic. The generals of an extended martial republic, far from the center of civilian authority, ally themselves with avaricious soldiers and civilians (Sulla, for example, accustomed his men to rapine, inducing new 'needs'). In Rome, civil war resulted.**

The same laws that encourage successful conquest do not, finally, cause good government. A politics of war can only appeal to a republic if it produces the material things which corrupts the necessary military characteristic: spiritedness. Avarice and war, compatible for a while, eventually conflict. The regime changes.

After the demise of the republic, the emperors adopted peace as their goal. Peace brought indolence (to Rome, whose most-feared enemy had been idleness). Some of the early emperors remained quite fierce — a remnant of republican militarism — but the empire at last

---

*The contradiction between the glory-loving Machiavellian Romans that Montesquieu presents here and the Romans whose underlying 'cause' is economic appetite need not be an unintentional error on Montesquieu's part. Perhaps Rome itself contained the contradiction, a contradiction that eventually ruined it. Notice that Montesquieu's analysis predates Marxist' logic of History.' Unlike Marx, Montesquieu does not imagine that these contradictions will vanish one day. He would balance some of them by establishing a political *concordia discors,* a mixed regime.

**Compare this with Tacitus, writing about a later period: "That old passion for power which has ever been innate in man increased and broke out as the Empire grew in greatness. In a state of moderate dimensions equality was easily preserved; but when the world had been subdued . . . and men had the leisure to covet wealth which they might enjoy in security, the early conflicts between the patricians and the people were kindled to a flame." [*The History,* Alfred J. Church and W.J. Brodribb translation, Modern Library, New York, 1942.]

succumbed to fiercer barbarian peoples.

Here, in a word, is the history of the Romans. By means of their maxims they conquered all peoples, but when they had succeeded in doing so, their republic could not endure. It was necessary to change the government, and the contrary maxims employed by the new government made their greatness collapse.

If greatness or grandeur is political strength or power, and virtue (especially the preeminently military virtue, courage) is the consciousness of strength or power, how does the power that wealth brings yield the decline of power? Apparently, consciousness is the most important defense. Luxury, Montesquieu may imply, obscures power-consciousness, and so does the poverty of artisans. This in turn yields Epicureanism for the rich and Christianity for the poor; power-consciousness, hence patriotism, declines or goes elsewhere.

*

Montesquieu, a modern, might reasonably be suspected of intentionally modernizing Rome.* His diagnosis, based as it is almost exclusively on material power, neglects the problem of justice, central to earlier political philosophers. Thucydides, the greatest student of the relationship between war and politics in ancient Greece, does not overlook the problem of justice.

To an extent, Thucydides too is a 'modernizer.' Like Montesquieu, he concerns himself with greatness. Unlike Plato, he remarks on "weakness of ancient times" and explicitly denies the existence of a Golden Age. The earliest Hellenes, he tells us, were nomads, and "consequently neither built large cities nor attained to any other form of greatness." Pirates, they satisfied economic needs and appetites. Tyrants ruled next, and safety, "the great aim of their policy, prevented anything great proceeding from them." Sparta defeated most of the Hellenic tyrannies; then Athens became powerful, making war "inevitable." Sparta and Athens concerned themselves with justice, as their predecessors did not.

Thucydides shows that the exigencies of war damage justice as conceived by Sparta and by Athens. The Corinthians, warning the Spartans of Athenian power, say that the Spartan *politeia* yields an *ethos* of moderation and a limited knowledge of foreign politics. "[Y]ou alone wait till the power of the enemy is becoming twice its original size, instead of crushing it in its infancy." Spartan justice, based on moderation and piety, informs an *ethos* that yields a conserving, cautious, procrastinating citizenry. The Athenian *politeia* yields an *ethos* that yields an innovative, adventurous and bold, restless citizenry. "[C]onstant necessities of action" necessitate "the constant improvement of methods," and "it is the law in art, so in politics, that improvements ever prevail." Montesquieu learned from this passage, perhaps; his Romans, however, combine at least some of Sparta's moderation with Athenian boldness. Justice and piety, clearly, do not determine the outcome of battles; moreover, in a world wherein the strong do what they can and the weak suffer what they must, imperfect justice becomes the best one hopes for, as the attempt to achieve perfect justice leaves one vulnerable to radically unjust adversaries. In Plato's *Republic,* Socrates wisely minimizes the realm of foreign policy.**

*I refer not only to some of his veiled allusions to Louis XIV — more prominent in the footnotes than in the text — but to the philosophic content of the book, which owes more to Machiavelli and Locke than to, for example, Cicero.

**See Leo Strauss: "On Thucydides' War of the Peloponnesians and the Athenians," in *The City and Man,* [Rand McNally and Company, Chicago, 1964]. Strauss follows Plato's insight, and remarks that for Thucydides injustice and immoderation do not necessarily lead to military failure; the loss of harmony between private interests and the public interest of the leaders causes military failure. Montesquieu regards that as one cause of military failure.

In war, there is no genuine ideal. One intends 'economical' victory, and such victory is a thing that can exist in the material world. In politics, there are ideals. By definition not achievable except in speech, they influence political life nonetheless — presented, in well-ordered countries, in the diminsihed forms of custom (laws, habits, institutions) and rhetoric. Philosophers usually do not seek the perfect war in speech.* War injures decent political life because at its best it is no ideal, only an instrument. Only in an extremely corrupt political order could war elevate political life. But an extremely corrupt political order rarely yields victory in war; war injures, sometimes destroys, decent political life but almost always destroys a certain kind of extremely indecent political life — namely, the kind characterized by indolence and cowardice.

Statesmen must then attempt to ready their countries for war (in peace and during a war) by balancing peaceful and war-like virtues. In Athens, for example, the populace sways from rashness (Nicias, trying to persuade the Athenians not to undertake the Sicilian expedition, describes the vastness of the effort it would require, unintentionally arousing their spiritedness) to fear (after the expedition's failure, "in the panic of the moment [the Athenians] were ready to be as prudent as possible.").

To remedy such inconstancy (typical of democracies, in which appetites or, at most, passions rule, oscillating from extreme to extreme), Pericles makes his celebrated funeral oration. He praises non-democratic virtues (honor, courage, glory) by invoking a democratic virtue: liberty. "In education, where our rivals from their very cradles by a painful discipline seek after manliness, we at Athens live exactly as we please, and yet are just as ready to encounter every legitimate danger." Moreover, "the palm of courage will surely be adjudged most justly to those who best know the difference between hardship and pleasure and yet are never tempted to shrink from danger." Pericles knows that the principle underlying democracy does not suffice to defend it, that liberty, another democrat's taste, is more useful. He contrives to en-courage the Athenians by simultaneously reminding them of their distaste for "painful discipline" (the opposite of liberty) and their love of pleasure in such a way as to appeal to the mean between pain and pleasure. With Pericles, Athens can achieve a political moderation distinct from Spartan inertia.

Pericles goes on to reconcile, in rhetoric if not in reason, the contradictory democratic tastes for individuality and for equality. The dead Athenians, in "this offering of their lives made in common by them all," received "each of them individually that renown which never grows old." (In fact, of course, the only dead Athenian that we remember from these pages is Pericles.)

The excitable democrats of Athens are not the only kind of democrats. The Syracusans have "a constitutional love of quiet," according to their foremost statesman, Hermocrates. When reports of an Athenian attack-force reach the city, this love of quiet inclines them to discount the reports. Athenagoras, leader of the democratic party (his name is therefore appropriate), assures his countrymen that the reports are invented, that Hermocrates attempts "to frighten your people and get into their hands the government." He assumes that the Athenians are as rational as he is (a typical democrat's misjudgment) — that they know they can't defeat Sicily and so will not try. Fortunately, a general decides to prepare, anyway.

Without a Pericles, or a prudent general, democracies seem unlikely to make war or peace successfully. (Thucydides, an Athenian, knows that democracies produce men who understand the reasons for the failure of democracies, that non-democracies produce men who defeat democracies while believing chimerical reasons for their victories.) In what is surely the reverse of Machiavellianism, the clear-sighted Hermocrates says that "A man can control his own desires, but he cannot likewise control circumstances . . . ." Well-ordered political life

*Two philosophers who use war as a metaphor for better things — Heraclitus and Nietzsche — partake of the anti-idealist and anti-rational tradition in philosophy.

inclines citizens to control desires (appetites and passions), thus allowing them to act appropriately in varying circumstances. Spartans remained the same in all circumstances; Athenians changed uncontrollably as circumstances changed. Both, then, were flawed. Statesmen who are neither simply oligarchic nor simply democratic can sometimes remedy such vices, more or less, and thereby defer disaster in war and in peace.

*

By Tocqueville's period, men attempted to control circumstances more than their desires. But Machiavellian passion had, in most of the West, become Lockean appetite. Montesquieu, thinking of the modern West rather than ancient Rome, writes that "the spirit of monarchy is war and the enlargement of dominion: peace and moderation are the spirit of a republic."

Writing less than three decades after Napoleon's death, Tocqueville contends that "If . . . a state of society can ever be founded in which every man shall have something to keep and a little to take from others, much will have been done for the peace of the world." He knows that American democracy resembles such a "state of society": "The ever increasing numbers of men of property who are lovers of peace, the growth of personal wealth which war so rapidly consumes, the mildness of manners, the gentleness of heart, the tendencies to pity which are produced by the equality of conditions, that coolness of understanding which renders men comparatively insensible to the violent and poetical excitement of arms, all these causes concur to quench the military spirit." A democratic populace in late modernity does not honor the military; such a military may or may not honor itself. If it does honor itself, the military in a democracy may endanger the regime by inciting war (the only condition that brings rapid advancement to soldiers) or by causing revolution. Protracted wars, especially, "endanger the freedom of a democratic country," and protracted wars are the kind modern democracies are most likely to win, as they are slow to make war (they are Syracusan rather than Athenian) but powerful when mobilized (Tocqueville writes in the period of the mass-army, as Clausewitz did).

Tocqueville's solution resembles that of Hermocrates. "Teach the citizens to be educated, orderly, firm and free, and the soldiers will be disciplined and obedient"; the nation's *ethos* will suffuse the army because the soldiers, after all, come from the nation. Tocqueville acknowledges ancient wisdom in that:

> Among the ancients none were admitted into the armies but freemen and citizens, who differed but little from one another and were accustomed to treat each other as equals. In this respect it may be said that the armies of antiquity were democratic, although they came out of the bosom of aristocracy; the consequence was that in those armies a sort of fraternal familiarity prevailed between the officers and the men.

The mass-armies of the early nineteenth century usually reflected a despotic political order. Tocqueville knows that a different military order could work better and threaten democratic regimes less.

But Tocqueville sees a more fundamental problem:

> If the love of physical gratification and the taste for well-being, which are naturally suggested to men by a state of equality, were to possess the mind of a democratic people and to fill it completely, the manners of the nation would become so totally opposed to military pursuits that perhaps even the army would eventually acquire a love of peace . . . .

"Nothing is more dangerous for the freedom and the tranquillity of a people than an army afraid of war," not only because other armies may not be afraid of war, but because such an army may retain its revolutionary inclination: surrender *and/or* revolution.

Tocqueville's solution recalls Machiavelli's remarks on the "effeminacy" of his time (attributed by him to Christianity, of course, not democracy). A democracy must preserve "the manliness of its character," its spiritedness. Like Pericles, Tocqueville recognizes that to do this liberty must be celebrated in a certain way.

> It should never be forgotten by the princes and other leaders of democratic nations that nothing but the love and the habit of freedom can maintain an advantageous contest with the love and the habit of physical well-being. I can conceive nothing better prepared for subjection, in case of defeat, than a democratic people without free institutions.

Without liberty, and the spiritedness (however limited) liberty requires (because liberty forces a citizen to assert himself or be victimized, whereas in the absence of liberty the subject who asserts himself is the one victimized), democracy's egalitarianism yields the unqualified rule of appetites, deadly in a world of countries that are not ruled by appetites. To those who object that the few may be as appetitive as the many, Tocqueville replies that "among [such] nations the enjoyments of civil life exercise less influence on the manners of the army, because among those nations [the few] command the army, and . . . however plunged in luxurious pleasures, [the few have] many other passions besides that of [their] own well-being, and to satisfy those passions more thoroughly [their] well being will be readily sacrificed." One might add that if a corrupt few rule, such sacrifices as need be imposed may often be shunted to the backs of the many. And as technology advances, especially in countries ruled harshly by the few, technology makes the many less capable of resistance.

*

That liberty, and appeals thereto, suffice to defend the regime of egalitarianism from the warlike, that they can prevent the 'feminization' of democratic politics, is at best a questionable thesis. They do, surely, help for a time. But even the skilful Pericles must appeal to non-democratic standards, making one suspect that Periclean democracy (essentially a popular monarchy) depended on principles remaining from non-democratic regimes.

Thucydides and Montesquieu finally advocate their versions of what Aristotle calls a "polity" or mixed regime — that is, a regime in which democratic, monarchic, aristocratic and oligarchic elements combine in a *concordia discors*. Such regimes — eventually unbalanced, corrupted, as surely as any pure democracy or oligarchy — nonetheless sustain themselves longer and (Aristotle would add) serve *humanitas* better than others.

FIFTH PART

CHAPTER 9

MÉMOIRES DE GUERRE (1954, 1956, 1959)

In the nineteen-fifties de Gaulle wrote his memoirs, dividing them into three volumes, with eight, eight and seven titled chapters, respectively. They are more than war-memoirs because de Gaulle, when he wrote them, was more than a soldier.

*   *   *

All my life, I have had a certain idea of France. Sentiment inspires it in me as much as reason. What there is, in me, of the affective naturally imagines France, like the princess of the tales or the Madonna of the frescoes, as devoted to an eminent and exceptional destiny. I have, instinctively, the impression that Providence created her for consummate success or exemplary disasters. If it happens that mediocrity marks, however, her acts and deeds, I feel the sensation of an absurd anomaly, imputable to the faults of the French, not to the genius of *la patrie*. But also, the positive side of my *esprit* convinces me that France is really herself only at the first rank; that, only vast enterprises are capable of compensating the ferments of dispersion that her people carries in itself; that our country, as it is, among others, as they are, must, under pain of mortal danger, aim high and stand straight. In brief, to my judgment, France cannot be France without grandeur.

In *La discorde chez l'ennemi* de Gaulle wrote that France ought to be based on *mesure*. But *mesure* supports an extreme — grandeur — and its absence yields another extreme —the exemplary disaster. Providence "created her" for these extremes; de Gaulle does not suggest that Providence guides France's destiny, but that it gave France its "genius," which guides that destiny. Otherwise, France's disasters could not be exemplary, as one does not instruct Providence. One instructs the French, who are not identical to France. The French carry "ferments of dispersion" within them, only compensated by "vast enterprises" (we recall, from *La discorde chez l'ennemi,* that the German leaders used this strategy). De Gaulle does not mention who it is that instructs the French, who it is that defines the needed vast enterprise; evidently, only those who understand grandeur can do that: writers, statesmen. But what is this grandeur, this thing without which France *is not*? *Mémoires de guerre* chronicle the Gaullist quest for grandeur, for France.

De Gaulle provides us with a partial answer immediately. As an adolescent, he writes, he felt "attraction, but also severity," toward the debates "in the forum . . . carried away as I was by the intelligence, the ardor, the eloquence," but "wounded to see such gifts wasted in political confusion and national divisions," even as war approached.* He describes the first world war in a way that implies its parallelism with the second: France, left undefended by a declining population, "hollow ideologies," "the negligence of the powers," nonetheless rose and, by "an incredible effort," won. The basis of the victory was the moral unity of the French, forged by Joffre, then by Clemençeau; if one recognizes the parallelism, de Gaulle was Joffre and Clemençeau, soldier and statesman. The French then "rejected grandeur and returned to confusion" — as they did in 1946, prompting de Gaulle's resignation.

---

*De Gaulle obviously does not subscribe to the sort of argument James Madison makes in the tenth *Federalist*. But Madisonian faction is, primarily, economic. The faction de Gaulle saw threatened the regime itself: not rich versus poor but the rich who were monarchists versus the poor who were socialists. Madison did not have to deal with that to the extent de Gaulle did, because the American revolutionary war eliminated most of the monarchists.

De Gaulle writes that from 1932 to 1937 he was assigned to the *Sécretariat Général de la Défense Nationale,* a permanent body at the Premier's disposal that supposedly prepared the state and the nation for war. Numerous changes of government allowed no policy to develop, save the one remaining from the 1920's. The ministers, "consumed and paralyzed" by partisan struggles, did little even during their brief tenures. The army was much more stable — ossified, even, enamored of old-fashioned strategies. The most notable of those was "the fixed and continuous front," embodied by the famous 'Maginot Line.'

> Such a conception of war accorded with the spirit of the regime. That, which weakness of [governmental] power and political discords condemned to stagnation, could not fail to espouse a system static to this degree.

De Gaulle here recognizes the architectonic nature of politics. It is the political system that shapes military strategy, more than military strategy shapes the political system. De Gaulle has made the transition from the military to the political.

He adds that "the state of mind of the country" found this "reassuring panacea" comforting. Those who espoused it were applauded and elected; no one *wanted* to notice "the revolution brought . . . by the force of the motor." In a parliamentary democracy, one infers, the mass opinion that rules does not necessarily rule well, and the nature of the regime allows it to continue to rule badly. The nature of another regime, in another place, may allow one country to defeat the parliamentary democracy in a war.

De Gaulle recounts his campaign to enlighten the French. After summarizing *Vers l'armée de métier,* he emphasizes that the Army would not transform itself unaided, that Army reform was only one part of a national renewal, including political renewal.* In 1935 de Gaulle enlisted the support of several deputies, including Paul Reynaud, but his proposal was defeated by powerful men who included Marshall Pétain and Léon Blum. The latter worried about a professional army's effect on republicanism — by which he probably meant parliamentarism. Again, de Gaulle was raising a question of regime, of 'who rules?' — of politics' deepest meaning. De Gaulle insists that such men opposed him uneasily, almost with a bad conscience, rendering to him "the sad homage of remorse."

Hitler took the Rhineland, and France could have stopped him, except that "our organization, the nature of our methods, even the spirit of our national defense, tempted toward inaction a power which was only too inclined [to be inactive] and prevented us from marching." In 1938 Hitler attacked Austria, then Czechoslovakia; "in these successive acts of the same tragedy, France played the role of the victim who awaits her turn." *La France et son armée,* published the same year, was "the ultimate warning that, in my modest place, I addressed to *la patrie* on the eve of the cataclysm." *La patrie,* not the French: by then de Gaulle could only address France, not the French.

The government declared war in September of 1939; de Gaulle implies that it did so only because Britain did. This stagnation resulted in *"attentisme,"* the "wait-and-see" tactic (if it can be called that) of the "Phony War" that ensued. Writing in 1954, de Gaulle finds himself capable of a kind of humor: "Conforming to habits, the regime, incapable of adopting the measures which would assure salvation, but looking to put itself and public opinion on the wrong scent, started a ministerial crisis." When Reynaud became prime minister on March 23, 1940, replacing Daladier, de Gaulle visited him and saw

> . . . to what point of demoralization the regime had come. In all the parties, in the press, in the administration, in business, in the trade unions, very influential cells were overtly devoted to the idea of stopping the war.

*He also refuses to claim that his ideas were original - as some propagandists claimed — but instead writes that he took several ideas and made them into "a whole for the benefit of France" [I, 17, *15*]: an original synthesis.

Some were Fascist or Nazi sympathizers, others were communists supporting the Nazi-Soviet pact of 1939. The masses were bewildered. Reynaud wanted de Gaulle as Secretary of the War Committee; Daladier, now Minister of National Defense and War Minister, blocked the appointment. 'Nothing personal' — but Daladier "had espoused the system" then in place. On May 10, the German offensive began.

> One can say that in one week destiny was sealed. On the fatal slope whereon an excessive error had, for a long while, engaged us, the army, the State, France, rolled now with a vertiginous rhythm.

De Gaulle was assigned to command the newly-formed Fourth Armored Division. It was at Laon, with his division, that he decided to continue the war until the enemy's defeat, regardless of France's defeat. The defeat corrupted the French military leadership.

> The crumbling of all of the system of doctrines and of organization, to which our leaders had attached themselves, deprived them of their energy [as always, to de Gaulle, faith yields energy, its loss weakens men]. A sort of moral inhibition made them, suddenly, doubt all and, in particular, themselves.

As they well might have doubted themselves before: their timing was unfortunate. De Gaulle, who didn't share their faith, and so didn't lose his, did well. At Abbeville his troops caused the Germans to withdraw. He does not fail to suggest that France would have done well, too, had an elite armored corps been constituted earlier.

This deficiency of material complemented deficient leadership. General Weygand, the Commander-in-Chief, was a defeatist not only in his judgment of the situation but by temperament. An excellent assistant to commanders, he lacked the character to be a commander: "To take action on his responsibility, to want only one's own mark on it, to face destiny alone, harsh and exclusive passion which characterizes the leader." Nor had he exercised command before. It was an error, "habitual in our politics," to give him command in those circumstances. Politics, again: de Gaulle continually returns to French politics in this first chapter.

> The regime, without faith or vigor, opted for the worst *abandon*]abandonment and/or lack of restraint]. France would therefore pay, not only [with] a disastrous military armistice, but also [with] the enslavement of the State. So true it is that, faced with great [*grand*] perils, salvation is only in greatness [*grandeur*].

Gaullist symmetry does not regard 'muddling through' as anything more than a muddle. Grandeur, always aspired to, becomes necessary when great perils threaten. Grandeur involves not only unity, but faith and vigor.

*

The first chapter of the first volume of *Mémoires de guerre* was titled *La Pente (The Slope)*: after *La Pente, La Chute (The Fall)*. In early June, Reynaud made de Gaulle Undersecretary of State for National Defense. In this capacity he met Churchill three times, and was impressed by his character and his rhetoric. Churchill had "a cordial reserve, seized already, and not perhaps without an obscure satisfaction, by the terrible and magnificent prospect of an England left alone on its island that he himself would conduct in the effort toward salvation." It is an extraordinary insight, perhaps into Churchill's character, surely into de Gaulle's.

De Gaulle wanted the French government to leave the continent and resume the battle in Africa. But Reynaud waffled, telling the French in a June 12 radio broadcast that if a miracle was needed to save France, he believed in that miracle. After quoting Reynaud, de Gaulle begins a new paragraph with this sentence: "It appeared to me assured that all would soon be consummated." Apparently, de Gaulle has a certain faith, but not in such a miracle. He considered resigning but allowed himself to be persuaded by Minister of the Interior Georges Mandel, who told him that France needed an "untainted man" to continue the fight.

On June 14 Reynaud seemed to decide that he would take the government to Algiers. De Gaulle went to London to arrange British help. Before leaving, he saw Pétain for the last time (Pétain, too, was in Reynaud's cabinet, and had a higher position than de Gaulle). They shook hands wordlessly, and de Gaulle takes the opportunity to give us his portrait of the Marshall. He thinks Pétain wanted glory, believing that Hitler was but another German conqueror who would withdraw after defeating the French.

> In the judgment of the old Marshall, the world character of the conflict, the possibilities of the overseas territories, the ideological consequences of the victory of Hitler, hardly entered into account. Those were not things that he had the habit of considering.

No, one supposes not. Moreover, "Old age is a shipwreck," and Pétain identified his old age with the shipwreck of France. Both, he thought, were irreversible, hopeless.

In Britain, de Gaulle and Churchill discussed the possibility of fusing the two countries in order to keep France in the war. Churchill persuaded his cabinet to approve the plan, but when de Gaulle returned to Bordeaux he learned that Reynaud had quit. He portrays Reynaud as a man who would have been effective in settled conditions, or even in an ordinary war. In 1940, in France, Reynaud's alternative to surrender was to retreat to Africa. "But that implied extreme measures: to change the High Command, to dismiss the Marshal and half of the ministers, break with certain influences [Reynaud's mistress, Hélène de Portes, was a Nazi sympathizer], resign himself to the total occupation of Metropolitan France . . . ." — in short, to jettison ordinary procedures in "a situation without precedent." Only two extremes were possible; Reynaud — habituated, perhaps, by parliamentary life — hoped for something in-between, and failed. He failed because circumstances were beyond compromise; they were, as Malraux would put it, manichean. De Gaulle does not neglect to insist on the political lesson:

> It is necessary to say that at the supreme moment the regime offered no recourse to the leader of the last government of the Third Republic. Assuredly, many men in office felt repugnance at the capitulation. But the public powers, struck by the disaster for which they felt responsible, did not react at all. While the problem was posed, on which for France all the present and all the future depended, the Parliament did not sit, the government showed itself incapable of adopting as a body a determined solution, the President of the Republic abstained from raising his voice, even in the midst of the Council of Ministers, for expressing the superior interest of the country. After all, this annihilation of the State was at the bottom of the national drama. By the light of the thunderbolt, the regime appeared, in its horrible infirmity, without any *mesure* and without any relationship with the defense, the honor, the independence of France.

If grandeur is the necessary salvation from great perils, only the state can be the instrument of grandeur. Parliament won't, can't, do it. These extreme circumstances required the extreme political act: the founding.

De Gaulle therefore went to London. "The departure took place without romanticism and without difficulty."

*

"Pursue the war? Yes, certainly! But for what end and in what limits?" Some of de

Gaulle's colleagues wanted merely to aid Britain in an organized way. Not de Gaulle: "For me, what was necessary to serve was the nation and the State" — his own. If France capitulated, after the war (whether it resulted in victory or in defeat), "the disgust that [the country] would have for itself and what it would inspire in others would poison its soul and its life for long generations." He decided to return to the war "not only the French, but France," which is both the nation and state because the state makes grandeur — the grandeur without which France is not France.

Such an effort necessitates sovereignty. De Gaulle, arriving in London, had no force or organization, no following or notoriety in France, no credit or justification abroad.

> But this very destitution traced for me my line of combat. It was in espous-
> ing, without reserving anything, the cause of national salvation that I could find
> authority. It was in acting as the inflexible champion of the nation and the State
> that it would be possible to group, among the French, consent, indeed enthus-
> iasm, and to obtain from foreigners respect and consideration.

Authority comes from espousing the cause of national salvation *(le salut national)*: enthusiastic consent from citizens, respect and consideration from foreigners derive from acting in accordance with that espousal. Authority comes from the espousal; sovereignty, which is consent and recognition, comes from acting authoritatively. De Gaulle's intransigence, which was to become famous, was a measured response to extreme circumstances: "all limited and solitary as I was, and exactly because I was, it was necessary for me to gain the summits and never descend." In this third chapter, *Le France Libre,* de Gaulle shows how he began to establish sovereignty.

De Gaulle publicly announced his espousal on June 18, 1940, over the radio from London. Repeating three times, "France is not alone," he insisted that France's Empire, the British Empire and "the immense industry of the United States" could win the war. "This war is a world war."

> Crushed today by mechanical force, we can vanquish in the future by a
> superior mechanical force. The destiny of the world is there.

Lucidity in chaos. But de Gaulle had known and written that the destiny of the world was in mechanized force; now, others listened. De Gaulle listened, too — not so much to what he was saying but to what it meant for him.

> In proportion that the irrevocable words flew away from me, I felt in myself
> a life ending itself, that which I had conducted in the framework of a solid
> France and an indivisible army. At forty-nine years of age, I was entering into
> the adventure, like a man that destiny throws outside all sequences [*séries*].

It is de Gaulle's second existential moment — the first being his first battle in World War One.

A historian has noticed that this famous "call" of June 18 (the first volume's title is *L'Appel*) was military, not political. The political announcement came the next day: "Before the confusion of French souls, before the liquidation of a government fallen under enemy servitude, before the impossibility of making our institutions work, I, General de Gaulle, French soldier and leader, I have the *conscience* of speaking in the name of France." Having attempted to persuade such French generals as Weygand, and Noguès to refuse to accept defeat, de Gaulle observed that "not one public man raised his voice to condemn the armistice."

> Before the frightening void of general renunciation, my mission appeared to
> me, at one single blow, clear and terrible. At this moment, the worst of her
> history, it was for me to assume France.

Thus he defends himself against the charge of arrogance — indeed, perhaps he is too defensive, in that we know very well that he relished the opportunity to lead France, even as Churchill relished Britain's role. De Gaulle never said *"La France, c'est moi,"* any more than Louis XIV said *"L'État, c'est moi."* He "assumed" France, spoke in France's name, because no one else was doing so.

"But there is not France without a sword"; speaking is never enough, to de Gaulle, and grandeur comes from action as much as from words. Although the military is subordinate to the political, it is still an inseparable part of 'France-ness.' He began to organize an army and a navy, hindered by the British destruction of Vichy-French ships at Mers-el-Kébir, on July 4. This act injured Free French recruiting efforts by injuring (somewhat misplaced) patriotic feelings of many anti-Vichyites still on French soil. But the men that did join formed an "elite," de Gaulle writes, characterized by a taste for risk and adventure, unity in action (and, frequently, disunity when idle — they were French), national pride, confidence.

In these early days de Gaulle avoided forming a government of any sort, not wanting "to cramp . . . the regrouping of the State." Instead, he formed a "National Committee."

*

The first three chapters of *L'Appel* contain de Gaulle's narrative of the defeat of France, including "the slope" that inclined toward the defeat, and his response to it: the formation of *La France Libre*. The following three chapter-titles are place-names: *L'Afrique, Londres, L'Orient*. Free France had no permanent base, and its odyssey had tragic as well as comic aspects.

De Gaulle chose Africa as the place to "remake an army and a sovereignty," while awaiting the United States' entry into the war. It was a good base for returning to Europe (near Italy, the Balkans, Spain); de Gaulle's presence there would establish "links of community" between France and French territories; it would help to prevent enemy annexation of those territories (to say nothing of their acquisition by allies); finally, it would end the exile of Free France, put it on French soil, if not on metropolitan French soil. Notice that, for de Gaulle, sovereignty is *made,* whereas authority, based on *le salut national,* is not made.

Although the North African territories were, *de facto,* in Vichy hands, "Black Africa" was not; the Gaullists arranged bloodless *coups d'état* where necessary, taking over friendly populations. West Africa's status was ambiguous, and the fortress at Dakar, controlled by Vichy sympathizers, was strong. Which lead to the Anglo-French attempt to win it: de Gaulle gives his side of that fiasco. Military-history enthusiasts can examine it carefully; for my purposes it suffices to note that initially de Gaulle preferred not to engage in this "vast collision" because, whatever the outcome, the shedding of blood between Frenchmen at that time would have "gravely reduced [Free French] chances." Presumably he means that Free France would have been injured by propaganda even if it had won the battle, because its legitimacy and Vichy's illegitimacy had not yet been sufficiently recognized by the French. Nonetheless de Gaulle and the British did attack Dakar, and failed to win it. Predictably, condemnations by the Vichyites, as well as by American and British newspapers followed: "the reactions to fear, both among adversaries who revenged themselves for having felt it, and among allies suddenly frightened by the check." (De Gaulle minimizes the charge made at the time, that indiscretions committed by some of the Free French in England forewarned Vichy and thus ruined the expedition; this charge served as justification or pretext for future Allied refusals to deal closely with Free France.) There were no defections among the Free French, however, and Churchill himself parried criticism of de Gaulle in Parliament.

This misfortune accelerated change in de Gaulle himself: his metamorphosis from a private to a public man.

> The fact of incarnating, for my companions, the destiny of our cause, for
> the French multitude the symbol of its *espérance,* for the foreigners the figure of

a France indomitable in the midst of trials, went to command my comportment and to impose on my personality an attitude that I could no longer change. This was for me, without respite, a strong inner guardianship [or tutelage: *"tutelle"*] and at the same time a very heavy yoke.

Earlier, de Gaulle told us of his decision to continue the war, then of his decision to "assume France." Now he tells us of the result of those decisions: with the stability of the old France gone, a renewed France replaces it, and this renewal centers on de Gaulle himself, takes place in his soul. By becoming a public man, a ruler, de Gaulle becomes a symbol. Psychologically this means that a new "attitude" imposes itself (but this imposition was chosen, hence not resented). This attitude is both a *tutelle* and a yoke; it guards, educates and burdens him. Before he left for Africa he told the French that "this great war . . . is also a great revolution." It is a revolution for the world, for France, for de Gaulle himself. For the latter it presents conditions that make self-metamorphosis a duty and, perhaps, an austere joy. "Events impose on me this sacred duty and I shall not yield it." Such jealousy, as we learned in *Le fil de l'épée,* does not arise from defending something that is merely burdensome.

In November de Gaulle had some successes at Libreville and at Port-Gentil. Before returning to London he established a military plan of action for Africa: to get Free France into the campaign in the Middle East at Eritrea and to get Free france into the North African campaign with attacks on Murzuk and Kufra. Responsibilities insisted upon: "So harsh were the realities, perhaps I could master them, inasmuch as it was possible for me, according to the phrase of Chateaubriand, 'to lead the French there by dreams.'"

*

Although he does not admit that he returned to London in order to receive needed assistance, de Gaulle does admit that Free France needed assistance from the British. The British themselves needed assistance in late 1940; the United States and the Soviet Union had yet to enter the war, but Japan had entered on Germany's side. De Gaulle had to rely on himself and his people, organizing a bank and an intelligence network, and continuing radio propaganda — which included his own speeches.

> . . . I spoke myself, with the moving impression of accomplishing, for the millions of listeners who heard me in anguish through frightful jamming, a sort of priesthood. I founded my allocutions on very simple elements: the course of the war, which demonstrated the error of capitulation; national pride, which, in contact with the enemy, moved souls profoundly; finally, hope for victory and for a new grandeur for 'our lady France.'

Remarkably, there is no mention of revenge. Indeed, in his numerous wartime broadcasts de Gaulle rarely used the word "revenge." — perhaps two or three times. De Gaulle's priesthood was not at the service of love, but it was at the service of grandeur, which is not vengeful. In *Le fil de l'épée,* also, the man of character seems to have a measure of magnanimity in him.

De Gaulle, who took words and ideas seriously, does not suppose that others do; "propaganda had, as always, only little value by itself. All depended on events." In March and April of 1941 the Axis took the Balkans and the Japanese attacked Indochina. French opinion did not rally to de Gaulle in such circumstances. The Middle East appeared to be the next battleground.

*

It was, but the battle, for de Gaulle, was between France and Britain. The Suez Canal was the critical point in "the Orient." Its loss would have exposed Asia Minor and Egypt; its retention would provide a base for attacks on Tunisia, Southern France and Italy. But Syria and Lebanon, French territories, were threatened by British or Turkish annexation. Britain especially wanted to give the impression to Syrians and Lebanese that if they received independence, they would owe it to Britain.

The expected German attack never came; on June 22 Hitler ordered the attack on the Soviet Union, instead. But he did want the Western allies preoccupied, so Rommel in Africa and the Vichy forces in the Levant busied themselves. The former had more success than the latter, and at Saint John of Acre the Vichyites transferred Syria and Lebanon to the British, under the guise of independence. This bypassing of Free France angered de Gaulle, who reminded listeners that France alone could grant independence. He went so far as to say that he would fight the British, if necessary, to assure French control of the Levant — while continuing to ally himself with them against the Axis! Britain backed down. During his visit to Beirut de Gaulle had occasion to notice, again, the importance of events.

> The majority had given to the system established by Vichy their concurrence, often their confidence. But, in making contact with them, I could verify, one more time, with what heaviness *faits accomplis* — when they are of just title — weigh on attitudes and even on convictions.

The previously-admitted acceptance of Vichy may reveal that *faits accomplis* are persuasive even when not of just title.

The British did not cease to press their interests, in different ways. De Gaulle returned to London, hoping to influence Washington and Moscow, to push the French Resistance forward, and to inspire and guide the worldwide mobilization of French resources.

*

L'Appel's last two chapter concern the outer and inner aspects of the Gaullist endeavor, respectively; they are titled *Les Alliés* and *La France Combattante*. France's allies were important for political as well for the obvious military reasons. Having established Free France's political, military and territorial reality by late summer of 1941, de Gaulle was ready to establish its reality in the diplomatic sphere. He saw that this had to be done before the war's "decisive shock," the point when victory would be decided. If it was not done, the victorious allies would please themselves, not France.

De Gaulle writes of Free France's relations with the United States, the Soviet Union, Britain and the exiled governments. De Gaulle wanted independence, and the United States, under Roosevelt, was least amenable to it among the allies. Although (because?) the United States recognized the Vichy government, it refused to recognize Free France, on the pretext of not wanting to determine the future government of France. "At bottom, what the American rulers took for granted, was the effacement of France." That winter (after the Pearl Harbor attack) de Gaulle reminded the United States that Free France existed by annexing two islands off Canada that had been under Vichy control. When the Americans protested, de Gaulle assured the British intermediary, Anthony Eden, that he'd fire on any American ships that threatened those islands. He did not think that would happen, however: "I have confidence in the democracies." American public opinion induced Roosevelt to reconsider.

Before that, in June 1941, Free France allied itself militarily with the Soviet Union.

> I obviously did not doubt that a victory in which the Soviets had taken a capital part would, because of that, raise other perils before the world. One must take them into account, even while fighting at their side. But I thought that before philosophizing it is necessary to live, that is to vanquish. Russia offered the possibility [of vanquishing]. On the other hand, her presence in the camp of the Allies brought to Fighting France, *vis-à-vis* the Anglo-Saxons, an element of equilibrium that I counted on serving me.

94

De Gaulle understands the distinction between living and living well. Balancing the Soviet Union against the United States and Britain allowed Free France to live well, or at least better than it might have lived; independence is a precondition of, perhaps a part of, grandeur. There is even a grandeur in totalitarianism.

> In M. Molotov [the Soviet Commissar for Foreign Affairs], who was and wanted to be only a cogwheel perfectly arranged in an implacable mechanism, I believe to have recognized a complete success of the totalitarian system. I saluted the grandeur. But . . . I sensed the melancholy.

Readers of *La discorde chez l'ennemi* recall the French-style garden, wherein each part sacrifices its prominence for the good of the whole, thus liberating a "noble melancholy." De Gaulle does not call totalitarian sacrifice noble — which suggests that totalitarian grandeur lacks the ethical worth of French republican grandeur. Totalitarianism yields a machine; France, whether monarchic or republican, is a garden, where liberty to grow, within limits, exists. Unity is part of grandeur, but the kind of unity, the kind of self-sacrifice, determines the worth of that grandeur.

As for the British, Churchill decided to "incline himself before the imperative of the American alliance," refusing to admit the independence of Free France. Continued difficulties in the Mideast, and similar difficulties concerning French territories in the Pacific resulted. *Mémoires de guerre's* account is, of course, for the public. Privately, de Gaulle was more severe. He told his young aide, Claude Mauriac, that he was

> . . . quite aware of the reasons that prompted [Churchill] to make that choice. But in doing so, he sacrificed his country's independence and turned it into an American dominion. When the Battle of the Atlantic was at its height and he sent out his S.O.S., asking the U.S.A. for fifty destroyers for which they no longer had any use and Roosevelt answered: "All right, but give me the Antilles for ninety-nine years," and Churchill agreed, he gave clear evidence of his irremediable defeat. If he had immediately spoken on the radio and explained the whole situation — "At this moment, as I speak to you, our convoys of supply ships are being destroyed one after the other and the U.S.A., which has fifty ships doing nothing, demands the Antilles in return for them; a demand to which I cannot concede with a clear conscience" — well, then, the weight of public opinion, even in America, would have forced Roosevelt to give way . . .
> Did I give away Dakar or Casablanca or Saint-Pierre-et-Miquelon [the islands off Canada] despite constant pressure from America? I did not part with a single French possession and God knows I had none of Churchill's resources.

De Gaulle knew that public opinion influenced the Allied rulers (the "Anglo-Saxons," at any rate), and he used his own public speeches and private conversations with the heads of the governments-in-exile based in London to influence public opinion.

> To speak truly, the governments of the Western countries no longer doubted, since the entry into the war of Russia and the United States, that their respective countries would be liberated. But in what state? That is what haunted my interlocutors . . . .

Greece, Yugoslavia, Czechoslovakia and Poland were especially fearful of communist takeover. By supporting them, Free France received diplomatic assistance in return, and additional support from the public. De Gaulle's public speeches encouraged this support. He mentions few of them in *Mémoires de guerre,* but many times in late 1941 and in 1942 he insisted, at rallies and over the radio, that the war was a revolution: in a speech at a British tank factory in October 1941; at a dinner of the "Royal African Society" ("Greek philosophy said that war gives birth"); at a demonstration by the "French of Great Britain" in November; in a radio speech in April 1942 ("National liberation cannot be separated from national insurrection"); in a declaration published in France in the underground journals of the Resistance in June ("a victory which does not bring a courageous and profound interior renewal will not be a victory"). Talk of revolution surely appealed to workers, colonials and others disgusted with the pre-war system. In *Mémoires de guerre* de Gaulle writes that this campaign was successful in weakening "Anglo-Saxon" hostility — or, at least, in making demonstrations of that hostility more circumspect.

In the Spring de Gaulle renamed Free France "Fighting France" (*"La France Combattante"*) This is the title of the last chapter of *L'Appel.*

*

During the previous autumn de Gaulle had instituted the National Committee, a body with the prerogatives and structure of a government, but not the title. He criticizes those among the French exiles who opposed the Committee; such people were merely attempting to continue the failed parliamentary regime. Admiral Muselier, who attempted to make the Navy independent of the Committee, was the most prominent of these. After being disciplined, he resigned. In metropolitan France dissidence also occurred; the communists entered the Resistance (doing so only after Hitler invaded the Soviet Union, thus revealing to whom they felt obligated). Their objective was "to establish their dictatorship by means of the drama of France." Nonetheless, de Gaulle assured their place within the Resistance.

> In the incessant movement of the world, all the doctrines, all the schools, all the revolts, have only one time. Communism will pass. But France will not pass.

De Gaulle evidently believes that nation-states count more than ideologies, that they ultimately determine the content of ideologies more than ideologies determine the policies of nation-states. "Before philosophizing it is necessary to live," and in politics the necessities of life moderate ideological passions: hence their impermanence.

In October 1941, Resistance leader Jean Moulin arrived in London to meet de Gaulle. The political parties, de Gaulle told him, could exist in the Resistance, and afterward; they should not control it. "To my mind . . . our misfortunes came, not from their existence, but from the fact that by means of institutions of decadence they abusively appropriated the public powers." Unity was necessary not only for military but for political reasons. After Moulin parachuted into southern France on January 1, 1942, de Gaulle had the occasion to speak to other young Resistants. He told them that

> The Resistance was not only the start of our defense reduced to extremity. It raised also the hope of renewal. Provided that after the victory it did not disperse, one could hope [or expect: *espérer*] that it would serve as lever for a profound change of system and a vast national effort.

Resistance leaders might, with de Gaulle, "direct a great human and French work" if they disciplined themselves, maintained unity, and thereby achieved "liberation in the complete sense of the term, that is to say that of man as well as that of *la patrie,"* based on liberty, dignity and security.* As if to assure democrats, de Gaulle also quotes from a November 1941 speech in which he used the old revolutionary motto, "liberty, equality, fraternity."

---

*In a speech to the *"Cercle Francais"* at Oxford University that autumn, de Gaulle identified liberty, security and dignity with "the triumph of *l'esprit* over matter," the triumph over the machine, which brings mass-life, "a sort of general mechanization" against which the individual should be safeguarded [*Discours et Messages*, I, 154-155]. Inasmuch as de Gaulle associates totalitarianism with machines, we know that this unity of which he spoke to the young Resistants was not a totalitarian unity.

Having described the National Committee and the metropolitan Resistance, de Gaulle turns to the military. Libya was the next theater of operations; Rommel plagued the Allies there. The British wanted to deal with him without French assistance, but when de Gaulle asked Moscow if he could be of any assistance to them on the eastern front, Churchill reconsidered. (The Soviets, recall, were "an element of equilibrium which I counted on serving me" "vis-à-vis the Anglo-Saxons.")

On May 27 Rommel attacked French troops at Bir Hakeim. "In his justice the God of Battles was going to offer to the soldiers of Free France [not yet Fighting France] a great combat and a great glory." The French troops broke the seige.

> In enterprises in which one risks all, a moment comes, ordinarily, in which
> he who takes part feels that destiny is fixed [recall the same thought, concerning
> Napoleon's career, in *La France et son armée*]. By a strange concourse, the thou-
> sand trials wherein he struggles seem to blossom suddenly into a decisive episode.

Bir Hakeim was such a moment for Free France. By mid-1942, Free France had 70,000 men under arms.

*   *

Mémoires de guerre's second volume, *L'Unité,* concerns the period from late spring of 1942 to the liberation of Paris in August 1944. Unity is central to de Gaulle not because it is an end but because it is the most important component of de Gaulle's end, which is (republican) grandeur.

*

He titles the first chapter *Interméde;* in it he deals with the period between the Bir Hakeim seige and "Torch," the Allied campaign in North Africa. Continuing the argument of the last chapter, de Gaulle writes that France needed unity in order to prevent subordination to the Allies after the war. If France remained prostrate until the war's end, the French would have lost faith in themselves and in France; loss of independence would have been the consequence of that loss of faith. But the Allies could not dominate a unified, faithful nation. The Allies' effort to divide the French and de Gaulle's effort to unify them comprise the subject of this volume, to which *Interméde* serves as an introduction.

The Americans considered two strategies: the immediate invasion of Europe (de Gaulle approved) and the invasion of North Africa, from which they would exclude de Gaulle. They chose the latter. But excluding de Gaulle wasn't easy. They needed a replacement, and they decided on a recently-escaped French general, Henri Giraud. De Gaulle saw that the Resistance would not accept the authority of a man who was no more than a career general, that Pétain would condemn Giraud, and that the Allies would take advantage of this disunity and injure France. In the summer of 1942 de Gaulle left Britain in order to be where French interests would be threatened.

In Cairo he met Churchill who, upon being reminded of his conscience in regard to safeguarding French interests, told de Gaulle, "You should know that my conscience is a good girl I can always come to terms with." He proved it in the Mideast, which de Gaulle visited next. There the British continued to undermine the French position in Syria and Lebanon, and de Gaulle continued to protest. The Allies' "political comportment"

> . . . had for its foundation sanctified egoism. Hence was I less than ever
> inclined to have faith in the ideological formulas they used for covering it. How
> to take seriously the scruples affected by Washington, which affected to hold
> General de Gaulle at a distance under the pretext of allowing the French the

liberty to one day choose their government and which, at the same time, conserved official relations with the dictatorship of Vichy and was preparing to deal with whomever would open to American troops the doors of North Africa? How to believe in the sincerity of the declarations of London which, to justify its interventions in the territories of the Levant where France had the mandate, invoked the right of Arabs to independence, at the same time the English put in prison, in India, Gandhi and Nehru, punished harshly, in Iraq, the partisans of Rachid Ali, and dictated to Farouk, the King of Egypt, the choice of his government? *Allons!* today as before, there was only the interest of France to listen to.

De Gaulle has an answer for those who would point to the inferiority of French resources in a struggle of nation-states:

> A *politique* is worth its means, In the Mideast, more surely than elsewhere, the relationship of the forces would end up determining [the outcome], not argumentation.

De Gaulle adopts the *realpolitik* argument, but uses it against the realists, claiming that power was really on France's side, despite appearances. In private conversation, de Gaulle was more frank: ". . . it was by bluff that I was able, in 1940 and the following years, to make the Allies sufficiently apprehensive of France's vitality that they didn't dare to assail our sovereignty." Not entirely bluff: the Allies (the United States and Britain, at least) depended on public opinion to bolster their power, and bluff counts in public opinion. It was public opinion that saved de Gaulle again and again during those years. Far from a simple democrat, de Gaulle used mass sentiment to the advantage of Fighting France against "the elites," as he called them. But that sentiment never served simple egalitarianism. It served things better than the ordinary: de Gaulle, France. It is this combination of democracy and aristocracy that underlies the exchange between Churchill and de Gaulle which occurred in London on September 25. To Churchill's "You are not France!" de Gaulle replied, "If, in your eyes, I am not the representative of France, why and by what right do you deal with me regarding her world interests?" Churchill's conscience, which was also partly democratic, partly aristocratic, was not always submissive, as Churchill had bragged.

When, in August, Pétain dissolved the French Assembly, the same parliamentarians who had instituted the Vichy regime became displeased with it. De Gaulle does not fail to insist on that irony. The Resistance grew.

*

The three chapters that follow this introduction, titled *Tragédie, Comédie, Alger,* concern the struggle in North Africa between de Gaulle and those the Allies used to counterbalance de Gaulle. The invasion occurred in early November. When the Allied troops reached Algiers they found Admiral Darlan of Vichy in control. Darlan negotiated with the Allies while deciding which side would best serve his interests. When the Allies, particularly the Americans, seemed to offer him power over the anti-Vichy French forces, Darlan chose to fight on their side. The United State's attempt to 'legitimize' Darlan, de Gaulle notes, only strengthened de Gaulle's popularity among the French, as did the concurrent German occupation of Vichy territory. To Churchill and Eden, de Gaulle argued that in modern war national suffering occurs; to use men like Giraud and Darlan antagonizes national sentiment. It would therefore be possible to win militarily but lose morally. After the war, Stalin would be the winner because the dissaffected French masses could turn to the one who, at least, claims to uphold nationality. The reason democratic sentiment served France and de Gaulle was not only because it was egalitarian (although anti-totalitarianism — which may or may not be egalitarian — was extremely important) but because it was national.

Disunity reigned among the French in North Africa. There was Darlan; there were the Vichyites who hesitated to support Darlan after Pétain condemned him; there was Giraud, more or less forced into Darlan's camp now, but embittered by the Allied switch from himself to Darlan; there were supporters of Fighting France. The situation became simpler when Darlan was assassinated in late December. De Gaulle implies that the United States had it done, having made use of Darlan as a "temporary expedient" — Roosevelt's very phrase — to gain Algiers.* De Gaulle expresses no pity for Darlan. "[I]n great moments, [the hard logic of events] only supports in posts of command men capable of directing their own course." Darlan's opportunism was, ultimately, inopportune — even as the Allies' realism and Vichy's realism were, ultimately, unrealistic. Darlan failed by not espousing France when the armistice was signed in 1940. To him the Navy, his "fief," was more important than France.

*

If Darlan is a figure of tragedy, Giraud is a figure of comedy. With the former's death, the latter was again the Americans' boy. In January of 1943 Churchill and Roosevelt 'invited' de Gaulle to the Anfa Conference in Morocco, where Giraud waited, assured by the Allied leaders that he would share power with de Gaulle. After making it clear to his readers that Churchill's threats did not impress him, de Gaulle recounts his arrival in Morocco, an arrival he delayed in order to demonstrate his independence. He met Giraud, who told him that he disliked the elementary, popular, revolutionary nature of the Resistance. Churchill said that the United States wanted Giraud to control military affairs, with de Gaulle and Giraud, along with another French general, as co-presidents of a French governing committee. De Gaulle met Roosevelt last. He describes him as a man possessed of "the most high ambitions," representing a country possessed of "a sort of messianism," and of "the penchant for intervention in which the dominating instinct cloaked itself." Roosevelt wanted to be the "savior and arbiter" of France. De Gaulle, needless to say, saw that as a usurpation. He refused any agreement. Giraud, under the pretense of not being 'political,' accepted Anglo-American hegemony, which in turn would have guaranteed his own power — subject to his superiors' approval — over the French.

De Gaulle's refusal prompted an Allied propaganda barrage that only augmented de Gaulle's prestige. Most amusing was Archbishop Spellman's visit to de Gaulle in London.

> This prelate, of eminent piety, approached the problems of the world with the evident solicitude to serve only the cause of God. But the most great devotion could not prevent *les affaires* from being *les affaires*.

The Archbishop urged de Gaulle to accept the coalition proposed at Anfa in the name of liberty, equality (co-presidents, you see . . .) and charity. However, de Gaulle did not submit to temptation. He knew that "it was indeed the future of the nation that was being played for in the dispute." The Anfa proposal allowed no political power to the Committee; "all would pass as if, insofar as it was a State, France no longer existed, at least until after the victory."

In May the leaders of the Metropolitan Resistance, organized by Moulin, publicly supported de Gaulle. On May 30 de Gaulle came to Algiers.

*

*Here I disagree with Milton Viorst's interpretation: that de Gaulle implies that Giraud was behind the assassination. Viorst's account. in general, is the best one available on de Gaulle's struggle with Roosevelt. [*Hostile Allies — FDR and De Gaulle,* The Macmillan Company, New York, 1965, p. 131].

On July 3 the French Committee of National Liberation was founded. By agreeing to the subordination of the military to the civil authority — that is, by proclaiming the Committee sovereign — Giraud assured his own defeat, as historian Milton Viorst has noted, and as de Gaulle implies. Moreover, de Gaulle soon persuaded the majority of the seven Committee-members to do things his way. This was aided by another Giraudian blunder: his trip to Washington in early July. Giraud, an unimpressive figure, bored the Americans. And, as de Gaulle puts it, "during this time in Algiers, the government, fatigued by its bicephalism, took shape." Not to forget the parliamentarians, de Gaulle adds:

> It is necessary [!] to say that, without parliament, parties, elections, the political game did not exist among the members of the Committee. My task of direction was facilitated.

With this Committee, the State reappeared. Its reappearance increased the ranks of Fighting France.

> A sort of tide of wills and sentiments consecrated this profound legitimacy, which proceeded from *le salut public* [the public safety, salvation, welfare] and which, always, France recognizes at the bottom of her great trials, whatever the "legal" formulas of the moment say. There was the elementary exigency of which, for being the symbol, I felt myself no less the instrument and the servant.

Legitimacy proceeds from *le salut public,* not from the wills and the sentiments of the people. That "tide" only "consecrates" legitimacy, that is, sets it aside as holy; it does not make it holy. And he quotes from his fine speech of July 14 in Algiers, wherein he asserted that French sovereignty never dissolved:

> *Envers et contre tout,* there has always been a French sovereignty in the war. French on all the fields of battle, belligerant French territories, French voices for explaining freely the will of the nation, *Envers et contre tout,* there has always been a Fighting France . . . .
>
> In the world, certain *esprits* have been able to believe that it was possible to consider the action of the French armies independently of the sentiment and the will of the profound masses of our people; they were able to imagine that our soldiers, our sailors, our aviators, differing in this from all the soldiers, all the sailors, all the aviators of the world, would go to combat without caring about the reasons for which they confronted death, the *esprit* in which they were to display their sacrifices. In brief, these theoreticians, pretended realists, were able to conceive that, for the French, and for the French alone, the war effort of the nation was susceptible of existing outside the national *politique* and *morale.* We declare to these realists that they ignore the reality.

Unsurprisingly, in his speeches de Gaulle tends to be less precise in distinguishing *le salut public* from the sentiment and the will of the "profound" masses.

As de Gaulle writes, "de Gaulle had won the match." Nonetheless, the Allies' negotiations with the Italians, after Mussolini's fall on July 25, excluded Fighting France. On Corsica, Giraud — acting in secret — had strengthened the communists among the Resistance leaders. (De Gaulle doesn't claim to know why, but hints that, for some reason, the British wanted it: a thesis in need of an explanation.) Fighting France landed on Corsica and took over. When de Gaulle told Giraud that he had proceeded in "a manner one could not admit," Giraud replied, "You are talking politics to me." "Yes. For we make war. But, war, it is a *politique.*" *Mémoires de guerre,* then, by definition, has for its subject a kind of politics. This kind of politics exists within the larger domain of politics proper. De Gaulle, unlike such men as Darlan and Giraud, knew and never ignored this fact. He made the transition from the military to the political life; many of his colleagues could not.

De Gaulle was soon the only president of the French National Committee of Liberation. *Alger* is the central chapters of *Mémoires de guerre.*

The next three chapters, as the preceding three chapters, form a group. Titled *Politique, Diplomatie, Combat,* they concern the readying of Fighting France for the finally-predictable day when France would be liberated.

The Consultative Assembly (a group composed of members of political parties, including the communist party, members of the Resistance both in the Empire and in metropolitan France, and general advisers from Algeria) had its first session on November 3, 1943. Unfortunately, many of the delegates were naive in regard to rulership; they believed it could be done without. De Gaulle, "sounding their souls . . .came to ask [him]self if, among all those who spoke of revolution, [he] was not, in truth, the sole revolutionary." For the eschewal of rulership was the most important characteristic of the old parliamentary regime. Many delegates wanted more, not less, "demagogy" — by which de Gaulle means that they believed the Assembly should have even more power than before, that the executive should be weakened or abolished. De Gaulle saw it was the wrong moment to discuss the topic publicly. He instead had them agree to keep the Consultative Assembly as the *de facto* government after the Liberation, then hold elections later. For the present, of course, the Assembly remained a deliberative body, with no real power.

Another problem with the delegates was their vengefulness. De Gaulle wanted to restrain the vengeance of the Resistance on the Vichyites, "to let justice only pronounce on the punishments."* De Gaulle, who would attempt to found a regime, saw beyond that satisfying passion; he recognized that lawlessness would only assist the communists and damage respect for any new laws — including a new constitution. In the many speeches de Gaulle made during the war, I count only three uses of the words "revenge" or "vengeance." In view of the rhetorical advantage de Gaulle might have gained from the invocation of that passion, and in view of what his own passions must have been, he reveals magnanimity in this.

Months before, Jean Moulin was captured by the Gestapo and tortured to death. The political consequence: increased disunity among the metropolitan Resistants whom Moulin had organized. De Gaulle never really could replace Moulin, and his death may have damaged France in ways not immediately obvious. "As long as the war lasted," de Gaulle writes, "I had the means, morally speaking, to unite the French people." But not after the war, when Moulin's work might have served de Gaulle uniquely well.

De Gaulle's manner of dealing with political questions combined distance with prudently-timed intimacy:

> The confrontation of points of view and the choice of the measures to take, I reserved, by design, for the councils of government. My nature admonished me, my experience taught me, that at the summit of affairs one safeguards one's time and one's person only by methodically remaining high and sufficiently remote.
>
> It was all the more necessary to make, at requisite moments, contact with people and things. I did it, as much as possible, by going to see them on the spot.

This manner of rulership served four political tasks necessary, de Gaulle foresaw, after the Liberation. The first was to establish the State's authority as an integral, responsible, independent body. De Gaulle appointed seventeen "Regional Commissioners of the Republic," who were to ensure the security of the French and Allied armies, to establish republican legality and to satisfy the population's needs by continuing needed services. He also

---

*One might object that de Gaulle's praise of *le salut public,* which he considers beyond "whatever the 'legal' formulas of the moment say," contradicts his law-abidingness here. I shall examine this seeming contradiction in the next section.

established a "Commission of Liberation" in each French department, an advisory body to be replaced after elections.

His second task was to establish a system of justice. The State should punish the collaborators; individuals don't have that right. He established "Courts of Justice," tribunals comprised of Resistants.

Economic renewal mattered politically:

> Many had the sentiment that the trials of war could lead to a vast change in the human condition. If one did nothing in this sense, one would render inevitable the sliding of the masses toward communist totalitarianism. On the contrary, by acting quickly, one could save the soul of France.

Inasmuch as a *laisser-faire* policy would yield inflation, and an anti-inflationary policy of strict controls would end growth — both leading to the wrong kind of revolution — de Gaulle chose the middle way: excess profit taxes, confiscation of illegal gains, moderate price controls and a thirty-percent wage increase. As de Gaulle needed the workers' cooperation, he decided to nationalize ownership of the coal, electric and gas industries and to provide unemployment and health insurance, old-age pensions.

Finally, de Gaulle wanted to transform colonial relations by giving more representation to the colonized peoples in those assemblies open to them.

*

> Diplomacy, under the conventions of form, knows only realities. To such degree that we were destitute, we could move men; we could seldom receive services.

French strength, supported by French unity, forced the world to recognize France again. A "political" France — that is, one divided by partisans — pleased foreigners because it was malleable. De Gaulle aspired to please foreigners even less than he aspired to please the French.

After a visit to defeated Italy (during which he described himself as "Christian, Latin, European" — note that nationality is central — de Gaulle returned to his diplomatic war with the Allies. Continued difficulties over Syria and Lebanon and the exclusion of France from the Teheran conference with Stalin ("before the exactions of Soviet Russia, America chose to be quiet. Great Britain searched for a formula. France had no voice in the matter") were mere skirmishes. The real conflict, for de Gaulle, was between himself and Roosevelt, and concerned de Gaulle's claim of authority over the French. Because Roosevelt could not dictate to metropolitan France (he had failed to do so in North Africa, where Fighting France was much weaker), "the intentions of the President appeared to me of the same order as the dreams of Alice in Wonderland." Roosevelt persisted in firing propaganda bullets, which ricocheted with minimal harm to de Gaulle.

He returned to London from Algiers in June 1944, in time for D-Day. After arguing with Churchill over French authority — Churchill supported the Americans, who wanted to govern France until elections could be held — he returned to metropolitan France on June 13, four years minus five days since his first radio message from London. The joy of the Bayeux crowds belied the Anglo-American propaganda.

> The proof was given. In Metropolitan France, as well as in the Empire, the French people had shown to whom it entrusted the duty of conducting it.

Roosevelt decided to invite de Gaulle to Washington.

Roosevelt wanted a four-power hegemony of the United States, the Soviet Union, Britain and China (!) to dominate the world after the war. De Gaulle replied that the West must revive because if it declined barbarism (i.e., Soviet domination) would result. Western Europe is essential to the West, and France is essential to Western Europe; therefore, to neglect France is to invite barbarism.

> The proposals of the American President completed proving to me that, in the affairs between States, logic and sentiment do not weigh heavily in comparison to the realities of power; that what matters is what one takes and what one knows [how] to hold; that France, in order to retrieve her place, could only count on herself.

Roosevelt believed de Gaulle egoistic, as de Gaulle believed Roosevelt egoistic. "I never knew if Franklin Roosevelt thought that, in affairs concerning France, Charles de Gaulle was egoistic for France or indeed for himself." De Gaulle is silent on the possibility of Roosevelt's being egoistic for America, merely writing that "As is human, [Roosevelt's] idealism cloaked the will to power." I am not sure if de Gaulle would not, secretly, have preferred to like Roosevelt. Perhaps it is a question of which country it is better to be egoistic for: America or France.

After visiting Canada, de Gaulle returned to Algiers.

*

We know from *La France et son armée* that the military is part of 'France-ness,' at least as much a part of it as politics and diplomacy.

> That our army would be at the head of all the armies of the world, our fleet one of the best, our air force at the first level, our generals the most capable, that, for us, was [France] being herself [*allait en soi*].
> Hence, the downfall of 1940 and the surrender which followed seemed to many monstrous and irremediable. The idea which the French always had of themselves, the historical opinion of their world on their account, were suddenly annihilated. There was no chance that France could recover her dignity *vis-à-vis* herself and *vis-à-vis* the others without rectifying her arms. But nothing could aid in remaking her unity and re-taking prestige as much as this surprising fact — that she could find, in her scarcely-assembled Empire, in her oppressed mainland, enough faith and martial valor to reforge an army which could fight, my faith! very well.

De Gaulle's faith, on the side of the heavier artillery, was confirmed by the effect of French military efforts in Italy and in metropolitan France: increased French unity.

> Politics, diplomacy, arms had together prepared unity. It was necessary, now, to reassemble the nation as soon as it emerged from the abyss. I left Algiers for Paris.

Paris: the last chapter of *L'Unité,* and the place where unity existed, momentarily, for France. In *Vers l'armée de métier* de Gaulle wrote that he who controls Paris controls France. Others knew that, too, and attempted to control Paris before de Gaulle could arrive. The Vichyite Pierre Laval wanted to arrange the empowering of the parliamentarians, who would then spare his life; de Gaulle tells us that Roosevelt favored this (although General Eisenhower, to his credit, did not). The scheme failed. De Gaulle writes that Laval was identified with the defeat of France, and the French were no longer defeatist. There were also the communists, who hoped for an insurrection, then a welcome of de Gaulle and his installation as a figurehead. De Gaulle's plans differed.

As he visited liberated cities, he "spoke, then, some sentences, not of pity which none wanted, but of *espérance* and of pride . . . ." One does not understand de Gaulle if he does not weigh that sentence. Just as de Gaulle avoided, for the most part, invoking the passion of revenge before and during the Liberation, he avoids invoking the passion of pity now. Far from being pitiless (as we saw in his sympathetic description of the suffering of the Italians — they were a *defeated* people) de Gaulle refused to speak *in public*. None wanted it; the French, in de Gaulle's account, were not self-pitying. There is a resentment that underlies revenge and a self-pity that demands shows of compassion from public speakers; de Gaulle regarded both as unproductive, not contributive to the rebuilding of a France of grandeur. For grandeur is a large thing; resentment and self-pity are small. *Espérance* and pride, if regarded as passions at all, are passions of what Plato called *thymos,* the spirited part of the soul: the part which defends the *polis.*

As for Paris,

> I had myself, in advance, fixed what I would do in the liberated capital. That consisted of reassembling the souls in one single *élan,* but also to make appear immediately the figure and the authority of the State.

He did both — symbolically and, to an extent, in 'reality' — during his walk down the Champs-Élysée on the afternoon of August 26. It was "one of those miracles of the national *conscience"*: unity, that rare thing: "only one single thought, a single *élan,* a single cry, differences effaced themselves, individuals disappeared." " . . . I felt myself filling a function that surpassed most highly my person: to serve as an instrument of destiny." De Gaulle at his most lyrical is here de Gaulle at his most ambiguous. What is destiny? Two paragraphs later he is back to writing of "History" as an instructor, providing lessons; if "destiny" means fate, such lessons are superfluous — one does what one has to do, lessons or no. In *Mémoires de guerre* de Gaulle leaves "destiny" undefined; in private conversation de Gaulle once used the word to mean 'potential' or 'purpose,' but that is hardly conclusive. If we could be sure that de Gaulle believed in divine providence or Hegel's 'History' (or Marx's) there would be no confusion; we cannot be sure. And if he means by "destiny" the combination of geography, national character and events he discusses in earlier books, it is hard to see why service to it would feel especially exalting.

We can be sure that de Gaulle took control of Paris, disbanding the Resistance units. (He had told the young Resistants that they could contribute to the renewal of the country, but when Moulin died the Resistance splintered, became more dangerous than helpful to de Gaulle.) Pétain, for whom resignation to *faits accomplis* was becoming habitual, sent a message to de Gaulle in which he offered reconciliation. De Gaulle never replied because Pétain's faction had neither force nor legitimacy.

Unity, for the moment: "One could believe that the French, now regrouped, would stay [regrouped] long enough so that the categories into which they divided themselves and which, by intention, strove always to impair national cohesion, could not carry it away anew until the immediate purpose was reached." De Gaulle's "role" (always the theatrical language) was to bend "to the common interest the diverse elements of the nation to lead them to *le salut* . . . ." Having been invited to admire de Gaulle as Man of Destiny, we are now invited to admire him as Maker of History. In earlier books he wrote that the ruler is both — that is, something in-between. There is no reason to think he's changed his thoughts now.

A nation-state achieves *le salut* only when diversity serves a specific kind of unity: the common interest. That miracle of the national *conscience,* the walk down the Champs-Élysée, was a moment in which diversity did not exist; the common interest and *le salut* were exactly consonant with popular sentiment. In ordinary politics miracles don't happen; ordinariness and the miraculous exclude one another. In ordinary politics diversity matters, as it does in the French garden. Republican statesmen bend diverse national elements to the common interest; they do not break or obliterate them. One way to bend those elements is to remind them of past, miraculous, instants of unity, in words and in gestures — that is, in speeches and books, in ceremonies and, occasionally, in political acts. If the war was a revolution, de Gaulle's attempt at founding came next, chronologically and logically. *Mémoires de guerre* is a three-volume book, not a two-volume book, because it is more political than military. For France, the military aspect of the war was disastrous, then modest. But politically the war was a profound thing; de Gaulle made it so. His attempt to found a new republic was an attempt to give political expression to the *mystique* of the Liberation. Such a *politique* need not be a mere corruption of a *mystique,* as Péguy thought. It would not be the same as the *mystique;* it could not be pure, perfect. But it would have its nobility, even if a nobility inseparable from melancholy: the melancholy of individuals who sacrifice part of their own individuality, but also the melancholy of those who know the remembered miraculous moment will not be duplicated often.

*   *

Le Salut, the third volume of *Mémoires de guerre,* is titled ironically. Although France's safety and salvation from the Nazis were achieved, its welfare — compared to what it was under the Vichyites — assured, the French returned to parliamentarism, to what endangered safety, salvation and welfare.

*

In the first chapter, *La Libération,* de Gaulle writes of the material destruction he saw and, more importantly, of the psychological unpreparedness of the French. The reigning illusions were that prosperity would soon return, that de Gaulle and the Allies, having done so much, could surely do more, that having done one thing (expelled the Nazis), they could surely do another (restore the economy). De Gaulle had to do a thing public men dislike; he had to disillusion the people. He insisted, in speeches, that the war wasn't over (as it wasn't). He attempted to maintain discipline when external restraints vanished. Restraining vengeance was especially difficult because de Gaulle used the men he could have used as police as soldiers, reasoning that France's place among the other countries — whose establishment depended on France's presence among those countries on the battlefield — mattered more, finally, than the commission of some unjust acts within France. Another internal problem was the communist hope of seizing power amid the disorder. All of this reduced de Gaulle's popularity. "My popularity was like a capital that would pay for disappointments, inevitable amongst the ruins."

In the autumn of 1944 de Gaulle toured many of the departments, noticing what they needed, economically and politically. Emphasizing to the crowds that liberation must not be confused with disorder, he saw that the people would have to "endure hard trials that would not lack exploiting by the demagoguery of the parties and the ambition of the communists." But also

> The nation discerned, by instinct, that in the trouble wherein it was plunged it would be at the mercy of anarchy, then dictatorship, if I did not find myself there to serve it as guide and center of rallying. It attached itself today to de Gaulle to escape subversion as it had done, yesterday, to be rid of the enemy.

The French recognized instinctively what de Gaulle recognized consciously: that de Gaulle was France's legitimate ruler, guarantor of *le salut.* The difference between ruler and ruled, to de Gaulle, seems to be the difference between this consciousness and this instinct; the ruler can guide the others, serve as the "center of rallying," the unifier, because he apprehends consciously what others apprehend instinctively: legitimacy, which he then identifies himself with (as opposed to identifying it with himself, the tyrant's nature). By contrast, there is the false ruler, a man like Albert Lebrun, erstwhile president of the Third Republic. "At bottom, as chief of State, two things he had lacked: that he was a chief; that there was a State." Lebrun lacked the intellectual and ethical virtues of the leader, as described in *Le fil de l'épée;* he also

105

lacked the institution on which a political leader, a ruler, stands.

De Gaulle possessed such virtues. He regretted the continuation of the war because he regretted the material and human losses it brought. But he did not regret the continuation of the war from the point of view of the larger interests of France. Because French military aid was needed, France's position after the war would be strengthened. Further, the continuation of the war resulted in continued national unity and increased French self-esteem; de Gaulle probably thought that a defeated country, saved by others, might still poison itself with self-denigration if it did not participate in battlefield victories. Again, not resentment or self-pity, but *espérance* and pride. The Allies didn't always help de Gaulle in this effort. They failed to equip all of the Frenchmen available for combat because, in de Gaulle's view, they preferred not to increase de Gaulle's post-war political leverage.

*

Such leverage is the principal subject of the second chapter, *Le Rang*. De Gaulle wanted France to be among the first-ranking countries. Toward that end he proposed the decentralization of Germany, which would have ended an old threat to France. He offered Churchill an alliance in which France and Britain would counterbalance the United States, on the one side, and the Soviet Union, on the other. But the Allies excluded France from the various conferences and committees that decided European questions, and Churchill refused a close alliance with France ("in politics as well as in strategy," he instructed de Gaulle, "it is better to persuade the stronger than to march to encounter him."). Noting that Britain had many chances for serving itself by following its 'American' strategy — especially in the Mideast and in the Balkans — de Gaulle tells his readers that "no trial changes the nature of man; no crisis, that of states." Those who take de Gaulle for a Hobbesian are partly right, but Hobbes was not a patriot, much less a Bergsonian.

Knowing the American and British policy, de Gaulle visited the Soviet Union, hoping to arrange French participation in the coming European settlements through Stalin. Before leaving, he did not neglect to upset the parliamentarians by saying that France was allied with these countries not because France approved of their forms of government but because they were fighting against those who invaded France.

In describing the Soviet Union, de Gaulle reveals that he is no 'conservative'; the prisoners there seemed no more passive, no worse-dressed, than the 'free' workers in France. Stalin was "accepted" by Russia (earlier, de Gaulle wrote that "in the long run, there is no regime that can hold against national wills"). True, "Stalin was possessed by the will to power," but so was Russia — which, de Gaulle writes, wanted to unite the Slavs, defeat the Germans, expand in Asia, gain access to the open seas. Russia tolerated Bolshevism in order to use it as a weapon for herself. What Stalin wanted more than anything at the moment was Russian domination of Poland, under the guise of the Lublin 'government.'

The hope for Soviet intervention on France's behalf, *vis-à-vis* the other Allies, in postwar negotiations dissolved in the first meeting between de Gaulle and Stalin. In later meetings, de Gaulle refused to recognize the Lublin Poles in exchange for a Franco-Soviet mutual defense pact. De Gaulle explains:

> The future lasts a long time. Anything could, one day, occur, even that an
> act conforming to honor and honesty appear, at the end of the reckoning, as a
> good political investment.

By which de Gaulle probably means that Russian and French interests, in this case, were not identical, and had, for example, the Soviets lost a war to the United States, Poland would have been in a position to remember France. Stalin had a different idea about the future: "After all, there is only death who wins." Stalin gave in; de Gaulle got the pact without recognizing the Lublin Poles.

In Paris, in January, de Gaulle spoke to Roosevelt's associate, Harry Hopkins. There is no more concise statement of Franco-American relations:

> For us, here is the essential: in the mortal perils that we French have gone through since the beginning of the century, the United States does not give us the impression that they hold their destiny as linked to that of France, that they wish her great and strong, that they do what they can to aid her to remain or to become so again. Perhaps, in fact, we are not worth the pain. In that case, you are right. But perhaps we will rectify ourselves. Then, you will have been wrong. In either case, your comportment tends to estrange us from you.

France was not invited to the Yalta Conference; de Gaulle refused to recognize the accords, which sacrificed Poland to the Soviet Union. He rejected Roosevelt's invitation to visit Roosevelt in Algiers because Roosevelt was returning from Yalta, from which France had been excluded, and because Algiers was French, and therefore not a place de Gaulle needed an invitation to visit. The criticism this decision aroused in France showed de Gaulle the extent to which communists, businessmen and others tended to exalt foreigners and denigrate their country.

*

La Libération concerned internal matters, especially the problem of civil order. *Le Rang*. concerned external matters, France's place in the international order. In *L'Ordre* de Gaulle links internal and external matters, showing how the state mediates between the two realms. Unlike, for example, Sartre, de Gaulle does not prize movement over order. Rather he agrees with the neo-classicist Buffon: style is order and movement; so is *la politique*. France in 1945 had movement; order was what was needed. And not only for France.

> To my eyes, it was clear that the stake of the conflict was not only the fate of nations and of States, but also the human condition. There is nothing in that, moreover, more natural. Always war, beneath its technical aspects, is a movement of societies. The passions which animate them and the pretexts which they invoke never fail to clothe a quarrel concerning the material or spiritual destiny of men. The victories of Alexander were those of civilization. It was the trembling desire of barbarism which made the Roman Empire crumble. No Arab invasions without the Koran. No crusades without the Gospel. The Europe of the Old Regime stood erect against France, when the Assembly proclaimed: "Men are born free and equal in right."

Modern war's modernity, then, is technical. As always, it is "a movement of societies" — inner and outer push each other. Not only economic and geographical — material — interests, but spiritual interests cause societies to fight. The catalogue of examples reminds us of *Le fil de l'épée:* he has replaced Salamis with Alexander's conquests; mentions the barbarian victory over Rome instead of Rome's legions; replaces the sword of Christianity and the scimitar of Islam with the *Koran* and the Gospel; mentions "Europe of the Old Regime" as well as revolutionary France; omits — understandably — mentioning that the French victory in the last war resulted in The League of Nations. The earlier passage emphasized the importance of force; this one emphasizes the importance of that for which societies use force. Oddly, many scholars and others quote the earlier passage without quoting this one. There is no contradiction; these are two poles of thought; the one does not cancel the other. De Gaulle, neither 'realist' nor 'idealist,' recognizes both force and *esprit*. When he told the Consultative Assembly that the Allies were allies because they fought the invaders of France, not because their political systems were admirable, he oversimplified things — deliberately, I suspect. He did not think that the British parliamentary system or the Soviet system were right for France (thereby annoying democrats and communists). But he did not deny the war's serious ideological content, nor that the beliefs of nations affect their foreign policy.

Specifically, de Gaulle recognized that mechanism "dominates the world," that "the great debate of the century" was: shall the working class by victim or beneficiary of mechanical progress? Socialism, communism and fascism, he writes, followed from the debate on this question. The war was a movement of societies regarding this "social question."

> How this was true for France! The war seized her in full class-struggle, the latter all the more alive in that our economy, gravely retarded, rejected changes and in that the political regime, destitute of vigor and of faith, could not impose them.

The political rules the social and the economic. And military or political service earns economic reward; as the working class resisted the Nazis, and the ruling class did not, many — including de Gaulle — wanted the economy to "serve the collectivity before furnishing profits to particular interests" and to "raise the condition of the working classes."

De Gaulle shows the link between the social/economic and the political (both in domestic and in foreign policy) with his comments on Vichy and on the communists. The Vichyites attempted to aid the laborers, but failed because they were capitulationists. Their lack of political independence allowed the Nazis to take whatever economic advantage they would. The communists also offered better conditions to the laborers, but they too submitted themselves to a foreign power, taking orders from the Kremlin.

De Gaulle's social/economic program improved the laborers' position without coming close to empowering them in the way the communists planned. He nationalized the Bank of France and other major credit establishments, as well as the airlines and the Renault works; he regulated and coordinated the fuel and oil industry; he improved working conditions by instituting social security and other such programs; he attempted to increase the birth-rate by giving family allowances. In order to grant workers responsibility, to prevent their remaining mere instruments, he attempted to promote the association of labor, capital and technology by instituting Committees of Enterprise, advisory bodies which included representatives from all three interest groups. These Committees were instituted for each large business establishment; without power, they were intended as a step toward real association, real laborer responsibility, in the future. By educating the interest groups to see their enterprise as a common one, not an arena for class-rivalry, de Gaulle treated each business establishment, in effect, like a miniature nation-state, constituted as a 'mixed regime' of democrats, oligarchs and technocrats. He did so in order to serve the larger country, to increase "the power of France," which is based on the economy's strength. Rivalry between business establishments may be economically worthwhile, but rivalry between classes within those establishments is not — or so I infer. The difference between a business establishment and a nation-state is that the former has no absolute sovereignty. Indeed, de Gaulle writes that the state should direct the economy for the benefit of the nation-state. Neither laborers nor capitalists nor technocrats necessarily have sufficient prudence and justice in them to run a country well. Their incapacity reveals the state's importance.

In order to give prudent and just direction the state must not be weak, parliamentary, a concatenation of interest groups. De Gaulle therefore instituted the National School of Administration, which was to supply men who were *of the state,* not of the interest groups. It is probable that such men, even if they shed their ties to whatever class they came from (which would rarely be the working class), would eventually serve the state alone, not the nation-state. Presumably, the Gaullist teaching on nationalism answers that; a realistic statesman will serve the nation's best interest — or at least take account of its desires, which is a different thing — if he wishes to retain his position. This is evidently not enough. Other institutional checks must be had, and de Gaulle will formulate them in a subsequent chapter.

As in Algiers, de Gaulle's new government included communists. He did this, again, to establish unity, believing that he could control them because he had the force to control them, that he had the force because of "the confidence in me the French people had." This superficial unity prepared a deeper one later on: "as soon as in place of revolution the Communists took for their goal preponderance in a parliamentary regime, society ran fewer risks."

Speaking of the parliamentary regime, "What struck me above all, in the parties which were re-forming, was the passionate desire to award to themselves, as soon as they had the occasion, all the powers of the Republic and their incapacity, which they displayed in advance, of exercising them efficaciously." Only when de Gaulle addressed the Consultative Assembly did the disunity abate.

> The grandeur of the subjects treated, the effect of the words, the human contact with de Gaulle, recalled in the delegates the solidarity which linked us all together and made them feel the attraction of the national community [de Gaulle, of course, already felt its attraction]. For an instant, we then felt ourselves more united, that is to say better.

Political unity is good not only because the shared ideal is good, better than any individual, but because unity itself is better, something higher or larger than the individual. Unity involves the sacrifice of the merely individual; men are political animals, whose nature is fulfilled in collective action. "These political animals," de Gaulle wrote in *Le fil de l'épée,* "have need of organization, that is to say of order and of leaders." This chapter, *L'Ordre,* defends the ethical status of order, without which unity does not exist.

Legal order supplements economic and political order. De Gaulle recounts the trials of some of the Vichyites, and defends his refusal to commute the sentences imposed on writers who had served the enemy; "in letters, as in everything, talent is a title of responsibility." And the Gaullist order is a unity based on responsibility, whether it be in the association of labor, capital, and technology or in the patriotism of men of talent.

Toward the end of the chapter de Gaulle returns to economics, explaining how this monetary policy was to have contributed to economic order. Two strategies were proposed. Pierre Mendès-France, the Minister of National Economy, wanted the government to freeze prices, freeze seventy-five percent of savings, and exact a major tax on capital. René Pleven, the Minister of Finance, wanted to allow expansion by exacting no major tax on capital, only a tax on "culpable profits" and, in general, favored a more *laisser-faire* approach. De Gaulle adopted Pleven's strategy, not because he was a *laisser-faire* capitalist, but because he thought circumstances, rather than theory, favored it. There was no reason to further restrict an injured population if the force of circumstances would tend toward recovery, anyway. De Gaulle wanted order; he also wanted movement. Moreover, because he regarded the force of circumstances as, frequently, more powerful than the force of planned human actions (recall his attacks on *'a priorism'* in military strategy), he designed a mixed economy, planning institutions for security and for justice, but allowed for partly-unmanaged growth when such growth seemed inevitable. It is characteristic of Gaullist thinking to establish this sort of reconciliation-in-tension of opposites.

*

La Victoire is the central chapter of *Le Salut,* as is appropriate. The Allies began a general offensive in November of 1944 which resulted in Germany's defeat. The French army participated, and de Gaulle showed how an army can serve political ends. When Eisenhower ordered a temporary retreat from Alsace-Lorraine by the French, de Gaulle intervened, saying that a retreat would damage hiw own prestige and further weaken French self-confidence. Alsace, he told Eisenhower, is "sacred" to France. When Eisenhower cited good military reasons for withdrawing, de Gaulle agreed, but insisted that armies should serve nation-states. Faced with injury to his own position as Allied Commander-in-Chief, Eisenhower relented; the

French held Alsace-Lorraine.

Recounting the Allied victory in spring of 1945, de Gaulle writes his thoughts on Mussolini and Hitler. The former's mistake was to oppose a European country to Europe; one cannot hurl a people into battle for a cause that is not its own: "is this not to force nature?" By attaching himself to Germany Mussolini was anti-European; his troops fought for him only so long as Germany advanced. When Germany weakened, Mussolini was finished.

If Mussolini provokes a lesson in politics, the nature of peoples, Hitler provokes a lesson in ethics, the nature of man. Hitler

> . . . encountered the human obstacle, that which one cannot overcome. He founded his gigantic plan on the credit he gave to the baseness of men. But they are made of souls as well as of mud. To act as if others will never have courage is to venture too far.

Now de Gaulle had to encounter the human obstacle, from the other direction. He had to struggle with the material part of human nature, reappearing with peace. "This flame of national ambition, reanimated under the ashes by the breath of the tempest, how to keep it ardent when the wind had fallen?"

*

Le Salut's final chapters — *Discordance, Désunion, Départ* — go together, as their alliteration suggests. Once more de Gaulle treats foreign, then domestic concerns, then shows their relation and what they resulted in.

After victory the states made their claims. De Gaulle's policy had four parts: to assure French security in Western Europe by preventing the rise of a new German Reich; to cooperate independently with both East and West; to make the French Union into a free association, thereby avoiding colonial upheaval; to persuade the states along the Rhine, the Alps and the Pyrenees to form a political, economic and strategic bloc, an arbiter between the Soviets and the Anglo-Americans. This last strategy was necessitated by the continued British attacks on French interests in Syria and Lebanon. De Gaulle suspects that Churchill instigated a dispute between the United States and France over French control of the Alpine territories won from Italy because that dispute would free Britain's hand in the Mideast. Britain did eventually control Syria and Lebanon, thus spoiling the possibility of a close alliance with France.

In August de Gaulle visited Truman in Washington. He found him less idealistic than Roosevelt (he'd abandoned the hope for 'world harmony') but rather simple — believing that independence alone would suffice to influence underdeveloped countries to favor the West. Truman believed that the question of peace was mostly of an economic order, that the standard of living mattered more to nation-states than frontiers, grievances and guarantees. De Gaulle, who saw economics as subordinate to politics, told him that France needed reassurances that Germany would not rearm. If these were given, the Eastern European satellites would not feel threatened, would eventually become less attached to the Soviet Union. Truman's later actions showed that he disagreed.

When the atomic bombs hit Japan, de Gaulle regretted that the means now existed to annihilate the human race, but did not allow himself to be so overwhelmed as to neglect sending Frenchmen back to Indochina, taken by Japan months before. De Gaulle saw possibilities of "free association" with the colonies, reconciling freedom for the 'natives' with French interests. "The will of the French would decide" if France would take this "opportunity for a role conforming to her genius": the "rays of a new sunrise" instead of "the last fires of the setting."

"As for me, who knew only too well my limitations and my weakness and who knew well

110

that no one man can substitute himself for a people, how I wished to make enter into the souls [of others] the conviction that animated me!'' But when he listened for echoes to his appeals, he heard that those of the multitude were "warm, but confused," and that those of the elites constituted "no other thing than the clamor of partisans."

*

Désunion is central to French postwar decline, even as unity was central to the French wartime victory. To de Gaulle it is always the French who are principally responsible for France's victories and defeats, not foreigners, however powerful. *Mémoires de guerre* provides its readers with a political education, and political responsibility is de Gaulle's primary ethical teaching, as political faith is its primary 'epistemological' teaching, and as grandeur is its primary political teaching.

With one-third of its wealth destroyed, with many young Frenchmen killed — often the more enterprising and generous ones who fought in the Resistance — France could still recover, de Gaulle thought, if the French remained united. Unfortunately, "political forces" divided the French. De Gaulle could have prolonged "the species of monarchy" he had instituted, "but the French people is what it is, not any other." Dictatorship would turn the French against de Gaulle because they "would no longer distinguish the reasons" for it; the communists would profit. A dictatorship lasts only when supported by a faction; de Gaulle had none. And de Gaulle needed either popular fear or popular ambition to survive; the French were then neither especially fearful nor especially ambitious.

De Gaulle preferred to establish a new republican constitution, one that provided for the national interest rather than for a factional interest or concatenation of such interests. The political parties were decadent because doctrinal passion, which led to their conception and nurturing, weakened in "this epoch of materialism indifferent to ideals"; they became mere interest groups. The new constitution would allow such parties to continue, but would counterbalance them with an executive whose power would not orignate in the National Assembly. This executive, designated by the people rather than by the parties, would have the power to appoint the Cabinet, to consult the nation by means of a referendum or the election of a new assembly, and would have the mandate to ensure France's integrity and independence if they were endangered. The parliament could cause the government to fall, but the government would have recourse to the nation. The parties, of course, opposed de Gaulle's proposed constitution. The nation was dubious:

> This people, beneath the moving testimonies that it exhibited to me but which expressed its distress as much as its sentiment, was it not tired, disillusioned, divided? These vast enterprises, this vigorous action, these strong institutions, that I proposed for its effort, did they not surpass its means and its desires? And me, had I the capacity, the skill, the eloquence necessary to galvanize it, seeing that all had been flattened?

The trial of Pétain and the public's reaction to it increased these doubts. The High Court failed to emphasize that the armistice Vichy signed was Vichy's principal error; all other abuses "flowed without fail from this poisoned source." Parliamentary and journalistic commentators failed to mark that. The French, both elite and non-elite, failed to perceive the political nature of de Gaulle's five-year war, which was the war *of France* — sovereign and independent — against the Axis after the *de facto* abdication of all members of the Fourth Republic's last government, except de Gaulle. January 1940 to January 1946, he told the press in April of 1947, was "a single and self-same effort on a single and self-same line: the war, the reassembling of the Empire, the reassembling of France, the liberation and then, the first measures of renovation . . . ."

De Gaulle began to campaign for the October referendum in May, after the Allied victory.

He gave his most important campaign speech over the radio on July 12. In it he blamed the "infernal cycle" of thirteen French constitutions in the last century-and-a-half for "imprint[ing] on our public life a character of discontinuity, agitation, improvisation, which has been, in total, disastrous." The last regime, the Third Republic, "no longer corresponded, over the years, to the conditions of our harsh epoch"; "the acceleration of the machine" brought a "rhythm more and more precipitous and complicated" to internal and external problems. Internally, government's tasks increased (the standard-of-living debate); externally, governments had to adapt to the existence of mechanized armies. In a July 29 speech to the Provisional Consultative Assembly de Gaulle said that the referendum's purpose is to "give to the French people a constitutional faith." Scepticism damages any constitution, especially one that has an element of democracy in it. By having the people themselves affirm the necessity for a new constitution, de Gaulle seems to imply, faith in the constitution they eventually would get would be more likely than if they did not affirm it.

The parliamentarians detested the referendum.

> Nothing showed me more clearly to what deformation of the meaning of democracy the spirit of the parties led. For them, the Republic must be their property, and the people existed, insofar as [it was] sovereign, only for delegating its rights and even its free will to the men they designated.

The parliamentarians wanted a weak state in order to "manage it and conquer it more easily." Although the Consultative Assembly rejected de Gaulle's proposal for a referendum by a vote of 210-19 (fortunately, the Assembly was only consultative), ninety-six percent of the voters agreed that a constituent assembly should be formed, and sixty-six percent agreed with the Gaullist proposal that the constitution should be ratified by universal suffrage. De Gaulle interpreted the latter result as an indication that the nation "as a whole" wanted him to continue to lead it, but also that its support for him had waned.

*

In November this new Assembly elected de Gaulle President of the Republic. By January 1, after a debate on national defense in which many parliamentarians opposed his proposals, he decided to resign. De Gaulle saw that he could not impose the constitution he wanted on this Assembly. It was important "to France and to the French" that de Gaulle "leave a man morally intact." He did, resigning later that month.

De Gaulle wrote *Mémoires de guerre* in the mid- and late 1950's, after his attempt to win power electorally by means of an organization founded in April of 1947, the *Rassemblement du Peuple Français*. The R.P.F. was to have been the instrument of a founding whose nature de Gaulle publicly described in what became known as the "Bayeux Manifesto."

> The Greeks, once, asked the wise Solon: "What is the best Constitution? He replied: "Tell me, first, for what people and in what epoch?" Today, it is for the French people and the peoples of the French Union . . .and in an epoch indeed hard and indeed dangerous. Take us as we are. Take the century as it is. We have to carry out, despite immense difficulties, a profound renovation which conducts each man and each woman of our country to more ease [or affluence: *"aisance"*], security, joy and which makes us more numerous, more powerful, more fraternal [note that these goods are parallel: increased population yields a stronger economy, more affluence; power brings security; fraternity brings joy]. We have to conserve liberty . . . .

More precisely, Solon said he gave the Athenians the best laws they could receive. De Gaulle, as founder, would give the French the best laws they could receive, given their national character and the epoch: a regime adapted to them, although, perhaps, not simply reflecting them. The postwar French, as de Gaulle wrote, concerned themselves more with *aisance* than with security — but here security is central, and in other speeches of the R.P.F. period de Gaulle speaks of security far more often and more urgently than he speaks of *aisance*. That may be why the R.P.F. failed.

In retirement, "how many hours flow away, where, reading, writing, dreaming, no illusion sweetens my bitter serenity!" Lack of illusions, for de Gaulle, is never identical to despair. He writes of the renewal of life in nature at his home in Colombey-les-deux-églises, and finds an analogy in his own efforts: "As all recommences always, what I have done will be, sooner or later, a source of new ardors after I have gone." He writes of the seasons, insisting that in winter the earth itself, which he makes speak, foresees "the marvellous return of light and life." He links the earth — old, ravaged by storms, shorn of vegetation, but always producing more living things — to France — also old, ravaged by deaths in wars and revolution, "but revived century after century, by the genius of renewal!" — and to himself — an "old man," also "worn out by trials," but "never tired of watching in the shadow the gleam of *espérance!*" Commentators have suggested that de Gaulle, writing this before returning to power in 1958 (the appeal to security had finally overweighed the appeal to *aisance*) predicted his return. Possibly: but a few sentences before he explicitly tells us that the "new ardors" will appear "after I have gone." Destiny, whatever it may be, readied one more cycle for Charles de Gaulle.

*   *   *

The best de Gaulle scholar, Stanley Hoffmann, writes that "ultimately, the great political leader is an educator," and that *Mémoires de guerre* is "essentially a treatise on rulership." It is not, of course, a treatise on rulership in the same way as *Le fil de l'épée* is a treatise on rulership; it is ordered chronologically, not logically. It is unsystematic. Presenting his political teachings within a historical narrative accords with de Gaulle's insistence on the importance of circumstances. Thus *Mémoires de guerre* is a more Gaullist book than *Le fil de l'épée*.

De Gaulle's student learns how a statesman may defend grandeur in a world that hates, fears, or ignores it. He may not easily see exactly what grandeur is. He must derive its meaning from de Gaulle's narrative. Professor Hoffmann has done that; I shall compare his understanding with mine, which is different, but not very different.*

Grandeur, Hoffmann writes, "was an attitude rather than a policy," which, "like natural law . . . was an imperative with varying (institutional or policy) content," and therefore "not an ideology" because it was "not unalterably tied to any specific policies or forms of power." There is some ambiguity in this language: attitude, law, imperative. But the negative point is sound; grandeur is not a specific policy, institution or combination thereof.

Hoffmann calls grandeur a "triple determination": it "implied a will to be an actor, not an object, a player, not a stake"; it "entailed a decision to be as ambitious, universal, and inventive an actor" as possible; it entailed the subordination of domestic politics to international affairs and rank, thereby exacting the sacrifice of some immediate pleasures. During the war, grandeur entailed independence, status and self-respect. Unity was its precondition.

I agree with most of that, but prefer to state it differently. De Gaulle associates grandeur with ethical and political unity, which result, along with the necessary power, in victory. Grandeur entails faith and vigor: it is the only salvation from great perils. It is anti-defeatist:

---

*The Hoffmann interpretation differs from mine in one important way not mentioned below. Professor Hoffmann tends to see de Gaulle's plans for France as having broadened gradually [p. 188-189] as, the war continued, whereas I think it's clear from *Vers l'armée de métier* that de Gaulle even then required nothing less than a re-founding of France. This is important because my interpretation denies the utility of any simple historicism in understanding de Gaulle.

not 'conquest' in the Machiavellian sense because it is not self-indulgent. Quite the opposite: for the state is its instrument in the political domain, and the state restricts self-indulgence. France is not France without grandeur and France has no grandeur without a strong state. A strong state exists only by sovereignty — the citizen's enthusiastic (faithful and vigorous) consent — which exists when the leaders speak and, more importantly, act authoritatively. Authority comes of their espousing *le salut publique* which, to this defender of nationality, is *le salut national*. In doing so the leader or ruler sacrifices his private self, becoming *grand* by becoming public, accepting the *tutelle* and yoke of rulership. (In order to do this, obviously, the ruler must be what de Gaulle names "the man of character" in *Le fil de l'épée*. Although it is not emphasized in *Mémoires de guerre,* character and the espousal of *le salut national* are related. A man of character may not espouse *le salut national* if he would be a religious or philosophical leader. But if he would be a military or political leader he must; only the nation gives adequate scope for his large ambitions.)

The self-sacrifice of the ruled is their consent to unite, to defer to the ruler in order to contribute to order, precondition of unity. Even totalitarianism has a kind of grandeur; de Gaulle believes that even it is consented to. But republican grandeur, based on liberty, is ethically superior to totalitarian grandeur because it enables responsibility. France's independence is a precondition of grandeur because responsibility is part of grandeur, and there is no responsibility without independence among nations and liberty among citizens. (Totalitarian grandeur, then, is a stunted grandeur.)

Sheer size is part of grandeur. An anthill might be unified and independent, but it is not *grand*. France is a *"grand pouvoir"*; that power may be ethical or cultural as well as military. There is also ethical and political size: the eschewal of vengeance and resentment. Pride, magnanimity and justice are not antlike. Nor is responsibility. De Gaulle's teaching in *Le fil de l'épée* — that men are political animals who need order and leaders — reveals that unity, both precondition and part of grandeur, serves *le salut national* because unity serves human nature, entailing human virtues even as parliamentarism and totalitarianism, finally, appeal to human vices. Grandeur is not the subordination of the domestic to foreign policy, but the subordination of that part of the domestic which is self-indulgent to that part of foreign policy which is responsible, that is, humanly virtuous. This sacrifice actually serves the citizens; in *Mémoires de guerre* de Gaulle shows how a war, foreign policy *in extremis,* might contribute to a founding, domestic policy *in extremis.*

If grandeur's vagueness persists, despite one's efforts to analyze it, that may be de Gaulle's intention. A specific definition is exclusive; definition implies exclusion. Perhaps de Gaulle wants to include some of the diverse understandings of grandeur that men uphold in order to gain their consent. If ordinary politicians use words so vaguely that they become catchalls, a statesman must balance precision and vagueness, principles and expediency.

CHAPTER 10

POLITICAL FOUNDINGS:
REFLECTIONS ON *MÉMOIRES DE GUERRE*

If "the political problem consists in reconciling the requirement for wisdom with the requirement for consent," the founding reflects that problem in its most comprehensive form. The politics of founding differs from ordinary politics because it is the series of acts and speeches by which all subsequent acts and speeches shall be oriented. Today's Americans and Soviets, their public and private lives imbued with different aspects of the political principle of equality, can know that.

Five types of founding have occurred: the ancient founding, based on religion; the tyrannical founding, based on force; the early modern founding, which is artistic, formulated by Machiavelli; the modern founding, which is legal-contractual, formulated by Hobbes, Locke, others; and the late modern founding, which is historicist, formulated by Burke, Hegel, Marx, others. There is also the classical founding, which is philosophic, formulated by Plato and Aristotle; no actual regime has been based on its principles.* It has not "occurred" in political history.

Fustel de Coulanges, the best portrayer of the ancient founding, tells us that "The religious idea was, among the ancients, the inspiring breath and organizer of society." The founding "was always a religious act" whereby the founder enclosed the souls of worshipped ancestors within the boundaries of the site, making it holy, a sanctuary. The founder was himself worshipped, his memory recalled by ceremonies and poems. "The *urbs* of the Trojans, the material part of Troy, has perished, but not the Trojan *civitas;* thanks to Aeneas, the sacred fire is not extinguished, and the gods still have a worship." The local and civic religion constitutes the ancient political bonds that unify citizens. Except in the case of tyranny, "It was not force . . . that created chiefs and kings in those ancient cities." Hence "We do not see at the origin of the ancient nations those fluctuations and struggles which mark the painful establishment of modern societies."

Most important "The ancient law never gave any reasons. Why should it?" For this reason, sophists and philosophers did it no good.

By Machiavelli's time, however, religiously-based regimes survived, having adapted some of the philosophic teachings to their own purposes. But whereas "the Philosopher," Aristotle, writes of habit, Machiavelli writes of discipline: the latter has more to do with a way of using force that is 'moderated' only by the necessity of not always using it openly; the Machiavellian founder 'moderates' his use of force only to augment the force he can use later. The Aristotelian statesman, had he ever existed, would have been architectonic, but not artistic in the contemporary sense. He would act to encourage virtue. "The ruler . . . must possess moral goodness in its full and perfect form, because his function, regarded absolutely and in its full nature, demands a master-artificer, and reason is such a master-artificer . . . ." We know that Aristotle does not regard reason as a generator of "constructs" in the contemporary sense; art, for him, is less the shaping of an artifact than the practice of mimesis, loosely translated as nature-imitation. Reason dis-covers nature, and the Aristotelian founder would artfully imitate the discoveries of reason, especially insofar as they regard human nature, the characteristic human virtues.

Machiavelli's founder is an artist-as-shaper who gives form to his malleable subjects. One

---

*Any typology that groups Plato with Aristotle, despite the latter's critique of Plato's ideal *politeia* — a typology, moreover, that groups Burke with Marx — needs subdivisions, to put it mildly. But for the purposes here these groupings are more accurate than inaccurate.

of his principal tools is "religion judiciously used" (a tool known to the classical philosophers, also): "In truth, there never was any remarkable lawgiver among any people who did not resort to divine authority, as otherwise his laws would not have been accepted by the people" — Moses in one of Machiavelli's examples. Real founding acts, Machiavelli assures us, are violent, criminal (in this Nietzsche follows, but also ennobles, Machiavelli). The Machiavellian founder uses force and craft (the celebrated lion-and-fox); he is an armed (force) prophet (craft) of pious cruelty who reverses the classical (Ciceronian) adage that it is better to be loved than feared by one's subjects.

The transition from the ancient to the early modern founding was eased by sophistry, with a certain measure of philosophy; the transition from the early modern to the modern founding was eased by modern science. Bacon, the artful defender of modern science, was perhaps the first philosopher in modernity to suggest that religion is politically unnecessary. In his essay "Of Seditions and Troubles" he identifies four pillars of government: religion is the first, along with justice, counsel and treasure. He follows that essay with "Of Atheism" and "Of Superstition." In the former, he writes that atheism is not politically useful, that religious belief has a good effect on human actions. But in the latter he writes that "atheism did never perturb states," and that "the times inclined to atheism . . . were civil times." Times of peace and prosperity, he writes, incline men to atheism. In other essays he declares himself a partisan of peace and prosperity, thus revealing that he would at very least risk increased atheism, and do so with a satisfied conscience. He artfully escapes censure by condemning superstition, which he may regard as identical to religion, but which religious men regard as the opposite of religion. In other, less popular, writings he proposes (as candidly as possible, given his circumstance) the replacement of dreams of heavenly paradise with what he believes to be the scientifically-realizable dream of a peaceful, prosperous earthly paradise. Science-as-art replaces religion-as-art; it serves comfortable self-preservation as much as it serves Machiavellian glory.

Hobbes (whose ruling passion, confessedly, was the fear of violent death) and Locke (of whom it is hard to imagine a ruling *passion*) supplied a political basis for Bacon's artful use of science as the means with which to conquer nature. Locke instructs us that "the great Question which in all Ages has disturbed Mankind, and brought on them the greatest part of those Mischiefs which have ruin'd Cities, depopulated Countries, and disordered the Peace of the World, has been, Not whether there be a Power in the World, nor whence it came, but who should have it." Who rules? It is the question asked by classical philosophers and Machiavellians alike; it is not a religious question ('whence came this power?' is the religious question). Unlike the harsh, spirited Machiavelli, Locke 'softens' the problem by formulating a contract-theory of founding. *Voluntary* consent is important to Locke, and to obtain the voluntary consent of the people one must appeal not to spiritedness but to appetite, and not to fear of violent death but to popular aversion to material scarcity. (Hobbes, then, is another transition-figure — a Machiavellian who has lost his nerve.) And like Bacon, the modern legal-contractarian political philosopher is more impressed with humanity's *realizable* capacity for reasonableness than previous philosophers are. Of course, "reasonableness" becomes different after Bacon; it is the passions' handmaiden, a vulgar-ized thing.

Rousseau eases the transition from the modern to the late modern founding. "It would take gods to give men laws," he tells us, before making it clear that a Rousseau will do. A founder/legislator, being an engineer (a prince is but a mechanic), "ought to feel himself capable, so to speak, of changing human nature" — substituting human morality, which is social, for human nature, which Rousseau believes to be solitary. Even with his doctrines of the *tabula rasa* and the social contract (formed voluntarily in the state of nature), Locke does not suggest that humann nature can be changed; he does say that parts of it can be redirected. But Rousseau's suggestion leads to historicism: "Most peoples, like most men, are docile only in youth; as they grow old they become incorrigible," and only violence and revolution can cause that "horror of the past" which "takes the place of forgetfulness." We are near the use of terror as an instrument for the re-making of human nature. Rousseau echoes Machiavelli, but metamorphoses him into a Machiavelli who has read Bacon and Locke — rejecting their economism, but retaining their belief in human malleability and their egalitarianism. Rousseau is almost the last political philosopher to advocate genuine foundings.

Burke, the first historicist, rejects founding because he disbelieves in the political efficacity of reason. His belief in the gradual accretion or growth of political regimes anticipates some aspects of contemporary nationalism. One suspects that his dislike of the modern use of reason — reason as the passions' handmaid, as the tool of engineers of the new social order — leads him to overemphasize the historicity of political life.*

Hegel, who is far more profound, more deeply wrong, rejects founding on epistemological grounds. He wants philosophy (the most comprehensive reasoning) "to relinquish the name of love of knowledge and to be actual knowledge"; he imagines that science can be exoteric, as the publicists of Englightenment did. But in order to imagine that, he needs to deny that ideas and ideals are radically different from everyday reality. "What is rational is actual and what is actual is rational," he insists. Ideals must be attainable; the state, he writes, is "inherently rational." Only "dialectic" reveals this — but the "dialectic" here is a Platonic word applied in a Machiavellian way. Founders, Hegel writes, *cause* morality to begin. They do

> . . . not do this as their recognized right, and their conduct still has the appearance of being their particular will. But as the higher right of the Idea against nature, this heroic coercion is a right coercion. Mere goodness can achieve little against the power of nature.

Machiavelli's founder-as-criminal; Bacon's conquest of nature; Rousseau's language of "right": Hegel deliberately synthesizes his modern predecessors and (unintentionally) prepares the way for Marx and other historicists, 'left' and 'right.'** Because Hegel is less materialistic than they, he ranks the founder higher than they do. But even for him the founder is only part of a larger, non-natural (indeed, anti-natural) process: history — soon to have a capital 'H' bestowed upon it. Soon the 'founder' becomes the most advanced of History's vanguard, and Hannah Arendt can write that "A fundamental difference between modern dictatorships and all other tyrannies of the past is that terror is no longer used as a means to exterminate and frighten opponents, but as an instrument to rule masses of people who are fundamentally obedient." Terror becomes an epistemological weapon. "Totalitarian policy claims to transform the human species into an active unfailing carrier of a law, to which human beings otherwise would only passively and reluctantly be subjected."

But this general summary needs a concrete foundation of its own.

*

Plutarch examines ancient foundings from a classical perspective. Although he is not a philosopher, he makes use of philosophic traditions. And if his founders are often mythical they nonetheless confront real and perennial difficulties; Plutarch apparently intends to

---

*Thus far, I have merely condensed and vulgarized the subtle argument of Leo Strauss in his *Natural Right and History* [University of Chicago Press, Chicago and London, 1953].

**One such later figure on the 'right' was Maurice Barrès, who criticized the "intellectuals" who praised the neo-Kantianism of France's Third Republic. "Intellectual: an individual who convinces himself that society should be founded on the basis of logic; and who fails to see that it rests on past exigencies that are perhaps foreign to the individual reason." [*Scenes et Doctrines du Nationalisme,* in *The French Right (from de Maistre to Maurras)*, edited by J.S. McClelland, Harper & Row, New York, 1971, p. 175]. "Logic, the analytical distinctions of thinkers, perpetuates the difficulties which the natural dynamism of things undertakes to remove" [*ibid.,* p. 188].

educate future statesmen.

Theseus wanted "to make himself popular." His action harmonized with his desire; he founded a democracy in Athens. Attica had been a collection of tribes; he united them, then re-divided them into three classes. The egalitarian principle underlying the democracy was the equality of these classes, each of which had its source of power. "[T]he nobles excel[led] the rest in honor [they cared for religion, chose magistrates, taught and dispensed laws, interpreted and directed sacred matters], the husbandmen in profit, and the artificers in number." Theseus seems to have intended that these classes would balance each other.

The regime failed. Theseus left Athens, and returned to see "the minds of the people . . . so generally corrupted, that, instead of obeying commands in silence, they expected to be flattered into their duty." Number and profit overbalanced honor.

Whereas Theseus's regime was too democratic, too 'libertarian,' Plutarch's Romulus (with whom Theseus is paired) became tyrannical. Romulus founded Rome by means of fraud (fake divination), violence (the murder of Remus) and religious ceremony. He buttressed the founding with another violent act: the 'rape' of the Sabine women. It is noteworthy that Plutarch refrains from condemning any of this — except for the murder of Remus, which he doubts that Romulus committed. Fraud, force (if not violence) and religious ceremony seem necessary to found a *polis* and a regime. In a later chapter, Plutarch writes that the "pretension to divine authority . . . if not true, assuredly was expedient for the interests of those it was imposed upon." Plutarch differs from Machiavelli in his insistence on the use of means that are not vicious at the service of ends that are virtuous. In Romulus's case, the tendency toward vicious acts overrode the tendency toward nobility, and tyranny resulted. It was followed, possibly, by tyrannicide.

Theseus and Romulus founded both the regime of a *polis* and the physical *polis* itself; Romulus, especially, caused a *polis* to be built where none had existed before. Another kind of founder founds a new regime or *politeia* in an existing *polis*. Such were Lycurgus and Numa Pompilius.

The source of Lycurgus's authority was his character. He had "a nature made to rule, and a genius to gain obedience." When he decided to fulfill that nature by founding a new regime in Sparta, he prepared things with care — beginning with himself. Traveling to Crete, he studied "their several forms of government." While there he also discovered Homer's poetry, and decided to use it as a source of citizen education in the regime he planned.

But he first used poetry to cultivate the rough ground of Sparta before his return. He had Thales, a poet, go to Sparta and compose lyrics celebrating

> . . . obedience and concord; the very measure and cadence of the verse, conveying impressions of order and tranquility, had so great an influence on the minds of the listeners, that they were insensibly softened and civilized, insomuch that they renounced their private feuds and animosities, and were reunited in a common admiration of virtue. So that it may be truly said that Thales prepared the way for the discipline introduced by Lycurgus.

This may be the first collaboration of a statesman and an artist. It was possible because poetry was then a source of authority; aside from its virtue-inducing measure and cadence, it owed that authority to religion.

Lycurgus also founded a tripartite regime. But instead of founding three classes, he founded three institutions: king, senate and popular assembly. The senate was "a central weight, like ballast in a ship, which always kept things in a just equilibrium," preventing the monarchy-to-democracy-to-monarchy swaying that might otherwise have occurred. Lycurgus thus avoided the mistakes of Theseus and Romulus. Moreover, although the people had the power to ratify the laws and proposals devised by the kings and senators, the latter could refuse to allow the former to pervert or misinterpret those laws and proposals.

Lycurgus also founded new economic, educational and social customs that harmonized with his governmental institutions. A new division of lands and moveable property made merit the "only road to eminence" in Sparta by blocking the usual road. He outlawed "all needless and superfluous arts" — no luxury, no oligarchy. He instituted the famous common meals and founded "schools of moderation," where youth "were instructed in [political] affairs by listening to experienced statesmen." He outlawed foreign travel and discouraged visitors, thus eliminating foreign moralities, habits and views of politics. He refused to commit his laws to writing, thinking that education is a better lawgiver than compulsion, and intending the laws' "manner and form" to be "altered according to the circumstances of the time, and determinations of men of sound judgment." Such allowance for circumstance anticipates Aristotle, and, of course, has nothing to do with historicism; Lycurgus intended his ethical and political principles to remain the same over the centuries.

Numa Pompilius remedied the conflict between oligarchs and democrats that devastated Rome after Romulus's death. Plutarch claims that Numa studied Pythagorean philosophy, not laws and poetry as Lycurgus did. He used not philosophy but "religious terrors" to induce Romans to feel "awe and reverence of the virtue of Numa." Religious dances and processions furthered "the task of bringing the hard and iron Roman temper to somewhat more of gentleness and equity." "The harder task was that of Lycurgus": inspiriting a decadent country being more difficult than gentling — 'civilizing' — a harsh one.

Solon is the last of Plutarch's founders. Founder of a new regime in Athens, he intended to "so fit his laws to his citizens" that all would understand it more advantageous to observe them than to break them. He failed because the Athenian character was difficult to govern and because he lacked the power Lycurgus enjoyed. "[W]hen he was afterwards asked if he had left the Athenians the best laws that could be given, he replied, 'The best they could receive.'" This is the only anecdote concerning the ancient founders that de Gaulle told publicly.

*

The American founding fascinates the student of founding because it combines many types of founding: although its largest single component is modern, it has ancient, classical and early modern components. This mixture of philosophic principles, and the regime's mixture of institutional principles (monarchic, aristocratic, democratic, oligarchic) has caused much scholarly and polemical ink-letting — both recently and from the beginning. The problem matters because the nature of a regime's *ethos,* in fact and in the intention of founders and of would-be founders, exists largely by reason of such principles and institutions.

A historian has identified two major competing *ethea* in early American politics. There was the vision of America as a "Christian Sparta," animating such men as Samuel Adams and Charles Lee. As its name implies, the Christian Sparta was to have been a regime based on a combination of two ancient *ethea;* as its name does not imply, the Christian Sparta was to have been a regime based on the principles of modern natural right, as well. At least one political scientist has noted that this would have been a problematic mixture.

The Christian Sparta's competitor was, of course, the commercial republic, familiar to readers of the *Federalist.* Commercial republicanism continues to inform America's *ethos* more than any other thing, but it would be a mistake to assume that the vision of the Christian Sparta, or various more-or-less secularized metamorphoses thereof, have vanished; they remain important, on the 'right,' on the 'left,' and even in the 'center.'

Everyone concedes that. Controversy arises when partisans of one *ethos* debate partisans of the other; it also arises when scholars (partisan or not) analyze the founding. One of the few scholarly debates worth considering matches Professor Martin Diamond with Professor Paul Eidelberg: the former contends that the American founding, based on modern political principles, established a democratic regime; the latter contends that the founding, based on a mixture of ancient, classical and modern principles, established a mixed regime or, at least, a well-

119

moderated democracy.* To consider the Declaration of Independence, the Constitution and the *Federalist* in the light generated by the Diamond-Eidelberg debate is to learn much about founding a regime in modernity.

The Declaration's first sentence begins, famously, "When in the course of human events, it becomes necessary for one people to dissolve the political bands which have connected them with another, and to assume among the powers of the earth, the separate and equal station which the Laws of Nature of and Nature's God entitles them . . . ." This "one people" is referred to as "they," not "it" — not merely a reflection of the grammatical rules of the day but a reflection of a political theory. For Jefferson believed that "the rights of the whole can be no more than the sum of the rights of the individuals." Nonetheless, on the international 'level' the Natural/Divine Law apparently operates on individuals through the medium of the "people" to which these individuals belong. The Declaration does not define the word "people" directly.

Nor does it tell us if "the Laws of Nature" really differ from the Laws of "Nature's God"; the founders' ambiguity makes possible the political toleration of politically tolerant religions. These Laws confirm "certain unalienable rights," such as Life, Liberty, the Pursuit of Happiness. To Jefferson, one pursues happiness by virtuous means; "good acts give us pleasure." The pleasure in doing good is the basis of the asserted self-evidentness of these natural rights, which has nothing to do with Lockean self-evidentness. For

> the true fountains of evidence [are] the head and heart of every rational and honest man. It is there nature has written her moral laws.

Such a "sense of duty" or "moral instinct" "is given to all human beings in a stronger or lesser degree." This synthesis of duty and natural right, made possible by a secularization of the Christian notion of conscience, was never endorsed by Locke, for whom only what he called "simple ideas" or sense-impressions are self-evident.** Eidelberg, who calls for a synthesis of the classical idea of duty with the modern notion of individual rights, in this respect resembles Jefferson; however, Eidelberg does not synthesize duty and rights on the secularized-Christian basis of self-evident moral sentiment. In that, Jefferson is a modern.

The Declaration's third sentence applies Jefferson's moral epistemology to politics. Governments are instituted in order to secure unalienable natural rights, which therefore exist prior to the institution of governments. Governments derive "their just powers from the consent of the governed"; consent is that which combines justice (unalienable natural rights) with political power. Given what Jefferson regards as the innate moral worth of most people,

---

*The relevant secondary documents are: Martin Diamond: "The Federalist," in *American Political Thought,* Morton J. Frisch and Richard G. Stevens, editors, Charles Scribner's Sons, New York, 1971; Martin Diamond, Winston Mills Fisk and Herbert Garfinkel: The *Democratic Republic: An Introduction to American National Government,* Rand McNally and Company, Chicago, 1966, 1970; Martin Diamond: "Ethics and Politics: The American Way," in *The Moral Foundations of the American Republic,* Robert H. Horwitz, editor, University Press of Virginia, Charlottesville, 1977; Paul Eidelberg: *The Philosophy of the American Constitution,* The Free Press, New York, 1968; Paul Eidelberg: *A Discourse on Statesmanship: The Design and Transformation of the American Polity,* University of Illinois Press, Urbana, 1974; Paul Eidelberg: *On the Silence of the Declaration of Independence,* University of Massachusettes Press, Amherst, 1976.

**See *An Essay Concerning Human Understanding,* I, ii, 18. Professor Garry Wills traces Jefferson's moral epistemology to Francis Hutcheson, among others. Wills's critics reply that the "moral sense philosophers" Wills cites owe much if not most of their doctrines to Locke. The point is that they don't owe *this* doctrine to Locke, although they do owe their language ("self-evident") to Locke. For Locke, morality is based on sentiment, but this sentiment has no cognitive significance. "Conscience," to Locke, is a myth; it is not "true," much less self-evidently true. Hence Locke cannot synthesize duty with natural right, although he seems to try in some books; duty withers, leaving only rights.

powers freely consented to are likely to be just; moreover, because of this innate moral worth, majorities who wield power will not use it to erase minority rights. Other signers of the Declaration did not share Jefferson's optimism in this regard, which may be why the Declaration never mentions democracy. Indeed, although a government's just powers are derived from the consent of the governed, this need not affect the form the government takes; if a people consents to establishing a monarchy, and if the monarchy respects its people's unalienable rights, that monarchy is as just as a republic. Even the majoritarian Jefferson did not imagine that unalienable natural rights could always be secured in practice. The natural right of self-government, "like all natural rights, may be abridged or modified in its exercise by [the people's] own consent, or by the laws of those who depute them, if they meet in the right of others." Jefferson had the good sense to see that in practice certain compromises secure rights more than they abridge them.

Any form of government can destroy (in practice, not in principle) the rights it should secure; in that instance, as Locke argues, the people have the right to alter or abolish the offending government and to institute a new one; this collective right corresponds to the asserted fact that the Natural/Divine Law operates on individuals in part through their existence as a people. In reforming or in revolutionizing their government, the people should lay the new law's or government's "foundation on such principles and organiz[e] its power in such form, as to them shall seem most likely to effect their Safety and Happiness." This is one of the rare metaphors in the Declaration, and it is a revealing one. To compare the founding of a government to the construction of a building implies that the original political act is artful. Nature supplies reason, speech and various sentiments, thereby inclining us toward society and endowing us with unalienable rights. Nature does not supply governments. This is not the classical view that political life is natural for man; it is a modern view, but not Locke's. For Locke, men are not naturally social or political; for Jefferson, we are naturally social but not naturally political. Other signers may have been more Lockean than Jefferson was.

To the signers, the principles underlying a just government are natural, as is the earth beneath the foundation of a building. The government's powers, however, are formed, organized, by the people as represented by political artists, founders.

The principles and form of the new polity shall be those that "seem most likely" to the people "to effect their Safety and Happiness." This moderate faith in popular wisdom accords with Jeffersonian moral epistemology, but notice the shift from Life, Liberty and the pursuit of Happiness to Safety and Happiness. The former are human rights, common to each individual. The latter are the hoped-for effects of the government, instituted by a people, a group of those individuals. Individual rights, natural and therefore unalienable, are objectified by the collective act of founding a government, and thereby metamorphosed into safety and happiness. Safety and happiness benefit individuals who are citizens; they would benefit individuals-as-humans, as prepolitical beings, were it possible to "effect" them without government. Locke holds that it is not, and Jefferson agrees.

Exactly what sort of government and exactly what governmental actions "effect . . . Safety and Happiness" has been known to provoke arguments. During such arguments, one often hears that the Declaration says government should guarantee the right to pursue happiness, but not happiness itself; one also hears that liberty and the pursuit of happiness mean property rights, or that liberty is good, but equality, or safety, is more important. The Declaration endorses none of that.

Still, what is a people? Perhaps a people is the concrete aspect of that whose abstract aspect is an *ethos:* an *ethos*-sharing group. If so, the Declaration both appeals to that *ethos* and shapes it. Like the poetry of Thales, the Declaration prepares for a founding. One must first establish one's independence, one's sovereignty, before promulgating one's laws; the king "has abdicated Government here, by declaring us out of his Protection and waging War against us." The King has made himself a foreigner, both by the standards of modern social contract theory and of ancient English law: in terms of the former, he has caused a state of nature, a state of war, to occur; in terms of the latter, he has refused to protect his citizens, thus annulling their duty to obey him. He is foreign in the ancient sense of the barbarian, who "brings on the inhabitants of our own frontiers, the merciless Indian Savages whose known rule of warfare, is an undistinguished destruction of all ages, sexes and conditions." The opposite of barbarity, to the founders, is not merely refinement of manners or high technology; it is the moral and political recognition of natural rights.

To the King's barbarity the revolutionaries oppose an *ethos* based on the principles of modern natural right, modulated by virtues not entirely consonant with modern natural right. These are not only Jeffersonian sentiments. The signers conclude the Declaration by "appealing to the Supreme Judge of the world for the rectitude of [their] intentions"; for this they cannot appeal to the opinions of mankind, the American people, or each other because men cannot, finally, know the rectitude of other men's intentions. They do so "in the Name, and by Authority of the good People of these Colonies," because the people would not be authoritative if they were not also good. Had the founders not thought the American people of 1776 were more or less uncorrupt (with a reasonable chance of remaining that way) they probably would not have argued as they did. As late as 1813, Jefferson contended that Americans "may safely and advantageously reserve to themselves a wholesome control over their public affairs, and a degree of freedom, which, in the hands of the *canaille* of Europe, would be instantly perverted to the demolition and destruction of everything public and private."

"And for the support of this Declaration, with a firm reliance on the protection of divine Providence, we mutually pledge to each other our Lives, our Fortunes and our sacred Honor." The rectitude of one's intentions can be judged only by God; the rightness of one's principles can be founded only in the Natural/Divine Law and perceived only by uncorrupt souls; the authority (that is, the justice and power) of a political action can be founded only on the consent of the people. But the support of a political action can come from only two sources: divine Providence and one's political friends. The names of these political friends follow; they tell us little. But their pledge tells us more.* In pledging their lives they show that, like democrats, they regard life as a worthwhile thing; in pledging their lives they show that, unlike democrats, they do not regard life as the most worthwhile thing. Most of the signers are sufficiently wealthy to be oligarchs and, like oligarchs, in pledging their fortunes they implicitly admit the worth of fortune. But unlike oligarchs, they are also willing to risk their fortunes. Many of the signers are also aristocrats in the conventional sense — 'well-born' men of refined manners. As such, they can value honor above life and fortune, designate it a "sacred" thing. Yet to pledge one's honor also means that one is willing to lose it, at least in the eyes of the world, despite one's decent respect for the opinions of mankind. In this sense the signers transcend the conventional aristocrat, who is frequently a merely touchy man. The virtues the signers admire are those of the mixed regime: Aristotle's way of making aristocracy possible in a world hostile to aristocracy.

A historian has argued that "the transforming democratic radicalism of the American Revolution" "contributed to [the] demise" of such men as these. The virtues needed to support the greatest political action, the founding, necessarily disappeared as the profound egalitarianism of the new republic's *ethos* pervaded the following generations. To judge his claim we must consider the founding itself, consider the kind of *ethos* that was being founded.

The founding progressed during the war for independence, as arguments and events affected public opinion; the Declaration contains the best of the arguments and alludes to the most famous events of that period. But the decisive acts were the formulation and defense of the Constitution.

---

*See Paul Eidelberg: *On the Silence of the Declaration of Independence* [*op. cit.*, pp. 102-103] for an analysis identical to this one at the outset but diverging from it toward the end. Professor Eidelberg and I have borrowed from one another here.

A founder must judge what can be done with those for whom he will found a regime; from the *Federalist* we learn what three of the American founders say they think of the Americans. John Jay, one of the three voices of Publius, defines a people as a human group that shares ancestors, language, religion, form of government, manners and customs; on that basis, Americans of the late eighteenth century constitute a people. Moreover, because this people has acted unitedly in war and in peace, Jay sees them as potentially united under a federal constitution.

If this potential is to be fulfilled, circumstance must cooperate. Madison recalls that "all the existing constitutions [i.e., the American state constitutions] were formed in the midst of a danger which repressed the passions most unfriendly to order and concord; of an enthusiastic confidence of the people in their patriotic leaders, which stifled the ordinary diversity of opinions on great national questions; of a universal ardor for new and opposite forms, produced by a universal resentment and indignation against the ancient government; and whilst no spirit of party connected with the changes to be made, or the abuses to be reformed, could mingle its leaven in the operation." For a founding to be republican and (relatively) wise, the founder must act when the people's concern with some danger overbalances their usual internecine squabbles, partisan or not — when the people (for that reason) unreservedly support "their patriotic leaders," the founders, and when "a universal resentment and indignation" against the existing regime animates them with "universal ardor for new and opposite forms." It is the rare instance of mass resentment for rulers combining with mass deference toward would-be rulers.

Fear and anger are, then, the passions that must be directed toward the establishment of a republican regime of order and concord. (This may surprise, even shock, purists of all hues — but what has political wisdom to do with them?) It is important to notice that Publius speaks to a predominantly modern people: when Jay invokes fear of external dangers, when Hamilton evokes fear of inter-state disorder, when Madison evokes fear of economic and other types of faction, there is little or no mention of divine retribution and no pretense of divine inspiration. The only 'religious' fears invoked are not truly religious at all; they are fears of the disorder that religion can bring.*

Nor is the defense against these feared dangers a religious one, in the usual sense. Political union under a republican constitution is the defense. Hamilton writes that "the science of politics, like most other sciences, has received great improvements" in modernity, including the discovery and/or elaboration of "the efficacy of various principles not known at all, or imperfectly known to the ancients," including division of powers, checks and balances, judges holding office during good behavior and, perhaps most importantly, representation. Eidelberg is correct to say the Founders knew that such principles were not *completely* unknown to the ancients; as Madison observes, the ancients knew of representation, the basis of republicanism. Madison goes on to observe that the ancients failed to apply this principle with sufficient rigor, as they allowed the people to participate to some extent in governments' executive parts.

The defense against political dangers is political, not religious. There is, nonetheless, a kind of religiosity attached to this modern republicanism; Publius tells us that disquisitions on political history, ancient and modern, are useful because "Experience is the oracle of truth," and "where its responses are unequivocal, they ought to be held sacred." The American Constitution — a product of such, as it were, religious experience — ought to be popularly regarded with "sacred reverence." If, as Eidelberg contends, the *Federalist* owes its lack of religiosity to the fact that religiosity was a needless-to-acknowledge characteristic of the American people, Publius's rhetoric suggests that religiosity was of a politically useful sort.

---

*The theoretical basis of the arguments from fear is the doctrine of modern natural right. According to Madison in *Federalist* #51, justice — "the end of government" and of "civil society" — is the securing of rights. In the "state of nature" "the weaker individual is not secured against the violence of the stronger."

This understanding of the nature of the people for whom they would found a regime, and this understanding of the effects of circumstance on that people, illuminates Hamilton's suggestion that one question to be resolved by the ratification vote is "whether societies of men are really capable or not of establishing good government from reflection and choice, or whether they are forever to depend for their constitutions on accident and chance." The founders cherish neither the early-modern dream of conquering events, history, nor the late-modern dream of letting 'History' conquer things for us. The founders were among those moderns who, with some of the classic thinkers, prudently regarded the founding act as somewhat artful and somewhat fortuitous.

Because "Constitutions of civil government are not to be framed upon a calculation of existing exigencies, but upon a combination of those with the probable exigencies of the ages, according to the natural and tried course of human affairs," the founder must understand human nature, especially as manifested in political life. The American founders regard human nature as partly rational, but not so rational that men can be governed by reason alone. Eidelberg finds this consonant with Aristotelian teachings; Diamond contends that Madison, for example, does not use reason in an Aristotelian way. Referring to the celebrated tenth *Federalist,* Diamond observes that whereas Aristotle would use reason to improve citizen opinion and (therefore) to improve citizen conduct, Madison uses reason to arrange a polity in which opinion shall be less religious, less attached to leaders, more attached to economic interest. But Diamond also admits, and Eidelberg insists, that Madison regarded the Bill of Rights as a kind of educative device with which public opinion could be elevated, counteracting mere interest and passion.

It is more precise to say that reason as conceived by Aristotle and reason as conceived by the American founders differ in nature more than they differ in use. Hamilton, who shares little else with Jefferson, does uphold a Jeffersonian epistemology. In *Federalist* #31 he writes that "first principles" are self-evident — including moral and political principles, which neither Aristotle nor Locke regarded as self-evident. Hamilton subsequently admits, now following Aristotle, that moral and political knowledge is less certain than such knowledge as one acquires by studying mathematics. But the founders are significantly to the 'left' of Aristotle; their epistemology allows (or requires) them to be there because it is a more democratic epistemology, one that holds fundamental truths to be self-evident to all uncorrupted minds.

The ethical result of the American founders' political depreciation of reason, according to Diamond, is the aforementioned depreciation of the classical emphasis on character-formation. Diamond's founders will leave human nature at a lower 'level' (that of "commodious self-preservation"), "deliberately tilt[ing]" the American regime so as "to resist, so to speak, the upward gravitational pull of politics toward the grand, dramatic, character-ennobling but society-wracking opinions about justice and virtue." Not only does Eidelberg disagree with this assessment of the founders' intentions regarding the people (citing Madison's intended use of the Bill of Rights), but he reminds us that an *ethos* includes the character-formation of statesmen as well as that of the people. Such men as Hamilton and Madison were not animated by economic motives, principally; Eidelberg emphasizes their aristocratic virtue, honor — an unMachiavellian virtue. But he quotes only the writings of James Wilson at any length on this point, and when he contends that honor in representative government bases itself on independence, which in turn bases itself on "the contemplative intellect," he ignores the problematic character of the relationship of judgment, which is practical, to contemplation, which is not practical.* Admitting that the Constitution is silent in

---

*Eidelberg also makes an argument based on a secondary source: Gerald Stourzh's *Alexander Hamilton and the Idea of Republican Government* [Stanford University Press, Stanford, 1970]. Stourzh cites Bacon's *Essay* 55, "Of Honor and Reputation," which discusses various kind of political honor and political greatness. Stourzh regards this essay as an exposition of an idea

(Cont.)

regard to such matters, he goes on to discuss the national university proposed by some of the founders, Madison's intended use of the Bill of Rights as "a political creed," and Witherspoon's eclecticism. He thus establishes that there is some potential in the American founding for something more than what Diamond sees; he does not establish — nor, I suspect, does he believe that he establishes — that this is the founding's dominant motif.**

With the probable exception of such men as Wilson and Witherspoon, and with the possible exception of the eclectic partisans of the "Christian Sparta," the founders were moderns more than anything else. But their predominantly modern view of human nature did not cause them to be democrats. Elbridge Gerry, who eventually refused to endorse the Constitution because he believed it too undemocratic, nonetheless insisted, during the first days of the Constitutional Convention, that "the evils we experience flow from an excess of democracy," that although the people do not lack virtue, they "are the dupes of pretended patriots." George Mason "admitted that we had been too democratic, but was afraid we should incautiously run to the opposite extreme." Mason hoped that the House of Representatives would be "the grand repository of the democratic principle of the government"; Edmund Randolph wanted the Senate to check and balance democratic tendencies, because the "evils under which the United States labored" originated in "the turbulence and folly of democracy." Madison agreed that the House of Representatives should be democratic. Arguing as he did later in the *Federalist,* he observed that pure democracy can only exist in small countries where the people live sufficiently near the legislature to vote on the laws; with representative government, the country can be larger — size being "the only defence against the inconveniencies of democracy consistent with the democratic form of government." He distinguished the Senate from "the popular branch."

The regime founded — "a system of government without an example ancient or modern" — is a republic. In the tenth *Federalist* Madison defines the republican and democratic forms as species of "popular government" — distinguished, again, by the use of representatives or the eschewal of their use. Pure democracy "can admit no cure for the mischiefs of faction." A republic can, because representatives "refine and enlarge the public views," and because its larger size makes it more difficult for corrupt representatives to act in concert. Madison assumes — or, at least, hopes that his readers assume — that good representatives will be able to do good (refine and enlarge the public views) while bad representatives will be stymied. Madison writes that the people in a large republic will be more likely than the people in a small republic to select representatives "who possess the most attractive merit and most diffusive and established characters." This is plausible; he does not go on to inquire as to *how* likely "more likely" is. The people of Madison's day, after all, chose Madison, and while "enlightened statesmen will not always be at the helm," Madison's slight 'Enlightenment' bias is understandable. This, perhaps, is the basis of his eventual alliance with Jefferson.

Madisonian republicanism, as Diamond sees, has a democratic cast to it. A republic "derives all its powers directly or indirectly from the great body of the people [not from "an inconsiderable portion or a favored class" of them], and is administered by persons holding their offices during pleasure, for a limited period, or during good behavior." The American

---

(Cont.) which linked classical with early modern thought. But Stourzh ignores the fact that Bacon, like Machiavelli (although significantly less than Machiavelli) admires spiritedness, and that Bacon's conception of reason is unclassical.

**The fundamental difference between Diamond and Eidelberg is this: Diamond is a scholar with a political intention; Eidelberg is something other than a pure scholar, although his intention is no less political. Diamond's political intention is to defend the founding against the charge that it is undemocratic; Eidelberg's political intention is more radical. Eidelberg would renew the American regime, and to do so he sees that he must overcome the dichotomy of the classic and the modern, and even that of the ancient and the non-ancient.

Constitution, Madison observes, outlines an *unmixed* republic (that is, all of its branches are republican, derived from the great body of the people, directly or indirectly — not as in England), but a *compound* one (wherein the branches are distinct, separated, hence — given human nature — competing).

Hamilton, who was not a democrat, preferred a mixed regime. At the Convention he said that

> In every community where industry is encouraged, there will be a division of it into the few and the many. Hence separate interests will arise . . . . Give all power to the many, they will oppress the few. Give all power to the few, they will oppress the many. Both, therefore, ought to have the power, that each may defend itself against the other.

In a republic, he continued, power originates in the people, but that need not yield democracy. Hamilton's untimely death prevented him from testing that argument with the oracle, experience. Jefferson, without political enemies of his stature, won, and America became more democratic than it might have been.

Both Madison and Hamilton knew how to arrange one part of the American *ethos*. Energy and stability in government, with liberty for the people, encourage confidence, deference, industriousness and what Tocqueville calls enlightened self-interest. Such are the virtues of an *ethos* of moderate tension, where duties and rights, religion and commerce, authority and liberty jostle one another in an enduring discord and harmony. Diamond calls this making democracy decent; Eidelberg replies, in effect, that to make democracy decent is to make it fundamentally non-democratic. Unlike Diamond, Eidelberg recognizes that although such a regime can survive periods without enlightened statesmen at the helm, those periods had better not be long — especially in this century, when the regime's survival depends on the wise direction of foreign policy. Knowing, after all, that the American founders did not sufficiently provide for the development of such statesmen, he would complete and overcome their work by emphasizing the noblest aspects of it.

*

For Lenin, as for any historicist, the problem of reconciling the requirement for wisdom with the requirement for consent causes less difficulty than it does for others. His epistemology allows this. Human knowledge, he writes, "reflects" nature; human social knowledge reflects society's economic system. Human knowledge is not subjective, a knowledge of one's feelings only, because sensation is "a direct connection of the mind with the external world," "the transformation of energy of external excitation into mental states." The external world is exclusively material, and matter behaves dialectically. The division of the one and the knowledge of contradictory parts is the essence of dialectics. These contradictory parts of matter can be seen in all 'branches' of science: mathematics has its plus and minus; mechanics has its action and reaction: physics has its positive and negative electricity; chemistry has its combination and dissociation of atoms; social science has its class struggle. Although these opposites may occasionally unify or coincide, such unity or coincidence is conditional, temporary, and relative. This struggle is not a stable *concordia discors*. It is leading somewhere, progressively, at least in human society.*

This is why any rejection of materialism is reactionary. "Fideism" and "idealism" are but

---

*Lenin avoids any speculation on where non-human matter is going. There is the basis for a 'religion' here, and Lenin might have been shocked (or disgusted) by that prospect.

means by which the bourgeois repress proletarians.* Marxism, a dialectical materialism, grew (Lenin's metaphor) out of all revolutionary experience and thought, throughout the world. Revolutionary thought is thought that supports whatever class is currently making its dialectically, materially inevitable advance to power: in Rousseau's day, the bourgeoisie, in Lenin's day, the proletariat. Such thought becomes most profound and clear not in a classroom or a library but during revolutionary activity, when the masses "learn each week more than they do in a year of the usual somnolent life" because they learn the aims of competing economic classes. With Machiavelli, Lenin finds extremes more revealing than the everyday.

As in epistemology, so in ethics. Lenin instructs a group of young communists that "our morality is entirely subordinated to the interests of the class struggle." To a communist, *all* morality lies in class struggle; there is no ethical standard beyond it. For Lenin, the right kinds of epistemology and ethics are simultaneously philosophic and rhetorical; they reflect the progress of 'History,' and assist it.

Lenin's materialism causes him to concern himself with mass. And for Lenin 'the people' are the proletariat, in part because of its mass. But the proletariat is also the only class "capable of manifesting courage and decisiveness" *as a class*, although of course individual bourgeois are courageous and decisive. Proletarian spiritedness contrasts with bourgeois fearfulness, and its evocations thereof. Lenin chides the bourgeois press for its use of fear-tactics. The American founders, as mentioned above, frequently appeal to fear. Lenin does not. Like Machiavelli, Lenin exalts spiritedness over timidity and its result, meekness. Unlike Machiavelli (and also unlike Plato, who also prefers spiritedness to meekness, but who does not deride deference), Lenin ascribes spiritedness to the majority.

He can do that because he believes in a historical dialectic. He can be an extremist, maximize the spiritedness of the majority, because he believes that 'History' advances toward an extreme. As its dialectic (seen in the "contradictions" or class-antagonisms of the bourgeois order) advances, there shall be no need for compromise and/or reconciliation. Politics means a struggle between classes — a struggle that ends only when classes disappear.** In the long term, the dialectic will prevent compromise, reconciliation.*** This is why Lenin argues, with Lassalle, that a genuinely revolutionary party "becomes stronger by purging itself," ridding itself of those who don't know where 'History' is going.

Knowing where 'History' is going is the job of the party leader/ideologist — philosopher/ rhetorician *and* politician, combined. Lenin writes that good ideologists foresee events, then direct those who do not foresee them. To foresee is to be "politically conscious," and "the conscious element *participates"* in the "interaction" of environment and people "in the determination of the path" that the people take. Because for Lenin consciousness is an exclusively material thing, the politically conscious leaders are those who detect underlying economic circumstances and trends, speaking and acting so as to make the people detect those circum-

---

*Today's adherents to a 'theology of liberation' — a combination of Marxism and Christianity — would arouse Lenin's contempt. He wrote to Gorky that Christian 'socialism' is distortion of socialism [Letter to Maxim Gorky, in Lenin's *Collected Works,* Progress Publishers, Moscow, 1966, volume 35, p. 127]. This is not to say that a Leninist would not use such a 'theology' for his own purposes at a given point in world history; one may always make use of the contemptible.

**Recall that Madison wanted to preserve the existence of (moderated) factions.

***For a — as Marxist-Leninists say — concrete example of this, see Lenin's *The Agrarian Question and the 'Critics of Marx,'* (1901), especially Chapter IX, "Dairy Farming and Agricultural Co-operative Societies in Germany" [*Collected Works,* Volume IV, International Publishers, New York, 1929].

stances and trends, also. In doing so, leaders make us partake of their belief that reality is dialectical. This allows them to contradict themselves in speech and action if such shifts contribute to raising mass consciousness (which in turn contributes to the dialectical progress of 'History'). But the ideology itself coheres logically, for to Lenin the vanguard fulfills its role by enacting an ideology that eschews the compromised middle course and 'objectively' and strengthens the proletarian class economically and politically. The dialectical twists and turns of the Leninist leader (the lying speech, the deceptive actions) are at the service of what Lenin believes is the 'logic' of 'History,' identical to Lenin's ideology.

The Leninist founder differs from other founders because he believes that he foresees the next move of this dialectic; earlier founders believed, or said they believed, that they foresaw the gods' desires; some founders claimed no foresight, contenting themselves with advocating certain doctrines. Lenin's 'founder' does not found so much as he leads; the military language is no accident, because Lenin would have the people move, change themselves radically, and not stop until 'History' stops. The promised land of a Moses exists within the realm of change; Moses, like all non-historicist founders, would arrange rest-within-change. To Moses, only God can make change cease. To Lenin, mankind will do what Moses thinks only God can do.

Getting mankind to do what it will do requires this new kind of political wisdom (foresight) and spiritedness. There is no contradiction in the fact that it requires a vanguard's foresight and spiritedness to cause the historically inevitable; that vanguard, with its foresight and spiritedness, is part of mankind, part of 'History.' The vanguard, too, are inevitable.

Lenin's writings give their readers a fairly accurate notion of how this is done. There is a certain period of waiting for the right circumstances to occur while writing polemics intended hurry events, organizing revolutionary cadres, and studying revolutionary and 'reactionary' political thinkers. As late as April of 1917 Lenin wrote that the proletariat in Russia was less organized, less prepared, and less class-conscious than the proletariat of other countries; socialism could not triumph there immediately. Lenin regarded Russia as a petty-bourgeois country, vacillating between bourgeoisie and proletariat. The petty-bourgeois are often democratic in their way; their way is determined by their "aversion to class struggle." They are born parliamentarians. Lenin said that parliamentary compromises only blunt mass-consciousness, weakening the proletariat. Parliaments can be useful, for a bourgeois revolution serves proletarian interests in a country ruled by a czar, but they are temporary; the bourgeoisie, along with its parliaments, shall be overthrown by military force — not within "institutions of one kind or another established in a 'lawful' or 'peaceful' way." Lenin says that force alone settles political questions, that the communists should use force "not only for defense but for attack." Lenin sketches a period of violence accompanying the death of capitalism and the birth of socialism, a period of wars — imperial, civil, and wars of national-liberation' — an "epoch of gigantic cataclysms" that has just begun.

Understandably, the First World War was the *deus ex machina* of Lenin's life. "War is a continuation of the policies of a class [Clausewitz, but via Marx]; to change the character of the war, one must change the class in power." The task of Marxist revolutionaries is to change this war from a quarrel among imperialists to a war between the classes. Because it is utopian to assume that the proletariat will achieve its aim peacefully, such revolutionaries must recognize that the war, too, is dialectically progressive. The Leninist 'founder,' a leader above all, thrives in military circumstances; insurrection, Lenin writes, must be treated as an art — as something that *makes,* in both senses of the word. A war is a gigantic purge, destructive and creative.

Purges make a revolutionary party stronger, but only if they are well-timed. One polarizes and purges after one is sufficiently powerful to benefit; before that, one may build coalitions. One may use parliamentarism; one may use nationalism or anti-imperialism (cf. "The Socialist Revolution and the Right of Nations to Self-Determination," written at the right time: 1916);

one may use the peasants. After the revolution, parliamentarians, nationalists and peasants will find themselves less welcome. In Russia the "democratic dictatorship" of the proletariat and the peasants was replaced by "socialist dictatorship," dictatorship by the proletariat alone, by what Lenin believed to be the more historically-advanced class.

The power being seized by the revolutionary party and the class it believes it represents belongs to the state. In *State and Revolution,* Lenin argues that the state is the product of irreconcilable class differences. State power is the stake in every revolution. The proletariat needs this in order to attack enemies and to organize a socialist economy. Using military language, Lenin wants the 'state of war' to continue after the founding act: dictatorship of the proletariat is "a state of simmering war, a state of military measures of struggle against the enemies of proletarian power." (The epistemological link with this is that "stubborn, desperate struggle in earnest is the only real teacher"; the state of war against proletarian enemies shall form the communist *ethos.*)

Lenin's 'founding' task, then, is not merely to establish a new state; that is only one step. The 'founding' shall cease only after the state he establishes is gone. The state shall, in Lenin's famous words, "wither away" because the state, which he believes to be the product of class antagonisms, is unnecessary and cannot exist in a society in which there are no class antagonisms. The way to abolish the state, to the dialectical Lenin, is to first strengthen the proletarian state.

The Russian proletariat should destroy existing state machinery and replace it with another one, merging the police, the army, and the bureaucracy with the people, who are armed. Having done that, he would make each one of the poor part of the bureaucracy, thus, in effect, eliminating the bureaucracy as a separate class. At the same time, this merging of the state with the people must not result in decentralization for small-scale production would only engender capitalism. Centralization prevents this. Lenin would centralize *and* make the state wither.

Proletarian dictatorship, or, as Lenin calls it, democracy without parliamentarism, can do this by making it possible to gradually abolish all bureaucracy. As more people perform the tasks of the state, the bureaucracy, "the functions of control and accounting, becoming more and more simple, will be performed by each in turn"; they shall "then become a habit," eventually disappearing as a specialized function of one economic group. In addition to being a hunter, a fisherman and a literary critic, communist man will be his own bureaucrat. The violence and subordination of life under the state shall disappear, replaced by peaceful (because habitual, unenforced) equality.

In the meantime, one must be firm. having rejected, as Machiavelli did, the ideal of meekness, Lenin substitutes, as Machiavelli did, discipline. His "proletarian dictatorship" requires the "firm" and "ruthless" "crushing" of "exploiters and hooligans," as well as "unquestioning obedience" to the party vanguard. This discipline, especially important because of the delay of the revolution in the West,* is "the discipline of comradely contact." The modern political philosophers associated economy with liberty; Lenin associates economy with discipline.

The moderns believe that in leaving men at liberty they allowed them to fulfill their nature.

---

*Lenin had hoped the proletariat would rebel in all the European countries in the late stages of the war. After that failed to occur, Lenin recognized that the greatest difficulty of the Russian revolution, its greatest historical problem, was the international problem, "the need to evoke a world revolution, to effect the transition from our strictly national revolution to the world revolution" [Political Report to the Central Committee (March 7, 1918), *Selected Works,* volume 2, p. 577]. Without that revolution, the Soviet revolution will not survive, he goes on to predict.

Lenin the disciplinarian is more ambitious. By *"compelling people to work"* he uses "means of control" that are "more potent than the laws of the Convention and its guillotine." "The guillotine *only* terrorised, only broke *active* resistance. *For us, this is not enough.*" It is not enough because passive resistance — liberty itself (Lenin would say bourgeois liberty) — must be broken. "We must organise the deepest foundations of the existence of hundreds of millions of people on entirely new lines."* These "lines," according to the Declaration of Rights of the Working and Exploited People, shall contribute to the revolution's "fundamental aim": "to abolish the exploitation of man by man, to completely eliminate the division of society into classes, to mercilessly crush the resistance of the exploiters, to establish a socialist organisation of society and to achieve the victory of socialism in all countries."

It is easy to deride the Soviet Declaration of Rights by contrasting its words with the political realities; this was done from the beginning. Lenin answered such critics by saying that the communists had to build communism out of the debris of capitalism, with all the limitations that implied. The debris of capitalism includes not only ruined capitalists but imperfect proletarians — imperfect because they lived under capitalism. The proletariat must overcome their own faults while fighting (and to an extent, probably, by fighting) the remaining capitalists, in and out of Soviet Russia.

This fight continued, dialectically, in Lenin's final years. In his later speeches Lenin emphasizes that the true revolution is many years away. His "New Economic Policy," a system of limited capitalism under socialist dictatorship, was the last of his dialectical maneuvers. Because capitalism — within and without — is technologically superior than socialism, socialism must adopt a system of personal incentive, borrowed from the capitalists themselves, in order to fight capitalism.** At the same time, Lenin requires centralization (the slogan "Communism is Soviet power plus the electrification of the whole country" refers to the use of technology for centralization) and purges (see "Purging the Party," published in September, 1921). Propaganda, too, is useful, but in the countryside it should not be communistic; as long as the countryside lacked the material basis for communism it would be "fatal" to propagate a pure communist doctrine there.

Despite the delays of 'History,' Lenin insisted that in the matter of "true, not paper, democracy," the communists had done more than was done or could be done by the best of the democratic regimes in hundreds of years. He offers no proof of this assertion; given his position as the leader of a group that regards itself as a vanguard, proofs are no longer required of him. He is his own 'proof,' a result of the 'logic' of 'History.'

Instead of ridiculing Soviet Russia's Declaration of Rights one might notice that it contains its own refutation. By calling it a declaration of rights "of the Working and Exploited People," Lenin appeals to resentment; he probably believes that such resentment will cease after the non-working exploiters disappear — having been, as he said, crushed. But by liberating resentment, by encouraging men to act on the basis of it, and by giving those men

---

*Socialism (the dictatorship of the proletariat) undertakes to abolish the difference between factory worker and peasant, to make workers of all of them. It does this by "the organisational reconstruction of the whole social economy, by a transition from individual, disunited, petty commodity production to large-scale social production." The proletariat, directed by its vanguard, "must separate, demarcate the working peasant from the peasant owner, the peasant worker from the peasant huckster, the peasant who labours from the peasant who profiteers"; "in this demarcation lies the *whole essence* of socialism" [*Economics and Politics in the Era of the Dictatorship of the Proletariat* (1919), *Selected Works,* International Publishers, New York, volume 3, pp. 278-279.]

**Lenin complains that no single book had been written about state capitalism under Communism. He hoped to restrain state capitalism. See his Political Report of the Central Committee of the Russian Communist Party (March 27, 1922, *Collected Works,* Progress Publishers, Moscow, 1966, p. 278].

130

dictatorial power, Lenin merely assures the systematization of vengeance. The resentful, becoming powerful, revenge themselves upon active and passive resisters, habituating themselves and their subjects to think and feel in those terms, even while wishing for something better. Children are educated within this *ethos,* and because every child resists actively or passively at times, few overcome it, and those few are aliens. Socialism never overcomes itself to advance to communism, and the once-proletarian dictators become debased oligarchs — bourgeois without bourgeois virtues.

*

For de Gaulle, too, a world war was a *deus ex machina.* Democratic politics had yielded the Maginot Line in military strategy — that is, the stagnation of parliamentarism yielded a static form of defense. The military disaster thereby allowed yielded *"abandon"* among apoliticians and citizens alike; this loss of *mesure* was predictable because parliamentarism teaches its creatures to talk and to compromise, but not to act with courage. The *ethos* of parliamentary democracy includes habits that render its citizens helpless (demonstrating once more that politics is architectonic).

Hence de Gaulle required a political revolution, which was a re-founding of France. After arriving in London, his first act aimed at establishing authority by espousing the cause of *le salut national.* His famous radio speech echoed the call of Vercingetorix, the Gallic chieftain who rebelled against the conquering Caesar, telling his people that "they should not be too depressed in spirit, nor alarmed at their loss; that the Romans did not conquer by valor nor in the field, but by a kind of art and skill in assault, with which they [the Gauls] were unacquainted." Hoping to forge "a general unanimity throughout the whole of Gaul," Vercingetorix called for courage, privation-bearing, and honor. To de Gaulle, an extended allusion to the first French leader is no mere historical ornament; it demonstrates his fidelity to France — in action and in principle.

Establishing one's authority (precisely the opposite of the 'personality cult') wins the enthusiastic consent of citizens, the respect and consideration of foreigners. De Gaulle's next act was to build Free France's military power; the military is also part of what France is. One does not *make* authority; one either adheres to France or does not. One does make sovereignty, which has to do with power. In addition to a military force, de Gaulle therefore organized a bank, an intelligence network, a diplomatic corps. The latter appealed to French and foreign public opinion, and worked well in Britain and the United States. It was irrelevant in Soviet Russia, of course, but the U.S.S.R. nonetheless proved a useful diplomatic counterbalance to the "Anglo-Saxons." "War gives birth," as de Gaulle says, quoting Heraclitus; de Gaulle used foreign policy during a war as a means of founding.

Upon returning to France, de Gaulle insisted that legitimacy proceeds from *le salut public,* not from the will or sentiment of the people. He restrained the sentiments of revenge and self-pity because the lawlessness they engender damages all laws, and would have damaged the new constitution he planned. With this legal renewal he planned economic renewal, including the "association" of labor, technology and capital. Legal and economic renewal were to yield unity, the precondition of grandeur: a political, not economic/individualistic ideal, and one that opposes revenge, self-pity and the other petty sentiments.

De Gaulle failed in 1946 because, without the pressures of wartime, unity disappeared. For the democratic French, only the desires for self-preservation and for liberty from the Nazis were sufficiently powerful reasons for unity. After self-preservation and liberty were assured, they used their lives and liberty to pursue the economic goal, *"aisance."* For the old elites these assurances meant the opportunity to return. Thus the next stage of de Gaulle's enterprise (a political founding, a national re-founding) — which was to have been "to give the French a constitutional faith" — did not occur.

This admiration for leadership may resemble a historicist's,* but de Gaulle would lead his people to rest-within-change, not to some eschaton or other. His real nature is closer to the early modern, classical and ancient models; he borrows from each of them.

*For a discussion of classical *rulership* and late-modern *leadership,* see Harvey C. Mansfield, Jr.: *Statesmanship and Party Government - A Study of Burke and Bolingbroke* [University of Chicago and London, 1965], especially pp. 210-211. To the extent that de Gaulle partakes of historicist leadership, he resembles Burke far more than he resembles Hegel or Marx. Burkean historicism has no eschaton, and de Gaulle regarded grandeur as a path to something unknown.

132

SIXTH PART

CHAPTER 11

MÉMOIRES D'DESPOIR (1970)

For de Gaulle, all of this led to the founding of the Fifth Republic. Perhaps it not only led to that founding but culminated in it. Hoffmann is probably right to suggest that the style of *Mémoires d'espoir* excites us less than that of *Mémoires de guerre* because de Gaulle's style reflects his subject; wartime fit this "crusader with great ambitions," whereas 1958-1969 was "a period resembling that of Louis-Philippe" wherein, eventually, the French themselves opposed the crusader. But in terms of politics the Fifth Republic was the culmination of de Gaulle's life. The attempt at a founding described in *Mémoires de guerre* barely started before it failed; it's easy to rule the French by radio from London if you don't have the power to actually rule them. (A heartless man might suggest that the war gave the French what they always wanted: a real government to hate and an imaginary one to love). Actual rulership is more problematic, and although de Gaulle never completed his founding, he'd got much further along in 1969 than in 1946.

De Gaulle's last memoirs are as incomplete as his last attempt to refound France. We have one of the three planned volumes, and two chapters of the second volume. I will use his speeches to supplement his memoirs, knowing that the missing volumes are not replaceable.

*   *   *

Volume I, *Le Renouveau,* contains seven chapters, the first of which, *Institutions,* begins with France and not with institutions.

> France comes from the depth of the ages. She lives. The centuries call to her. But she remains herself through time. Her limits can be modified without changing the relief, the climate, the rivers, the seas which mark her indefinitely. There live the peoples that embrace, in the course of History, the most diverse trials, but which the nature of things, utilized by politics, mold unceasingly into a single nation.

Note well that it is politics, not economics or 'History,' that "utilizes" the nature of things, and contributes to the molding of the French nation.

> France comprehends many generations — past, present and future — "But, by the geography of the country that is hers, by the genius of the peoples that compose her, by the neighbors that surround her, she reveals a constant character that makes the French of each generation depend on their fathers and pledges them to their descendents." It is the state, "which answers for France," that has responsibility for maintaining France's "heritage of yesterday, its interests of today and its hopes of tomorrow." By titling his book *Mémoires d'espoir, Memoirs of Hope,* de Gaulle links past and future by remembering and hoping. Obviously, he intends his autobiography as a book for the future as much as a book about the past.

> Such a beginning is an invitation to comparison. The opening paragraph of *Mémoires de guerre* also concerned France. But it was more subjective: "All my life, I have had a certain idea of France." Here the "I" is gone and only France remains. There is less passion, less extremism, here: no consummate successes or exemplary disasters, no mention of grandeur or of Providence. De Gaulle chooses, more modestly, to emphasize unity, grandeur's precondition. Still, he emphasizes the state's importance, as he did in *Mémoires de guerre.*

> Vital necessity, which in case of public peril is indispensable sooner or later to the collectivity! Since then, for a power, legitimacy proceeds from the sentiment that

it inspires and from that it has incorporated national unity and continuity when *la patrie* is in danger.

All the major French dynasties "received and lost this supreme authority" by their conduct when *la patrie* was endangered. And, indeed, de Gaulle here makes legitimacy and authority the same thing, whereas in *Mémoires de guerre* he wrote that a man could have legitimacy without having authority, justifiable consent. De Gaulle himself, he continues, received authority in days when *la patrie* was in danger, during the second World War, and reintroduced order, progress and liberty (he does not write liberty, equality and fraternity), during and after that war.

He did that by re-establishing the state; "several months after the victory, the State was upright, unity re-established aspiration reanimated, France in her place in Europe and in the world." The state is the institution of and for France. "[A]s long as *la patrie* was immediately in question" de Gaulle had few obstacles. Once *la patrie* was safe, however,

> . . . all the pretensions, ambitions and outbiddings of the past were raised . . . . For the parties had reappeared . . . with the same names, the same illusions, the same clienteles, as before.

Worse, "I must say that, in the public, there did not manifest any current to the contrary." No authority: he resigned.

De Gaulle rejected, of course, the notion that popular sovereignty "could be parceled out between the different interests represented by the parties." (In a radio speech on June 13, 1958 he said that the "fractions" don't add up to the "general interest.") The parties should express opinions, deliberate and vote on laws, but the state is "the instrument of French unity, of the superior interest of the country, of continuity in national action"; far from being a mere "fraction" (as 'interest-group liberals' would have it) the state, to de Gaulle, is the supreme institution, the one whose existence proves that the whole is more than the sum of its parts. Therefore he "held it as necessary that the Government proceed, not from Parliament, in other words the parties, but, above them, from a head [of state] directly mandated by the *ensemble* of the nation and put in position to will, to decide and to act." It would seem that the popular mandate may put a man in place as head of state, but that it must then allow him to will, to decide and to act; this is no pure democracy. De Gaulle's power derives from his appeal to a democratic standard which the interest-groups — the "elites," as he called them — could not publicly reject. He used that power to weaken the interest-groups, but not merely to register popular sentiment.

In 1946 de Gaulle "could not deceive [him]self that, the danger past, such as renovation would not be realizable before hard and new experiences." Moreover, because of Vichy's injustice, "the political game . . . called democratic," appealed to the French. To defeat the communists, then powerful in France, without becoming a dictator, he decided to let the party system do its worst, smothering the communists and preparing popular sentiment to incline again toward de Gaulle. Before leaving office he prudently instituted the referendum, thereby arranging the (democratic!) means by which he might regain power in the future.

For twelve years "the derisory figures of this ballet," the parliamentary system, failed to govern the country. In domestic matters the civil servants, technologists and the military worked from day to day (de Gaulle refuses to praise the regime's economic policy because the needs of reconstruction stimulated activity, which the Planning Office he instituted directed); in foreign matters other countries got what they wanted, as the regime merely tried to "satisfy others" (an "effacement" cloaked by ideologies — 'European unity' or 'Atlantic solidarity' — that "submitted France to the hegemony of the Anglo-Saxons"). The Fourth Republic's fatal incapacity, however, was neither exclusively domestic nor exclusively foreign; it was its incapacity to deal with the overseas territories.

After losing Indochina, the French had the Algerian independence movement to deal with.

The French *colons* threatened civil war if the metropolitan French didn't support them. The regime, the Fourth Republic itself, was endangered, and de Gaulle writes that "it was necessary for me to fix the moment when, closing the shadow-theater, I would make come forth 'the *deux ex machina,'* in other words when I would enter the scene."

André Malraux predicted that *Mémoires d'espoir,* like *Mémoires de guerre,* would be "a Roman simplification of events." The description of the maneuverings of Spring 1958, which ended in de Gaulle's accession to power, is very much a simplification, mixed with disdainful remarks about "the politicians" and praise for those who admitted the inevitability of de Gaulle's return. Historians have measured the difference between de Gaulle's account and history; my interest is in de Gaulle's teaching. His investiture, he writes, was "a profound transformation, not a revolution," because the Fourth Republic's institutions remained. Public acceptance of de Gaulle allowed him to make the revolution, to found a new regime; "the somewhat mythical character with which my personage is decorated contributed to spreading the idea that the obstacles, for all others insurmountable, were going to smooth down before me" (he sensed that feeling in 1945, also). "Eminent dignity of the leader, heavy chain of the servant!"

The most important characteristic of the new constitution de Gaulle proposed was the role of the President of the Republic. He was clearly superior in power to the parliament; parliamentary 'democracy' ended. De Gaulle suggests that the parliamentarians hoped they would gain *de facto* control, anyway, but de Gaulle himself became the first President of the Fifth Republic in order to establish the constitution as he wanted it to be. Circumstances forced this to be an ongoing founding.

On September 28, 1958 the French adopted the new constitution by referendum. After reforming the electoral law (abolishing proportional representation and replacing it with single-member constituencies),* de Gaulle was elected President on December 21 and took office on January 8, 1959.

> . . . I saw open the horizon of a great enterprise. Certainly, by contrast with that which encumbered me eighteen years before, my task would be stripped of the exalted imperatives of a heroic period. People, first of all ours, no longer felt that need to elevate themselves above themselves that danger imposed on them. For almost all, — we [French] are of those — the immediate stake was no longer victory or collapse, but a life more or less easy. Among the statesmen with whom I would deal with the problems of the world, most of the giants had disappeared, enemies or allies, which the world had made stand erect. Remaining were political leaders, assuredly watchful for advantages for their countries, even indeed to the detriment of others, but anxious to evade risks and adventures. How in these conditions, was the epoch propitious to the centrifugal pretentions of the feudalities of the present: the parties, money, the syndicates, the press, the chimeras of those who would replace our action in the world by international effacement, to the corrosive denigration of so many *milieux,* of business, journalistic, intellectual, worldly, delivered from their terrors! In brief, it was [in] a time on all sides solicited by the mediocre that I would act for grandeur.

This is the most important passage in *Mémoires d'espoir* because in it de Gaulle shows that he saw his dilemma: how could he found a regime, refound France, in modernity on the basis of a

---

*With this system de Gaulle got a majority of his supporters in the Assembly. He also caused representation to be less fragmented; obviously, proportional representation maximizes the power of minority-party candidates. Single-member constituencies, as in the United States, moderate the parties by forcing them to appeal to many kinds of voters, various interest-groups.

principle — grandeur — which is not entirely modern? The means of this renewal were to be "the State, progress, independence," and the central one, progress, is itself a modern principle; renewal was to come "according to the genius of the times." Seemingly, de Gaulle intended to set the genius of modernity against its mediocrity, hoping that the resulting battle would cause men to feel the need for grandeur.

De Gaulle intended to write what he called a "'philosophic'" chapter in the second volume of *Mémoires d'espoir;* his death prevented it. Perhaps he would have elaborated on the problem of founding a not entirely modern regime in modernity. While acknowledging the risks of attempting to speculate on the content of such a chapter by examining speeches, the importance of the problem induces me to present that kind of speculation. Before continuing to discuss *Mémoires d'espoir* I will discuss two speeches de Gaulle made early in his first term, one at *La Cité Universitaire* of Toulouse, the other at *L'École Polytechnique.*

In the first he applauds the "conjunction" of "fundamental research" and "applied research" as being in "the human interest and in the national interest." "The rivers of discovery" flow to "the unknown lands of progress," and this is "the general movement of our species."

> Man, at grips with the Universe, that is to say first of all with himself, man searches to emerge from himself, to accede to that new world, where desires remain infinite, but where nature ceases to be limited. This modern man regards with passion and admiration what is discovered in the laboratories, and what is finally applied by modern techniques.

Except, perhaps, for his acknowledgement that to be at grips with the universe is first of all to be at grips with oneself, de Gaulle sounds like a typical modern, praising science and progress. Still, there could be irony in the phrase "that new world, where desires remain infinite, but where nature ceases to be limited" — especially in view of de Gaulle's earlier writings, his insistence on the limits of human nature. And he continues:

> But, at the same time, [modern man] is guided by his demon, for the rivalry of States, the struggle of ideologies, the ambition to dominate, or even the spirit of independence, rise, gradually as arms of war, as the new means destined to ameliorate life. Eternal conflict of the Archangel and Lucifer.

Curiously, although de Gaulle always reproved the struggle of ideologies, he often praised, in his own way, the spirit of independence, the ambition to dominate and the rivalry of states. Unless we are to conclude that he was at least partially on Lucifer's side, we may decide that this is very much a speech to an audience of intellectuals, unwitting disciples of Hobbes.

Be this as it may, we see that de Gaulle isn't simply a modern; he does not advocate a purely modern education. "This [conflict] is why it is indispensable that, concurrently with scientific and technical formation, pure thought, the philosophy that expresses it, the letters that assert its worth, the arts that illustrate it, and also the morality that proceeds from *conscience* and reason inspire and orient this immense effort of evolution." Progress, de Gaulle evidently thinks, is far from inevitable. It depends on "the development of the *esprit,* by the understanding of what is beautiful and the cult of what is good." He does not intend to allow the scientific establishment alone determine the parameters of beauty and goodness. The state "has the duty to maintain in the nation a climate favorable to Research and to Education." The "enthusiasm for what is modern," which de Gaulle wants the French to have, will exist if the state gives both "direction" and "autonomy" to researchers; he apparently means that the state will decide what public needs are, fund research, then let the scientists do their work. Politics will not defer to science; the rulers will rule, and not only according to modern principles. De Gaulle reveals the balance he would arrange between the modern and the unmodern in his peroration.

Yes! nothing is better than lightening the burden of man. Nothing is more noble and more great *[grand]* then to offer them hope.

We know that if de Gaulle wanted to lighten material burdens he wanted to do so in order to make the French responsible in other ways. De Gaulle was no burden-lightener.

De Gaulle insisted on that in his later speech at *L'École Polytechnique.*

> . . . the conditions in which we live, the incredible flight of our industrial era and all of that which is connected with it in the case of technique, of researches, of realizations, all that which relates to energy, mass, vitality, envelop us in material conditions which tend to carry us away. That is why it is essential that, the more that these material conditions elevate themselves, unfurl, seek to govern, the more must persist and impose itself the domination of *esprit*. In our times, what France asks of *Polytechnique* is . . . men whose intelligence and whose character are capable of mastering matter and, by consequence, of using it in the general interest, in place of letting the world submit to its law.

The "grandeur" of *L'École Polytechnique* comprises "scientific knowledge, discipline and solidarity, personal work . . . capital for assuring the triumph of *esprit* over matter." For *esprit* to master or triumph over matter differs from Baconian nature-conquest in that the latter served the material *telos* of comfortable self-preservation. Gaullist grandeur does not:

> Gentlemen, I would end these few words by inviting you to elevate with me your thought, justifiably, toward France. What she expects of you is in the measure of what she gives you and of what she has given you.

To do so brings "the honor of responsibilities." France is unmodern; to be responsible to France is to be responsible to something beyond "a life more or less easy." The man who told students that "nothing is better than lightening the burden of man," was using a modern belief against modernity, baiting moderns with their own beliefs in order to catch them on the salutary hook of unmodern principles. A devoured fish contributes to a better life than its own.

*

De Gaulle's enterprise intertwines with the crisis of the overseas territories; without it he would have stayed at Colombey, writing and pacing the grounds. He used the crisis not only to begin his founding but to nourish it, as he demonstrates in the second and third chapters.

In *L'Outre-mer* (Overseas) he writes of decolonization much as he wrote of the World Wars.

> One can think that I did not do it with, as one says, gaiety of heart. For a man of my age and of my formation, it was passably cruel to become, by his own lead, the master-worker of such a change.

Another 'existential' moment: the third de Gaulle has written of. Colonizing had been a consolation for the losses incurred in the seventeenth and eighteenth centuries, the defeats of 1815 and 1870; it began "modern development" in those areas. "What a moral trial it would therefore be for me to transfer our power, to fold our flags, to close a great book of History!"

De Gaulle nonetheless saw reason for *"espérance."* Burdens on the colonial powers increased as 'progress' continued: more demands for economic and social improvement, for political independence, intensified by the competing ideologies of Russia, the United States, and China. France could do without these burdens, especially because certain links would remain; the ex-colonies would speak French, would feel "the attraction that the angels and demons of France exercise on . . . all those who are brought near them."

In Algeria, de Gaulle explains, the French *colons* hoped to retain their position and expected de Gaulle to help them; the Moslems expected de Gaulle to help them; the Army expected de Gaulle to help them. De Gaulle claims he had no fixed plan at the beginning, but that he did want association, not French dominion. It was too late for "integration," so de Gaulle intended to allow self-determination as long as it was a self-determination granted by France, not forced on France by military reverses, outsiders or parliamentary agitation.

> . . . such was my strategy. As for tactics, I would regulate the march by stages, with precaution. It was only progressively, by utilizing each concussion as the occasion to go further, that I would obtain a current of consent strong enough to gain all. On the contrary, if point-blank I proclaimed my intentions no doubt that, on the ocean of alarmed ignorances, scandalized astonishments, coalesced malevolences, would raise in all the *milieux* a wave of stupors and furors that would capsize the ship. Without ever changing course, it was therefore necessary to maneuver until the moment when, decidedly, good sense would pierce the mist.

This necessitated, among other things, a strong military position — no defeats in battle: a fact that escaped de Gaulle's left-wing critics at the time. As for the right wing, de Gaulle confused them by telling the *colons,* in June of 1958, "I have understood you!": a statement that was, de Gaulle assures us, calculated, not spontaneous, intended to rouse enthusiasm for de Gaulle "without taking me farther than I had resolved to go."

For more than a year de Gaulle hinted; in September of 1959 he announced that the Algerians themselves would vote on independence. "As the catalyst thrown into boiling liquid precipitates crystallization, so the position on self-determination provoked in opinion the radical separation of tendencies." In January of 1960 right-wing *colons* attempted an insurrection, which de Gaulle caused to be smashed. He ends the chapter with an expression of democratic piety.

> It was necessary for me to surmount the discord which gripped me while I deliberately put an end to a colonial domination, once glorious, but which would henceforth be ruinous. It was necessary for me, with great difficulty, to carry elsewhere the national ambition. I sensed that France called me to accomplish this task. I believe that the people listened to me. When the day came, I would ask them if I was given it rightly or wrongly. Then, for me, its voice would be the voice of God.

*

Vox populi vox Dei? Hardly: near the beginning of the third chapter, *Algérie,* de Gaulle writes that "I would lead the game in such a way as to accord little by little the sentiment of the French with the interest of France while evading what would ever rupture national unity." (This, from he who wrote that legitimacy derives in part from popular sentiment: it does, but only from right sentiment.)

When de Gaulle toured Algerian military bases in March of 1960 the journalists, failing to understand his strategy of keeping French forces strong until their departure, misinterpreted his speeches of encouragement as a reversal of opinion. By December, the time of his next tour, the war was "almost over"; in January a referendum on self-determination yielded an overwhelming vote in favor of de Gaulle's policy. (Gaullist) good sense, decidedly, had pierced the mists. De Gaulle's extraordinary political accomplishment was to increase his authority while jettisoning those whose rebelliousness had enabled him to achieve power in the first place. He was now unencumbered by any who would presume to claim an obligation. He refrains from mentioning that, of course.

The right-wing *colons* and army officers desired revenge, forming the *Organisation de l'armée secréte* (O.A.S.). De Gaulle learned of their plans for civil war. "It was necessary to reduce dissidence without compromising or deferring, by affirming in all its rigor the legitimacy which was mine and thus leading the people to uphold the law and the army to uphold discipline.'' De Gaulle invoked Article 16 of the constitution whereby the President of the Republic may assume dictatorial powers if the country is endangered. The coup attempt dissolved two days later.

Negotiations with the Algerian nationalists continued for a year, and the O.A.S. took to setting bombs and assassinating enemies (de Gaulle claims that they killed 12,000 Algerian civilians and several hundred non-civilians). "It is true that, the more my action appeared as clear and right, the more the gang of the professionals of objection presented it as obscure and tortuous to readers and to voters.'' De Gaulle thinks this had a bad effect on foreigners who were accustomed to seeing French governments fall when criticized; Bourguiba, for example, demanded that France withdraw its forces from Tunisia, in the hope of extracting an advantage from the embattled de Gaulle. When de Gaulle refused, Bourguiba's men attacked the French outpost at Bizerte; de Gaulle ordered a successful counter-attack. The political parties and the United Nations were appalled; de Gaulle ignored them.

In March of 1962 the negotiations ended. A month later ninety-one percent of the voters approved the agreements, confirming de Gaulle's legitimacy.

*

Critics faulted him for ignoring economics, but de Gaulle gives *L'Économie* the central place in *Le Renouveau.* He allows no one to believe that he did not subordinate economics to better things, however.

> Politics and economics are linked to one another as are action and life [and in *Le fil de l'épée* it is clear that life should serve action]. If the national work that I undertook exacted the adhesion of *esprits,* it evidently implied that the country had the means.

At a press conference de Gaulle said that "one cannot take any important economic measure without committing a political act.'' In the contemporary world, he writes,

> . . . every individual is constantly in prey of the desire to posses the goods newly created by the modern epoch; because he knows that in this regard his lot depends in a direct manner on what occurs globally and on what is decided at the summit; because the rapidity and extent of information makes each man and each people able at every instant to compare what they have relative to their fellows. Thus it is the principal object of public preoccupation. There is no government which manages outside these realities. The efficacity and ambition of politics have joined with the force and aspiration of the economy.

Because he "would consecrate a good half of my work, my audiences, my visits, my speeches'' to "economic and social matters,'' de Gaulle regards as "derisory'' the frequent complaints that he neglected them. (Knowing, I suspect, that many of his critics would have regarded anything less than a score of ninety percent of his work, audiences, visits and speeches as insufficient: "It is true that the results, whatever they be, would not fail to be contested in a matter where, by definition, the wishes of all are infinite and where nothing ever appears, to anyone, as sufficient.'')

De Gaulle set his "good sense'' against the irrational. Characteristically, he used modernity against modernity, serving grandeur by insisting that the French economy be in accord "with its epoch,'' which is industrial, competitive, scientific and technical. Already, "elements of solidarity'' existed, owing to "the diversity of [the French] and their territory and to the individualism which marks their national character.'' Unfortunately, "the same traits, having failed to be adapted to the times and rectified, tend now to slow the march . . . .''

141

"Expansion, productivity, concurrence, concentration, here, very evidently [are] the rules which must henceforth be imposed on the French economy, traditionally circumspect, conservative, protected and dispersed."

Mere modernization would have involved effort, but little risk. De Gaulle was far more ambitious for France.

> . . . for a long time, I was convinced that modern mechanized society is wanting in a human resource which assures its equilibrium. The social system which relegates the worker — if comfortably remunerated — to the rank of instrument and cog-wheel is, according to me, in contradiction with the nature of our species, indeed with the spirit of sound production. Without contesting what capitalism realizes, in the profit not only of some, but also of the collectivity, the fact is that it carries in itself incentives for a massive and perpetual dissatisfaction. It is true that palliatives attenuate the excess of the regime founded on *'laissez faire, laissez passer,'* but they do not heal its moral infirmity. On the other hand, communism, if it opposes in principle the exploitation of men by other men, permits an odious tyranny imposed on the person and plunges life into the lugubrious atmosphere of totalitarianism, without obtaining, by a great deal, with regard to the level of existence, the conditions of work, the diffusion of products, the *ensemble* of technical progress, results equal to those obtained in liberty.

De Gaulle faults capitalism because it contradicts human nature, not because it contradicts 'History.' (Indeed, the only reference to "the determinism of History "de Gaulle makes in *Le Renouveau* regards his necessary use of the Élysée Palace — i.e., in regard to a trivial matter.) Human nature is social and political, not purely individualistic. The admitted individualism of the French intensifies under capitalism, causing "massive and perpetual dissatisfaction" or, as one historian puts it, "protest as a national way of life." Extreme individualism is a "moral infirmity" which yields social and political instability. Communism, which might be regarded as an extreme anti-individualism, also contradicts human nature, and is *therefore* immoral (de Gaulle, I think, refuses to completely separate the 'is' from the 'ought,' while also refusing to meld them, as Marx did; de Gaulle rejects both poles of modern ethics).

> Condemning the one and the other of these opposed regimes, I believe therefore that all command our civilization to construct a new [regime], which regulates human relations in such a way that each participates directly in the results of the enterprise to which he brings his efforts and is endowed with the dignity of being, for his part, responsible for the advance of the collective works on which depends his own destiny. Is not this the transposition on the economic plane, making allowances for the *données* which are its own, of what are in the political order the rights and the duties of the citizen?

Stanley Hoffman suggests that the French seized on the modern theories of natural rights because the notion of pre-political rights, the un-naturalness of politics, conforms to French ambivalence toward authority and to *"l'horreur du face-à-face"* described by the sociologist Michel Crozier. De Gaulle wants to counterbalance the modern theory of rights, of individualism, with the ancient theory of political duties, of man as political animal (in one respect, then, de Gaulle was deeply un-French). "Participation" is against *"l'horreur du face-à-face,"* against a part of modernity; it is for responsibility (and hence for grandeur). It is not democratic insofar as democracy is egalitarianism. There would still be rulers in politics and executives in business.

De Gaulle is careful to show that "participation" wasn't something he first thought of after the insurrection of May 1968. In 1946 he formed work committees; in the R.P.F. days (and before) he spoke of the association of labor and capital; after 1958 he instituted some profit-sharing. After 1968 "participation" was

. . . what raised against me the determined opposition of all the feudalities, economic, social, political, journalistic, whether they be Marxists, liberals or immobilists. Their coalition, in obtaining from the people that, in its majority, it solemnly disavowed de Gaulle, would break, for the moment, the chance for reform at the same time as [it broke] my power.

This defeat was eleven years away when de Gaulle took power in 1958. In that year, he tells us, the French economy was weak. The alternatives were "miracle or bankruptcy"; "but the psychological reversal which my return to power entailed — did it not render the miracle possible?"

It did, along with sound policy. De Gaulle appointed Antoine Pinay, "symbol of reasonable management," as Minister of Economy and Finances: a man with whom the administrative and business types would cooperate. Under Pinay the government instituted a loan, uncoincidentally reminiscent of the "Liberation Loan" of the 1940's, and "took a series of decisions of which the least one can say is that, for the common salvation, they went against all the particular interests." These were: freezes on civil servants' wages and on farm prices, taxes on companies and on luxury goods, increased gasoline prices, and the reduction or suspension of credits for building. These actions reduced government expenditures, increased exports, decreased domestic consumption and lowered prices; inflation slowed without loss of production, although, of course, jobs were lost. Moreover, "even in France virtue sometimes has luck," and the concurrent economic decline of other countries, the United States in particular, helped France. Especially because France chose this period to liberalize foreign trade: de Gaulle calls this revolutionary, as France was protectionist.

There was, as always, an ethical and political point to de Gaulle's policy. De Gaulle wanted the French to become less secure, less mediocre, more competitive and desirous of risk; "it was what the project had of the coherent and the ardent, at the same time that of audaciousness and ambitiousness, which transported my judgment." economic development, he told the French in a radio speech, is "the route that leads us toward the summits." Economics — even economics — may contribute to grandeur; if heroism is beyond economics, at least economics needs not be dismal.

*

Le Renouveau has four chapters on foreign policy, three on domestic, with the first chapter on domestic policy, the second and third on foreign policy, the fourth on domestic, the fifth and sixth on foreign, the seventh on domestic.* De Gaulle titles chapters five and six *L'Europe* and *Le Monde,* respectively.

De Gaulle formulates what he calls his "philosophy" of foreign policy; needless to say, it has three parts: the interior effort of transformation (i.e., the founding), political stability and social progress, leading to "a world responsibility" for France. His policy was, simply, independence** — which the elites, the parties, resisted. His strategy was to avoid a centralized Europe which, historically, led to nationalistic backlashes (he is thinking of, among other phenomena, Rome, the Napoleonic wars, Hitler). He preferred evolution toward confederation. To get that he had to fight any 'Atlantic' system, which was what Britain wanted; he had to induce Britain and the others to orient themselves toward the Continent,

---

*One might quarrel with the classifying of the chapters on decolonization as "foreign," but the point is that it was a decolonization, a recognition of foreign-ness.

**Independence is the exterior counterpart of liberty. Both served responsibility. De Gaulle told an audience in San Francisco that "one cannot be responsible if one is not free" [*Discours et messages,* III, p. 221, April 27, 1960].

away from the United States; he decided to set the example of *détente,* then *entente,* with the Eastern bloc on the basis of "peace" and "progress," above "propaganda" and "parties."

Aside from France, Germany matters more than any other country to a European 'continentalist.' Accordingly, de Gaulle met Adenauer as soon as possible and, thereafter, spoke to him as often as possible. It is reasonable to think that de Gaulle believed the combined gravity of France and Germany would force other Europeans into the orbit de Gaulle wanted them in.

Gaullist confederation's principal competitor was the doctrine of European 'integration,' based on the already-existing Commission of the Economic Community. De Gaulle's most trivial reason for opposing it was its chairman, a German who concerned himself as much with German advantages as with true integration. De Gaulle's important reason for opposing it was his refusal to think that politics can exist above the states. The proposed federation was a federation without a federator (and de Gaulle, a founder, did not believe that political institutions evolved by themselves). At a 1962 press conference he said that there was no "federator who has today in Europe sufficient force, skill, and credit" to succeed. Spurning the notion of the assemblies as potential federators, he thought that if the parliamentarians tried it, "there would perhaps be a federator, but it would not be European": America, of course. More than the rejection of *de facto* American rule, de Gaulle's policy was political in the most comprehensive sense modernity allows — both nationalist and statist. In 1960, he told the press that anything above the state is "a chimera," except "certain organisms" (e.g., the Commission of the Economic Community) which "have their technical value, but . . . do not have . . . cannot have, authority, and, in consequence, political efficacy." Authority is legitimacy plus consent, power. The supranationalists of Europe lacked power:

> To what profound illusion or prejudice was it necessary to plunge, in fact, to believe that the European nations, forged over long centuries by efforts and sorrows without number, each one having its language, its traditions, its institutions, could cease to be themselves and form a single [entity]? To what summary views responds the comparison, often brandished by *naifs,* between what Europe could do and what the United States had done . . .?

And in his statements in the early 1960's, de Gaulle insisted that supranationalism lacks legitimacy as well as power. The "competition of peoples" is something "without which humanity would give itself up to going rotten and to dying" (similarly, in *Le fil de l'épée* de Gaulle wrote that the leader deprived of ambition would give himself over to decadence).

> . . . I do not believe that Europe could have any living reality if she did not include France with the French, Germany with the Germans, Italy with the Italians, etc. Dante, Goethe, Chateaubriand, belong to all Europe by the same measure whereby they were respectively and eminently Italian, German and French. They would not have served Europe well if they had been stateless and if they had thought, written, in some integrated 'esperanto' or 'volapük' . . . .

The events of the time (the withdrawal from NATO, the *entente* with West Germany, the Fouchet Plan, the rejection of Britain's request to join the Common Market, and so on) were, recognizably, tactical maneuvers in defense of de Gaulle's "philosophy," policy and strategy.

*

The smaller countries of the Common Market resisted Franco-German gravity, rejected the Fouchet Plan, what de Gaulle terms a "European Europe." De Gaulle ascribes this resistance to fear of French supremacy, but also to the 'Cold War,' the desire for American protection. The very love of statelessness only expressed the desire to be subordinated to America. "They still saw things as they were fifteen years ago. We saw them differently." *Détente* was one of de Gaulle's ways of trying to end America's domination of Europe.

In 1958 de Gaulle believed that the Soviets would not try to conquer the West. It is interesting to contrast the reasons he gave at a 1959 press conference with those he gives in *Le Renouveau*. In each case he gives five reasons, three of which do not change: a war with nuclear weapons would destroy both sides; China threatens Russia, will threaten Russia more in the future; Khrushchev's realism. In 1959 he added that "a better life and liberty" are what "man wishes by nature" and that the East Europeans burden Russia. In *Le Renouveau* he summarizes the earlier press conference statement, then adds that whereas communism requires a national calamity to succeed, the Western countries were stable, progressing; he also argues that dominating 300 million foreigners, in addition to the East Europeans, would be too difficult, and that it is impossible to maintain "a state of bellicose tension among peoples who think they will not fight." The 1959 statement is more optimistic-sounding; after the invasion of Czechoslovakia it was clear that the Russians would carry the burden of Eastern Europe, and after the referendum of 1969 human nature could have seemed less inclined toward striving for a better life and liberty, more inclined toward avoiding fights.

De Gaulle moved to acquire the power that enables a country to be independent. Now that the Soviets had nuclear weapons, the 'super-powers' would not attack each other directly, at first. They might, however, attack each other in Europe. "For the Western Europeans, NATO had therefore ceased to guarantee their existence." De Gaulle began a program to develop nuclear weapons, the "modern means of dissuasion." When Eisenhower objected that France would never have armaments in the same quantity as the Soviets, de Gaulle replied that it is sufficient to kill the enemy once, although he could kill you ten times. Consistent with his aim of independence, he withdrew French troops from NATO.

In order to justify *détente,* de Gaulle had to minimize the power of ideology, for an ideological Russia would not fail to persist in its competition with the West. Hence he told Dulles that Moscow's interests were as much Russian as they were communistic, and that Russia's true interest was peace. He told Eisenhower that ideologies and political systems should not be considered more important than "national realities" — that, for example, Peter the Great might have acted as Stalin did after the war in regard to the establishment of Russia's borders. Therefore a gradual "*rapprochement* between one European nation and another" would contribute "little by little to conducting the totalitarians toward relaxing their rigor."

At the time, de Gaulle argued that political systems would also contribute to *détente.* At a 1960 press conference de Gaulle said that the totalitarians "impose on their peoples a system that is contradictory to human nature." Not 'History' but the unnaturalness of totalitarianism makes its (very slow) change inevitable.

Evidently, de Gaulle was far from being naive in his conduct of *détente.* His report of his talk with Khruschev represents de Gaulle as a man undeceived by Khruschev's rhetoric, understanding the national reasons behind it. Khruschev's feigned optimism concerning Sino-Soviet relations and his droll proposal to ban nuclear weapons but to disallow inspection do not pass unexposed. And in fact, Gaullist *détente,* as de Gaulle explained in public statements in the early 1960's, involved not only cultural, economic and touristic exchanges to "create an atmosphere of appeasement," but an "excluding [of] provocative acts and speeches" and, at first, the insistence that the "free peoples" "agree and discipline themselves enough" to block the totalitarians. To contribute to that agreement and discipline, de Gaulle said, for example, "that the ambitions of the Soviet system, the excitations that it is so prodical of on all who, on the earth, tend to disorder and hate, the danger of atomic war that it makes hover over the human species, the provocations it multiplies outwardly in the measure of its interior dramas and, notably today, in this sort of Thermidor where it affects to condemn the past series of its abuses and its crimes without renouncing their cause, which calls itself totalitarianism, all this obliges us to put ourselves on guard, to provide for our defense and to maintain difficult alliances." And when, at the 1960 Paris Summit Conference, Khruschev used the Gary Powers incident as a pretext for ruining the conference — or, de Gaulle suggests, for winning concessions from a guilty West — de Gaulle offered no apologies, blamed the Soviets and not the Americans, and derided Macmillan's spinelessness. In short, de Gaulle recognized the distinction between a provocative act or speech and acting with courage, speaking with candor. He was not afraid of offending the Soviets — or others, for that matter.

It is also evident that de Gaulle's anti-ideological cloak disguised an ideology. After the 1960 Summit he told the French that he wanted "organized cooperation between the East and the West consecrated to the service of Man . . . ." No territorial or doctrinal controversy "holds, in relation to the necessity of exorcising this monstrous peril," nuclear war. France wants "to unite, not to divide, to ennoble, not to debase, to free, not to dominate . . . ." Cooperation, Man, safety, unity, nobility, freedom: we may conclude that an "ideology" or a "doctrine" is a set of beliefs one disbelieves.

De Gaulle's most precise statement of his understanding of the relationship of ideology, ambition, nationality and human nature was his lecture to John Kennedy on Indochina.

> The ideology you invoke will change nothing. Even more, the masses will confound it with your will to power. That is why, the more you engage yourself there against communism, the more the communists will appear there as the champions of national independence, the more they will receive of cooperation, and, then [cooperation] of despair.

De Gaulle advised Kennedy not to ruin those countries but to provide them with the means to escape "misery and humiliation . . . the causes of totalitarian regimes."

De Gaulle understood that, in the early 1960's the ideology-ambition-nationality-human nature equation consisted of the United States and Europe, which were constants, and one variable: the Soviet Union. *Détente,* he wrote to Kennedy, "depends solely on Moscow." To ask a totalitarian regime to cooperate in ending the causes of totalitarianism is to ask it to prevent totalitarianism, perhaps to undermine itself. Gaullist *détente* and *entente* would depend on deep changes in Soviet politics, some changes in American politics, few changes in Gaullist politics.

*

If, as de Gaulle told the students of *L'École Nationale d'Administration,* "the most important and most noble function that is the temporal order [is] service of the State," the Chief of State's function is the noblest of the noble. That de Gaulle thought so is obvious throughout *Le Renouveau's* last chapter, which contains de Gaulle's thoughts on his own function. The Chief of State symbolizes renewal, *le renouveau,* and as such a discussion of the Chief of State concludes the first volume appropriately.

De Gaulle explains that, upon becoming the Chief of State, his authority was neither hereditary nor mandated by popular vote; "only the appeal, imperative but mute, of France" constituted his authority. His function resulted from "my initiative and what took place in regard to me in the national *conscience.*" This was why he needed to "maintain between the people and myself a fundamental accord": hence the referenda.

De Gaulle's normal function was to direct policy, not to involve himself in day-to-day administrative matters. This necessitated an attempt to balance non-interference with careful overseeing: "I kept my distance, but not in an 'ivory tower.'" Indeed, the chapter shows de Gaulle applying the principles enunciated in *Le fil de l'épée:* defending one's authority by maintaining distance and using silence judiciously (e.g., whereas de Gaulle occasionally telephoned his ministers, they were never allowed to telephone him) while always watching circumstances as they shift.

To circumvent the "elites" that professed democracy, de Gaulle needed majority consent, expressed in the referenda. Television, the best means of direct contact with the French, was therefore his most important resource. But this seeming democracy had an aristocratic (as distinguished from oligarchic) tendency: "Always I spoke to them much less of themselves than of France." As France cannot be France without grandeur, de Gaulle — insofar as he spoke to them of France — appealed to the masses with an aristocratic standard. As we have seen, that is problematic. It may have caused his defeat in 1969, when his appeal for another renewal jarred on self-interested oligarchic *and democratic* ears.

Those who interposed themselves between de Gaulle and the French did not earn de Gaulle's gratitude. He throws lances at "the politicians" in every chapter; as for the journalists, theirs is a *"métier* [that] blunts human values." "But, if I am little sensible to the blows brought on my person by speeches and writings, I am more so to the impression that through me it was the very idea of national recovery which provoked such denial and cholers in the notable *milieux* of the nation." Their suspected preference for decadence made de Gaulle think seriously about the problem of his successor, because he knew that the "elites" would prefer someone they could dominate.

*   *

De Gaulle titles the second volume *L'Effort*. Renewal was achieved by 1962; before the next attempt at renewal (which would be social and economic as much as political) de Gaulle had to buttress an authority which was questioned as soon as the immediate danger of the Algerian crisis was gone. Some people — the "elites," mostly — disliked the unity of power; de Gaulle, on the contrary, wanted to destroy the worst kind of faction, the faction that destroys regimes.

> How to doubt . . . that this profound transformation, given to the Republic by a head that organically it had never had, would tomorrow be breached by all the feudalities? How to assure it a character and a luster so strong that it was made possible to maintain it in *droit* [right and/or law] and in practice, when the dramatic circumstances and the exceptional personage which had, once, imposed it, would disappear?

De Gaulle was less concerned with the possibility of the election of a weak president as by the destruction of his new system by the parties if a weak president were elected shortly after de Gaulle's founding.

> . . . in any time and in any domain, what the infirmity of the leader has, in itself, of the irremediable cannot be compensated for by the value of the institution. But, inversely, success is only possible if talent finds its instrument, and nothing is worse than a system such that quality decays in impotence.

The Third and Fourth Republics, for example. It was to protect present and future men of quality, therefore, that de Gaulle fought for the institution of a national referendum for the Presidency. The President would then be "'the man of the country,'" and not the creature of the interest groups. Although he does not write it, de Gaulle obviously hoped that such a national referendum would give men of quality scope for their ambition.

He did not institute the presidential referendum in 1958 because he did not want to endanger national unity by raising the ghost of Bonapartism; again, this was an ongoing founding, even if some periods are described as "renewal," and others as, merely, "effort." By late 1962 the parties were reviving, and de Gaulle wanted to limit their power. De Gaulle took politics too seriously to allow what he called "political games" to dominate French public life.

In calling for a national referendum on the question of whether to amend the Constitution so as to allow national election of the President, de Gaulle, in the opinion of the parties, violated that Constitution. Critics cited Article 89, which specifies that a constitutional amendment "must be passed by the two assemblies in identical terms" before its submission to the people. De Gaulle cites Article 11 — that the President of the Republic, "on the proposal

147

of the Government during [Parliamentary] sessions . . . may submit to a referendum any bill dealing with the organization of the governmental authorities . . . ." Significantly, de Gaulle referred to his proposal as a "modification of the Constitution" during a Cabinet meeting, but his official announcement merely called it a "proposal" — surely a more prudent choice of words. The key word is "organization." De Gaulle was obviously correct to argue that the mode of election *has bearing* on organization; the question is whether it *is* organization.

'Broad construction' versus 'strict construction': Americans have heard those arguments. De Gaulle's more substantial argument is that the election of the President by universal suffrage is in the spirit of the Constitution and of its founder's intentions (therefore de Gaulle's remark that he, after all, knew what the Constitution meant because he was "the principal inspirer" of it is not as preposterous as it seems; de Gaulle obviously does not expect us to question his honesty). He is right to say that "in sum, one looked at the collision of two republics": parliamentarian versus presidential. The parties' opposition to de Gaulle's proposal "would have clarified for me, not certainly a good faith which I did not expect on their part, but the inextinguishable nostalgia that an absurd past inspired in them."

The *Conseil d'état,* instituted to judge the constitutionality of such things, sided with the parties; de Gaulle ignored them (Americans may recall Andrew Jackson's famous: "John Marshall has made his decision; now let him enforce it."). The National Assembly voted to censure de Gaulle; de Gaulle, as he could under the Constitution, dissolved the National Assembly and called for new elections. "In truth, it was high time to prove that the political, professional and journalistic fiefs, were they added together, would not express the will of the people any more than they defend its collective interest." And the simplest way to demonstrate that was to defeat them in a national referendum, which he did; over sixty-two percent of the voters approved de Gaulle's "proposal."*

This left the elections for the (still-dissolved) National Assembly. The *Association pour la Nouvelle République,* "born under the ardent aegis of André Malraux," resulted from the marriage of the two principal Gaullist parties. It won the November elections, giving de Gaulle a useful legislative majority.

*

Having established the Fifth Republic's foundations, de Gaulle had to choose the appropriate Prime Minister. Michel Debré, who wrote the Constitution, was appropriate in the first stage of the founding. Knowing that the early, crisis-provoked unity would not return, despite the parliamentary majority, de Gaulle chose a prudent man, Georges Pompidou, to replace the excitable Debré. Pompidou, de Gaulle implies, was appropriate for "the relative respite" from immediate crises that now ensued. Pompidou's character suited the period; it suited the contemporary French, who saw "themselves constrained, not without pain, to a

---

*In his account of this controversy de Gaulle writes a sentence which begins: "Chief of State, invested by the most hard History with a legitimacy, by my function with a mandate, by the referendal vote of the people with a legislative mission . . . . " Earlier in the chapter he wrote: " . . . a supreme authority, legitimized by events and supported by the confidence of the people." [See *L'Effort,* page 52, *329* for first quote, page 11, *305* for the second]. The notion that History, events, legitimize is inconsistent with previous Gaullist statements, some of which lead us to think that consent legitimizes, some that justice, the general interest, legitimizes. De Gaulle's inconsistency on this point is odd, perhaps sloppy. One could argue that de Gaulle thinks legitimacy combines events, justice and consent (making it identical to authority, or nearly so). Or one could point to *Le fil de l'épée* and *Mémoires de guerre,* noting that de Gaulle argues in the latter that events are the strongest single determinant of consent, and that in the former he argues that a good leader knows how to use events. I choose the latter possibility as being the most consistent with all of de Gaulle's writings, but the simplest explanation is that de Gaulle was being inconsistent this time.

mechanized, agglomerated life." Earlier Frenchmen, whether farmers or artisans, tradesmen or *rentiers,* enjoyed an "individualistic existence"; such a people might easily rebel against mass-life, "in some irrational crisis." This was so because desires increased with development. "All the strata and categories, pursuing in haste to see their standard of life raised, but bruised by the brutal privileges of the capitalist system, are in a permanent state of reproach and suspicion in regard to the more or less distinct interests which appear to them to be opposing their elevation." Paradoxically, mass-life yields faction.

> Without doubt the *malaise* of souls, which results from a civilization dom-
> inated by matter, would not be cured by whatever regime that it be. More or less
> it could be alleviated by a change of moral condition, which would make Man
> responsible instead of being an instrument. Besides, in order that the inevitable
> inequalities, mutations, taxes, which comprise a modern economy would appear
> in the eyes of all as regular and justified, there would be necessary an organiza-
> tion wherein each one would be a partner at the same time as an employee.
> I must, meanwhile, coldly recognize, in the atmosphere of *immobilisme* which
> was at the end of the dramas and the removal of perils and where routines,
> egoisms and sectarianisms stiffened themselves, the pacific revolution of partici-
> pation could not be started in motion with the *ampleur* [abundance, elevation,
> dignity, volume] that it exacts. But, after all, it was not overnight that I had been
> able not long ago to reassemble the country on the side of the Resistance, or lead
> it to give itself a regime worthy of itself, or to decolonize the overseas terri-
> tories and emancipate Algeria. The consent which renders the laws fecund often
> appears, I know, only in a flash of thunder. Without desiring that the storm
> should raise itself, I must therefore turn it to account if it came one day to break.
> In politics, as in strategy, in affairs or in love, the gift is surely necessary. The
> occasion is also necessary.

Thus de Gaulle waited, with ambivalence, for a May 1968 (a few pages later he asks, apropos of the 1963 miners' strike, "Is it not the frequent penchant of the French, each one in his specialty, to crave the march forward while wishing that nothing budge?").

Stanley Hoffmann describes the problem with de Gaulle's strategy: the "storm" that allows a ruler to reform institutions provokes citizens to challenge his very authority, if he's in power when the storm occurs. Hence "the hurricane of 1968, far from bringing consent [to reform], only provoked a backlash of conservatism," except in the educational system. Hoffmann does not suggest, as he might, that de Gaulle's ambivalence toward the "storm" might have owed something to his understanding of just that danger. Moreover, de Gaulle's judicious balance of distance (which brings the chance to deny responsibility) and authority (which allows one to demand responsibility) nearly enabled him to get what he wanted; the educational system, after all, was reformed, and he lost the 1969 referendum by only five points. Finally, Hoffmann's own suggestion — a sort of gradual evolution — depends on even broader consent then de Gaulle needed, and is even less consistent with the French national character than Gaullist "participation."

The "respite" of the mid-1960's was only "relative"; the French did not allow their agitational skills to fall into complete disuse. Despite the coming-of-age of the postwar babies and the arrival of more than half a million immigrants and French Algerians, employment was high. But the miners, farmers and public-service employees had grievances; de Gaulle attributes the disturbances they caused to the lack of responsibility which poorly-structured economic institutions allowed.

Educational reform was especially difficult because it involved the government in ideological struggles as well as economic ones. Teaching is "an incomparable national duty"; "in all my sayings and writings that accompanied my action, what was I ever if not someone who strove to teach?" Indeed: a founder would educate a people in new political 'first principles,' even as a statesman who is not a founder would educate a people in political 'first principles' already established.* Consonant with this, de Gaulle tells us that his educational views were no less "political" than "ideal." In order to adapt students to the new France, de Gaulle wanted "utilitarian, scientific and technical" education, as well as education in the liberal arts. Although he does not write it, I think it fair to suggest that de Gaulle wanted to give some non-ideological ballast to the French ship; he was aware, as we've seen, that modern science itself is not without philosophical weight.

In his reform attempts de Gaulle encountered "a dull and passive resistance" from the educational establishment. "It would be demonstrated to me one more time, that unless by making a *tabula rasa* by dictatorship or by revolution, no institution can be truly reformed if its members do not consent." During and after the crisis of May 1968, de Gaulle was blamed for neglecting educational institutions; his reply, obviously, is that the educators were to blame.

De Gaulle has been thinking of the end of his presidency, and he now discusses regionalization, the political side of "participation." The old French *departements* were now too small for a modern economy in this "modern life where economy dominates all." De Gaulle wanted to re-institute the old provinces on the economic plane, calling them "regions" and having them ruled by councils composed of politically-elected members and of spokesmen for professional and social organizations. At the same time the French Senate, then moribund, would be reformed to consist of regional representatives and delegates from economic institutions. Obviously, de Gaulle intended to make economic groups politically responsible. Economics would still dominate modern life, perhaps, but there would be political (de Gaulle would probably say "national" — political in the good sense) checks on economic activity.

It is unintendedly ironic that the last subject de Gaulle treats in what became the last chapter of *Mémoires d'espoir* is an economic one: inflation. Inflation usually accompanies expansion; it did in the early 1960's. De Gaulle does not fail to insist on its political effect. The "solidity" of a country's money "measures in the world the reality and efficacy of the economy of the country, on which depend those of her policy." Monetary solidity affects internal matters, also. It is,

> . . . in the interior, the essential condition of honesty of relations, modera-
> tion of desires, serenity of destinies, of social and moral order. It is, for the
> State which marks its pieces with its effigy — the king, the emperor, the repub-
> lic — the attestation of its capacity, the justification of the authority that it
> exercises and the confidence it requires, the argument which is necessary to it in
> order to demand effort, impose sacrifice and to repress abuses.

Psychologically, modern expansion induces people to gamble more than they possess in credit, investment and wages; while de Gaulle admired risk-taking, he only admired it when it had the chance to succeed.

Accordingly, in September of 1963 de Gaulle introduced budget economics, credit restriction, price stabilization, and demanded that the United States pay its debts to France in gold, not dollars. There were objections, a few strikes, "but how could I have not learned that what is salutary for the nation does not go without blame in public opinion, or without losses in election?"

In a letter to the man who assembled documents for his use in writing *Mémoires d'espoir*, de Gaulle wrote that the second volume, *L'Effort*, would have seven chapters: two

---

*Alternatively, a statesman might prudently avoid raising 'first principles,' knowing that to raise them will attract questions, even criticism, that could damage the regime. Burke teaches this lesson, one that the British learn more readily than the French, generally speaking.

"'political'" (we have one of them), two "economic and social" (we have one of them), two on foreign policy and "a chapter of the 'philosophic' order, wherein I will formulate *my* judgment on the situation of France, Europe, the world." By putting the word "political" between inverted commas, de Gaulle may be insisting, again, that politics is more than what most people call politics: partisan fighting. By putting the word "philosophic" between inverted commas, he demonstrates that he knew what he was and what he was not.

*   *   *

The last three volumes of *Discours et Messages,* de Gaulle's collected speeches and press conferences, parallel the existing and planned volumes of *Mémoires d'espoir.* The latter's first volume is *Le Renouveau,* corresponding to *Avec le renouveau* of *Discours et Messages.* Volume II of *Mémoires d'espoir* is *L'Effort,* corresponding to *Pour l'effort.* The last volume of *Discours et Messages* is *Vers le terme.*

Instead of treating the last seven years of de Gaulle's presidency as a historian might — chronologically — I will treat them thematically, as years wherein he elaborated familiar ideas. The traditional distinction between foreign and domestic policy is convenient and misleading; as it's more convenient than misleading, I'll retain it.

*   *

Independence remained the purpose of de Gaulle's foreign policy. In a 1965 radio/television speech he told the French that "the capital fact of these last seven years is that we have resisted the sirens of *abandon* and chosen independence." The "temptation of renouncement," if yielded to, would bring "a decadence without return"; we recall his diagnosis of Germany. Two years later he still decried "this strange passion for abasement," "the apostles of decline," "these adepts of denigration," and exhorted the French to "repress doubt, that demon of decadences." The opposite of doubt is faith; de Gaulle's enterprise, whether animated by religion or not, depended on faith, "constitutional" and extra-constitutional.

This faith was not an illusion of strength. De Gaulle recognized, and stated publicly, that France's "scientific, technical and industrial" capacities contrasted badly with those of the United States and the Soviet Union. But, as he told an audience in Guadeloupe (perhaps with a touch of cruelty?), "the most expensive, the most ruinous *politique* is to be small, it is to ask for something from all the world without being able to obtain it." The ideal Gaullist international system would combine responsibility and mutual assistance: "the superior interest of the human species commands that each nation be responsible for itself, disencumbered of infringements, aided in its progress without preconditions of obedience." Because he knew that ideals by their nature are not realized ("Perfection is not of this world," he said, in another context), de Gaulle tried, with limited power, to force and persuade others to respect French independence. Continued efforts at Franco-German *entente;* continued building of nuclear weapons; the denial of British entry into the Common Market (Britain was firmly bound to non-European powers; the Commonwealth and the United States); the spurning of European parliamentarism ("Any system which would consist of transmitting our sovereignty to international areopaguses would be incompatible with the rights and duties of the French Republic"); the criticism of the United States' war in Vietnam; the tour of Latin America (with mild 'anti-American' rhetoric); the withdrawal from NATO; the refusal to accept U.S. dollars as equivalent to gold;* *"Vive le Quebec libre!"*; the criticism of Israel in

---

*Later in his presidency, de Gaulle again criticized U.S. economic policy: "President Johnson has not yet done the necessary things such as restricting consumption in the United States in order to avoid the danger of inflation. Any serious inflation in the United States could have dangerous repercussions in Europe." [C.L. Sulzberger, *An Age of Mediocrity,* Macmillan, 1973, p. 339. Interview held on January 22, 1968].

1967: all of these assertions of French independence gave de Gaulle's France a unique if not pre-eminent place among nation-states in the 1960's. But it was *détente,* more than any other policy, which revealed the difficulties of Gaullist foreign policy; I return to it.

Although he told the Iranian parliament that strategy is ideology plus geography, he claimed that "the banner of ideology in reality only covers ambitions." But underlying those ambitions are nations. He told Sulzberger that

> Europe remembers all too well the danger of Germany. This memory remains in the popular mind. And people are stronger than regimes. If the tsars still ruled Russia they would oppose German reunification just as the communists do.*

Nationality weakens both hegemonies: "the monolithism of the totalitarian world is in the course of being dislocated"; the United States' power in Europe has also declined. Even after the Soviet invasion of Czechoslovakia de Gaulle insisted that "it is too late for any ideology, notably communism, to sweep away national sentiment."

Too late for ideology, but what of technology? De Gaulle, contrary to his critics' assumptions, knew what atomic weapons meant for nationalism. As early as 1948, in private conversation, he said:

> No problem presents the same facet since the atom bomb. I even begin to wonder whether it's worth trying to do anything nowadays. No action one takes has any meaning any more, nor has any humane project. The conception of individual nations has lost all significance. What does *France* mean now?"

De Gaulle exaggerated, but the problem was there; throughout presidency, behind all the actions and speeches, he knew it. And surely he saw that the *force de frappe* was at best a long-term gamble.

There was also the rhetorical problem: persuading a modern audience that independence is worth the expense. One can tell a Guadeloupe audience that the costliest policy is to be small and expect agreement, but a French audience requires more subtlety — and, perhaps, less realism. In a 1967 radio/television speech de Gaulle listed the three purposes of his foreign policy. Peace was "the first of these ends, which commands the others." Independence was the second, and it buttresses peace. Finally there was progress, "for independence, today, cannot go without progress." Except for his central purpose, independence, de Gaulle here resembles Thomas Hobbes.

Several years earlier, at *L'École Militaire,* de Gaulle said another thing. Independence is not for security; security is for independence. The discrepancy between the two statements need not reveal a changed opinion or genuine inconsistency. It could reveal his adjustment to the nature of the audiences. When Sulzberger asked him, "What is the primary force governing men in their actions?" de Gaulle replied:

> One must draw a distinction between the individual and the collective masses. For the individual it is ambition and a taste for adventure. I think the real motivation, the primordial motivating force for the individual is ambition, but for the masses it is fear. There Stalin was right. And this applies to the masses of all countries.

Hobbes, the individual, was governed by the mass-emotion, fear, and his political philosophy,

---

*He made the same point in a later interview with Sulzberger on July 1, 1965. Explaining his much-repeated phrase, "Europe from the Atlantic to the Urals," he said: "The real Russia stops at the Urals. All the rest — Turkistan, Siberia, parts of Mongolia — these are all colonies." Eventually, he believed, China would acquire them.

based on his theory that fear is the ruling passion of human beings, is fundamentally a political philosophy of the masses. To appeal to the masses, de Gaulle thought, one appeals to fear, whether directly ("De Gaulle or chaos" was one of his campaign slogans) or indirectly ("peace," "security"). The students at *L'École Militaire* were not of the mass, and to them de Gaulle represented security as an instrumental good which contributes to the attainment of independence (itself the precondition of the fulfilment of ambition). We know that independence is for grandeur, and that grandeur is, in part, an ethical category. To use modernity — the Hobbian desire for peace, fear of violent death — against modernity: de Gaulle's sympathy for Chateaubriand is understandable.

> [Chateaubriand] knew that France had lost the secret of [her] power with the passing of the Ancien Regime — but he was aware that the Ancien Regime had vanished for ever. Whence comes the pathos of his attempts to give France a foreign policy, in spite of everything, when, as he was the first to realize, it was no longer possible.

De Gaulle enjoyed more success than Chateaubriand; he had more political power. But the nature of modern power — which is a thing of technology and of mass sentiment — makes it cumbersome to use for unmodern ends, and few men have known that as surely as de Gaulle.

*

One cannot be responsible if one is not free; liberty is independence's counterpart. For de Gaulle, "participation" is liberty. This is un-French of him; to the French, Hoffmann writes, liberty "is freedom *from,* not freedom *to.*" One has rights by nature, and duties are impositions. In 1946 de Gaulle told Claude Mauriac that

> . . . the people are difficult to know and difficult to handle. They want to be guided but they don't want to support whoever wants to guide them. They want to be captured but they refuse to give themselves up. They hate weakness but they can't bear the idea of yielding to strength.

They are, he concludes, like women. (A poll taken sometime after de Gaulle's resignation in 1969 showed that fifty-one percent of the French regretted de Gaulle's resignation, but sixty-two percent didn't want him to return. They were not asked about alimony).

The French ambivalence toward rulers may account for their political disunity. In private conversation de Gaulle listed their five political groupings, which have not changed for centuries: the apolitical; the revolutionaries; "the envious, the cuckolds and the failures" ("today's socialists and yesterdays radicals"); the propertied classes; and a group he didn't name, which surely must have included, in its latest metamorphosis, the Gaullists.

To ambivalence toward rulers and faction, add economism, a more recent political problem. In 1964, with the regime established and the Algerian rebels crushed, de Gaulle is alleged to have remarked:

> Frenchmen have nothing more to fear, neither paratroopers, nor scamps, nor a third world war, nor hunger. And so they want to enjoy life. De Gaulle stands in their way. They are tired of making an effort.

At the same time, François Mauriac, writing an otherwise adulatory tract, admitted that "what embarrasses me in Gaullist France is a disproportion between the policy of greatness as General de Gaulle conducts it abroad and the indifference to the deterioration of the French spirit, the neglect of the youth of France . . . abandoned from adolescence to all the basest stimulations of sexuality and violence." Indeed, "the whole of French society reveals preoccupations and tastes that in no way correspond to the notion of greatness its leader incarnates." It was an accurate, if banal, observation, and later Mauriac deepened it:

We must have the courage to confess that the young are not attracted to de Gaulle. the young are attracted to those who flatter them, who satisfy their desires for violence . . . . De Gaulle rises above such eddies: it is not from the young that he derives his strength, as Hitler did, but from the whole people . . . .

Mauriac might have added that youth-in-politics is a modern theme. We know that Plato would educate men before allowing them to rule, that Aristotle thinks political philosophy inappropriate for anyone under thirty. It was Machiavelli who glorified youthful traits; in this, de Gaulle was deeply un-Machiavellian. If he wanted a larger French population it was for youth's strength, not for its putative wisdom.

De Gaulle publicly acknowledged the problem of economism in 1965. During a televised interview he was told that the French thought de Gaulle preoccupied with French affairs "on a very elevated level," and less with day-to-day economic problems. De Gaulle replied that the French must exist if France is to exist, that he concerned himself with prosperity because it yields strength in this "economic and social epoch." He objects to any advantage for one group: "That is very convenient, it is vulgarly convenient!" "Yes, *mon Général,*" his interviewer said, "but it is also what the French individually say to themselves." And de Gaulle did not try to refute that.

De Gaulle said that the machine produced the modern economy. It contributed to "these excessive systems," *laisser-faire* capitalism and communism. It moved society faster than society moved it (this was de Gaulle's refutation of Marx).* The rebellion of 1968, he explained in another interview, was caused by "unprecedented transformations," wrought by the machine, of things that had "not stirred since Antiquity." France had been agricultural and rustic, was now industrial and urban; France's social, ethical and religious foundations weakened; two world wars had occurred, as well as other shocks; "colossal" means of communications existed, whose directors were "against all authority" and presented "the sensational, the dramatic, the sorrowful, the scandalous"; the people know atomic weapons could destroy them: "How is it that one could imagine that this society would be placid, and be, at bottom, satisfied?" Although "modern mechanical society" "spreads among us material goods in quantity and in quality," and "elevates the life of all," and although technology affords us "miraculous perspectives," *machinisme* "entwines man" — "for example the worker," making him, in both capitalist and communist regimes, "like an ant in an anthill or a termite in a termite nest." "How to find a human equilibrium for civilization, for the mechanical modern society? There [is] the great question of the century!" We know that for de Gaulle *humanitas,* at its best, is grandeur; we know that for de Gaulle equilibrium is the ancient idea of the *concordia discors.*

A constitution, de Gaulle said, "is an *esprit,* institutions, practice." In 1967 he predicted that "a day shall come, without doubt, when our Constitution with all that it implies, shall become as our second nature"; one thinks of Plutarch. Among the things implied by the Constitution was, evidently, that equilibrium between capital and labor known as "association": one part of the larger *concordia discors,* "participation." The state, whose function is to guarantee unity and whose power to do so is not merely implied but insisted upon in the Constitution, "rejected . . . an abusive capitalism and a crushing communism,"

---

*In 1947 he told Claude Mauriac that technology, "new forms of energy" — this was not long after the invention of the atomic bomb — may refute Marxist predictions by "reduc[ing] manpower to a minimum and mak[ing] the conditions of our everyday life extraordinarily easy" [Mauriac, *op. cit.,* p. 237, February 2, 1947]. Indeed, this had already happened to some extent. Marx obviously believed the revolution would occur before technology developed much further, making mass-uprisings difficult. Marx overestimated the rapidity of mass-movements, underestimated the rapidity of technological advance. Today we know that communism is unlikely to defeat capitalism unless the communists use technology — i.e., weapons — to defeat the capitalists.

preferring an "evolution" directed by it. Addressing the Greek Chamber of Deputies, de Gaulle said that

> In our epoch, science, technology, the machine imprint on certain of our activities a more and more agglomerated and certain character, submitting to totalitarian systems, tending even to give one to believe that in modern times life, production, prosperity exact servitude. But the Greek and French people, who know very well and who prove today how fecund are the cohesion and continuity of the State, safeguard, across all the machinery, the soul and dignity of men, the liberty of citizens.

De Gaulle saw no necessary contradiction between state power and liberty because to him liberty was "liberty *to*," not mere "liberty *from*." He knew that the French would easily supply the discord, and therefore emphasized the unifying concord within which discord is productive. It was a political answer to the questions modernity poses.

The ethical basis of "participation" was the worth of man's "participat[ing] actively in his own destiny," of not being a "passive instrument." (In this de Gaulle and André Malraux were identical; both were resisters of destiny. Indeed, this explains the deeper importance of the Resistance for them.) If the Constitution became the second nature of the French — if it became the French *ethos* — state direction and national participation would serve one end — grandeur — and such discord as would exist would prevent decadence, not be a symptom of it. Lenin, Stalin and Mao would have re-made human nature; de Gaulle would have added to it, brought it to its fullness. There is no more obvious contrast between late-modern and ancient.*

Gaullist economics reflected Gaullist ethics. Free enterprise, de Gaulle said, "must not be a rampart of immobilism, but . . . on the contrary must be a base for *élan,* for risk, for development; the international competition which exists perfects it [note that discord serves an end other than itself]; the [State's] direction . . . which chooses the means and roads, arranges the means and harmonizes efforts." A satirist might call this a heroic economics, but the animating purpose, France (which cannot be France without grandeur) would fructify discord by minimizing the petty absolutism of self-righteous interest-groups.

Labor-capital association, "participation's" economic aspect, was neither capitalistic nor communistic (and thus complemented Gaullist foreign policy). "Association" "changes the condition of man in the *milieu* of modern civilization" by allowing men to "form together a society . . . where each has interest in his production and in his good functioning, and a direct interest." The worker shares profits, is informed "in a sufficient manner of the course of the enterprise" and participates, by means of elected representatives, in the society in order to advance his interests, points of view and proposals." The enterprise would have a director, as the state has a president; de Gaulle does not say that this director would be elected. That would have ruined all bourgeois support (much of which he lost, anyway). If de Gaulle planned that such elections would eventually occur, making French enterprises microcosmic Frances, I would not be surprised. I doubt that he would have wanted collective decision-making, however, inconsistent as that is with the Gaullist theory of leadership, and de Gaulle's practice.**

---

*These economic reforms were only partly realized. De Gaulle got most of what he wanted only in the educational system, and even there genuine "participation" was ignored, and a quasi-parliamentary system introduced. It is true that "participation," unlike some of de Gaulle's other plans, doesn't work 'in the short run' if citizens do not consent to it.

**In a May 24, 1966 speech at the *Congrès International de la Responsabilité Medicale,* held at Versailles, de Gaulle quoted Bacon, who wrote that a doctor is "A man who adds himself to nature" [*Discours et Message,* V. p. 37]. Bacon was a modern who exhorted men to master nature with applied science; de Gaulle, characteristically, selects one of the more modest exhortations. We have seen that de Gaulle did not find the human mastery of nature unproblematic.

"Participation's" national aspect was regionalization. In 1964 de Gaulle instituted the Commission of Regional Development, "conjugated" the plans and credits of the state "with local initiatives and resources." In 1966 he said that "in the future and when evolution in its course shall reveal the opportunity, we must without doubt bring together in a single assembly the representatives of the local collectives with those of the great social and economic orders of the country in order to deliberate on affairs of this nature before the National Assembly, political representation, solving them by voting laws." The 'events of May' 1968 and their aftermath revealed what de Gaulle hoped was that opportunity. He proposed to re-institute the provinces, calling them "regions," and to refound the French Senate as a consultative body comprised of regional representatives and delegates from economic and social organizations, as well as deputies. The fifty-two percent negative vote in the 1969 referendum, in which this reform was proposed, induced de Gaulle's resignation. Whatever the merits or demerits of the proposal (Hoffmann criticizes it thoroughly and soberly),* it follows from de Gaulle's ideal, the *concordia discors.*

> Even as the French nation formed itself by a long effort from the very varied
> populations of the provinces, thus, in modern times, our economic power shall
> depend on the outlay of value in all our regions. For each one . . . it must pro-
> ceed there according to its own character and its own capacities, but in such a
> way as the national *ensemble* be coherent and balanced. As always, it is by con-
> jugating multiple diversities that one realizes unity. As always, it is the State
> which is in charge of [the unity] of France.

"Participation" might work, were it consented to. De Gaulle failed to induce that consent. Previously he had succeeded in inducing consent, partly by actions and partly by words. Why did he succeed for ten years, then fail in one?

A frequently-suggested answer is that de Gaulle's proposal was ill-timed — that, as journalist Michel Droit suggested in an interview with de Gaulle televised two weeks before the referendum, the reaction to the 'events of May' was conservative but de Gaulle's proposal was not. I think this is correct, and that it points to the fundamental irony of de Gaulle's career. One sees this irony, of which he was entirely conscious, in a characteristic speech he made in April of 1964.

De Gaulle was scheduled to undergo an operation, but recorded a speech for radio and television beforehand, to be aired at the time of the operation. Thus De Gaulle arranged to be present in the minds of the French even while temporarily absent from his own. The speech began with the *concordia discors* theme: "France is one in her diversity." Noting that "certain people" fail to see the whole beyond the particular interests when they discuss French affairs, he let his audience understand that he was not one of those people.

He discussed internal matters first. "The purpose toward which we march has never been more evident"; it is development, "the spring of modern civilization, the desire of the entire people, the condition of French independence, power and influence." Many statistics later, he concludes: "The law of our epoch is no longer the permanent and systematic struggle of interests [the sort of thing he condemned in the parliamentary regime and in *laisser-faire* capitalism], but indeed the organization of our economic and social solidarity" — which meant, at the time, unpopular anti-inflationary measures. Inasmuch as everyone, except a de Gaulle, belongs to some particular interest-group, it doesn't surprise one to learn that de Gaulle's domestic policies were frequently disliked by the majority of the French.

He then discussed foreign matters. He justifies the expense of nuclear weapons by citing the "danger of destruction and invasion" and the alternative of "entirely placing [France's] defense, thereby her existence and, finally her *politique,* under a protectorate that is foreign

*See Hoffmann, *op. cit.,* pp. 179-184.

and, after all, uncertain." He uses fear to overbalance the desire for comfort or gain. He justifies foreign aid — not as expensive as nuclear weaponry — by appealing to national pride and, indirectly, to fear (the desire for peace being, usually, the mirror-image of the fear of violent death). In his peroration he calls on France to be France. De Gaulle's foreign policies were frequently admired by the French.

The causes of those reactions are obvious. In domestic matters de Gaulle flattered no one in particular and offended everyone slightly. Whereas his policies raised the living-standard, the many-who-are-bourgeois could never believe that their benefactor regarded comfort as a worthy end. In foreign matters de Gaulle appealed to national pride and to fear. He achieved power at those times when fear overrode the desire for comfort, economism.* He lost power whenever the bourgeoisie found leaders who quieted their fears *and* promised comfort: the parliamentarians in the late 1940's and early 1950's, Pompidou in 1969. He is said to have remarked in 1969, "General de Gaulle was not born to reassure the masses," but he knew that fear was the most powerful mass-sentiment, that he came to power precisely because he did reassure the masses, sometimes.

*   *   *

The irony of de Gaulle's career, then, is the irony of modernity, which attempts to square the circle of Hobbian geometry. How to reconcile wisdom and democracy? The Leviathan is the regime that maximizes equality; all are equal but one, the ruler. But that ruler had better serve the mass-sentiments whose ends are comfort and security if he wants to remain the ruler. De Gaulle, whose *eros* was radically un-Hobbian, nonetheless attempted to rule a modern, that is to say egalitarian and individualistic, people in a modern political system which necessarily made much of majority rule and of individual rights. He defeated the old quasi-democrats, the parliamentarians, by invoking what seemed (and what in some respects was) a purer democracy. When it was then necessary to train a new elite, whose ends would have been anything but purely modern, and to train a new citizenry that would defer to if not partake of the ends of that elite, he failed. "We defeated Vichy, we defeated the O.A.S., but we failed to make nationals of the bourgeoisie." To have been national in de Gaulle's view would have been to admire grandeur, but the many rarely defer to anything beyond themselves, to any ends beyond comfort and security.

---

*As late as 1968, de Gaulle won by invoking fear, telling the French that "France is menaced by dictatorship," "communist totalitarianism" [*Discours et Messages,* V, p. 320, May 30, 1968]. The speech in which he made that argument swayed mass-opinion against the insurrectionists, assured his continued rulership. It was when he tried for more than retaining his power, when he tried to introduce reforms a year later, that he lost the referendum and resigned.

CHAPTER 12

FOUNDING AND EDUCATION: REFLECTIONS ON
MÉMOIRES D'ESPOIR

"All revolutions are failures," Orwell remarks, "but they are not all the same failure." The Gaullist revolution failed, if not in the way predicted by many of de Gaulle's contemporaries.* De Gaulle wanted to metamorphose the French *ethos*, which encouraged oscillations between radical individualism *("incivisme")* and radical patriotism. These oscillations, made possible by the disjunction between state and society, accompanied an odd, theatrical individualism whose gratification depended on the approval of others. By insisting that he was de Gaulle, not Charles de Gaulle, he attempted to dilute one cause of French inebriation. The 'events of May' in 1968 demonstrated that many of the French hadn't learned.

De Gaulle told Malraux that while most contemporary French intellectuals had nothing to say worth listening to, Montesquieu would have told him important things. Under questioning, Montesquieu first might have told him that "the natural means" of metamorphosing a country's *ethos* is not law (lawgiving often resembles tyranny) but *moeurs* and customs. By introducing new *moeurs* (morals, manners) and customs, the legislator "engage[s] the people to make the change themselves." Montesquieu criticizes some ancient legislators for "confounding" laws, which "regulate the actions of the subject," with *moeurs*, which "regulate the actions of the man."**

But if questioned further, Montesquieu would admit that laws do contribute to forming the *moeurs* and customs of a country; laws that do not rigorously limit citizens' actions produce a more passionate citizenry than other laws do, for example. At this point he would introduce the topic of the laws relating to commerce.***

De Gaulle also knew that simple lawgiving is not enough. While Montesquieu would extend commerce by appealing to what he regards as feminine vanity, the desire of women to own things that enhance the esteem with which others regard them, de Gaulle appealed to the

---

*Example: on March 29, 1967 the left-wing partisan leader Pierre Mendès-France predicted that de Gaulle and his constitution would go simultaneously, and that a leftist partisan alliance would replace them [C.L. Sulzberger: *An Age of Mediocrity*, Macmillan Publishing Company, New York, 1973, p. 318]. By this measure of political success, de Gaulle's revolution succeeded: "The game he has played for twenty-four years, which seems to have been won at the moment I write [1964], will be won for sure only on the day when de Gaulle's successor, elected by universal suffrage, governs without any deletions having been made in the institutions of the Fifth Republic" [Francois Mauriac: *De Gaulle,* Richard Howard translation, Doubleday and Company, Garden City, 1966, pp. 42-43].

**If Montesquieu has Plato in mind, he misreads him. The Athenian Stranger warns against legislation of minutiae; unenforceable petty infractions habituate citizens to break the laws and invite ridicule. Rather, 'unwritten laws' — precepts, customs, admonitions — should underlie formal laws.

***As he does in *The Spirit of the Laws,* today's explorers of Montesquieu's subtly-written book have the advantage of being able to engage a reliable and discreet guide: Thomas L. Pangle: *Montesquieu's Philosophy of Liberalism* [University of Chicago Press, Chicago and London, 1973]. This superb book underlies much of what I have to say about Montesquieu in this chapter.
  On the influence of law on *ethos*, Tocqueville writes that "the function of law is not to eliminate crime (which is usually the product of deranged instincts and of such violent passions as will not be halted by the mere existence of laws). The efficacy of laws consists in their impact on society, in their regulation of matters of daily life, and in setting the general temper of habits and ideas" [*Letters exchanged with Gobineau,* in *"The European Revolution" and Correspondence with Gobineau,* edited and translated by John Lukacs, Doubleday, New York, 1959, p. 212].

feminine attraction to a certain kind of masculinity — that animated by fatherliness and tradition.* Simple lawgiving, in order to effect revolutionary ends, requires more power than de Gaulle enjoyed. The Athenian Stranger recommends that the founder change the composition of the citizenry by means of exile, death and/or colonization, that he redistribute property (which belongs to individuals but also to the *polis* and to the goddess, Earth) by dividing lands and abolishing debts, that he not disturb the local gods but add some, and that he keep the population small (5,040) because "trust presupposes acquaintance." De Gaulle had to act circumspectly.**

"France is a Republic," his constitution proclaims, "indivisible, secular, democratic and social." Following Montesquieu, not Plato, de Gaulle produced a constitution that does not include explanations for its provisions; such doctrines as the Rights of Man and the Citizen are only referred to. De Gaulle aimed his iconoclasm at the parliamentarians, preferring not to disturb too many local gods. He added a few — publicly distinguishing the people's "mandate" from "national legitimacy," for example, a distinction not sanctioned by the 1798 Declaration. But both he and André Malraux knew that the Fifth Republic's constitution, while giving the President of the Republic the means of authoritative action, did not by itself sufficiently re-form the French *ethos.* ***

Foreign policy, a means of using constitutionally-provided authority to metamorphose the French *ethos,* raises the problem of republicanism that Lincoln saw: "Must a government, of necessity, be too *strong* for the liberties of its own people, or too *weak* to maintain its own existence?" "Democracies never attack; they never react to imminent mortal danger," de Gaulle told young Mauriac. And as Montesquieu teaches, "Democracy . . .has two excesses to avoid — the spirit of inequality, which leads to aristocracy or monarchy, and the spirit of extreme equality, which leads to despotic power, as the latter is completed by conquest." To restrain the spirit of exteme inequality is to restrain the spirit of democracy itself, to insist on a mixture of other-than-democratic principles in the regime.

De Gaulle's understanding of this problem underlaid his characteristic use of foreign policy. He criticized NATO, for example, because he "questioned the integration of [military] forces as taking from the people a sense of responsibility for their defense, and losing the impetus of patriotism." Responsibility and patriotism: *self*-government, not egalitarianism, animated de Gaulle's founding.**** This contrasts with Montesquieu, for whom confederation

*Roman Catholic women supported him more fervently and more faithfully than any other group, according to many public-opinion polls conducted in the 1960's. See John S. Ambler: *The Government and Politics of France,* Houghton Mifflin Company, Boston, 1971, p. 31.

**Only careless readers image that Plato's 'idealism' prevents him from understanding practical political realities. One of the few observers who seems to really *think* about de Gaulle as a founder is Jacques Soustelle. He calls his former ally, then enemy, a "legislator and founder," comparing him to "a legislator of antiquity" — Solon, Lycurgus. But he inconsistently demands that de Gaulle act as a modern, contractarian founder/legislator. [Soustelle: *Vingt-huit ans de gaullisme,* La table Ronde, Paris, 1968, p. 175].

***Malraux, who served as de Gaulle's Minister of Culture, understood de Gaulle's enterprise better than any of de Gaulle's other associates. He devotes extensive sections of his 'auto-biography,' *Le Miroir des limbes,* to de Gaulle; he also made numerous speeches in defense of Gaullism, collected as *"Malraux: Paroles et ecrits politiques,* 1947-1972," in *Espoir: Rêvue l'Institut de Charles de Gaulle,* January 1973.

****And not only in military matters: a Gaullist deputy in the National Assembly answered the European economic integrationists in the same terms." . . . [Y]ou are claiming to be building political Europe with a group of purely economic and functional institutions, and you are instituting European commissions of high officials without any responsibility, which we do not want at any price. To the extent that we accept the Europe that will arise from the consent of the peoples, from the consent and true agreement of governments, to this extent . . . we do not at any price want the Europe of M. Jean Monnet" [Raymond Triboulet, quoted
(Cont.)

160

requires the abandonment of sovereignty. But Montesquieu wants to replace much of politics with economics, commerce.

Here Montesquieu and de Gaulle clash. Modernity, as Montesquieu foresees, and as de Gaulle knew, brings interdependence among industrialized countries; economics and technology are inter-national.* "The problem here," as the astute Hoffman observes, "is how any nation can preserve its character and retain individuality while the social order is standardized across all frontiers." Commerce, left to itself, yields cosmopolitanism; the world is "but one single state" insofar as moveable property "belong[s] to the whole world in general." Technology, also, yields cosmopolitanism, according to one of Montesquieu's profoundest students:

> In modern times the poor and barbarous find it difficult to defend them-selves against the opulent and civilized. The invention of fire-arms, an invention which at first sign appears to be so pernicious, is certainly favourable both to the permanency and to the extension of civilization.

Technological conquest (both in its economic and in its military aspects) assures modernity's dominance, what Adam Smith calls "civilization."**

De Gaulle resisted interdependence, but surely knew the limitations of such resistance. Those who assume that he believed he could permanently defeat the economic integrationists of the 1960's overlook his rhetoric of the 1940's, his assertion of France's "independence" and status as "a great power" when Hitler ruled Paris and de Gaulle resided in London. We know he bluffed then; why assume he didn't bluff twenty years later? A bluff might slow the worldwide shift from politics to economics while buttressing de Gaulle's founding. Once established, that founding might exemplify a life that makes all *necessary* compromises with modernity while reserving certain unmodern principles for use against the weaknesses of modernity.

His effort did not fail entirely. Contrary to impressions, French military spending in the 1960's declined in relation to the total of economic goods and services the French produced. Spending for 'social' programs increased, but demand for them increased even more. A scholar who contends that this modern, economic appetite caused de Gaulle's loss in the 1969 referendum cites the fact that support for his legislative reform proposal declined when de Gaulle made its passage contingent on his continuation in office. He fails to reflect sufficiently on another fact he cites: the French approved of de Gaulle's foreign policy while criticizing his domestic policy. The French wanted greater material prosperity, liberty *and* independence, simultaneously.

(Cont.) in F. Roy Willis: *France, Germany and the New Europe 1945-1963, Stanford Press,* Stanford, 1965, p. 264]. Notice the use of an egalitarian appeal to undermine the egalitarianism of the purely economic Monnet.

*For a detailed picture of this, see Edward L. Morse: *Foreign Policy and Interdependence in Gaullist France,* Princeton University Press, Princeton, 1973. One of the few flaws in this informative book comes to view when Morse writes that interdependence is affected and effected "very little by ideology" [p. 45] — failing to see that modernity is *also* an ideology.

**Hans Jonas writes that "Compared to the extreme artificiality of our technologically con-stituted, electronically integrated environment and corresponding habits, the Greek *polis* — this supreme work of collective 'art' wrested from nature in the first flowering of Western man — has almost the naturalness and intimacy of an organic fact. For this reason, alas, its wisdom is lost to us and its paradigm no longer valid. Technology is stronger than politics. It has become what Napoleon said politics was: destiny." [Jonas: *Philosophical Essays — From Ancient Creed to Technological Man,* Prentice-Hall, Englewood Cliffs, 1974, p. 79]. Jonas overstates this, of course.

In domestic politics, de Gaulle's founding confronted less serious problems initially, but more serious problems ultimately, than in the domain of foreign politics. De Gaulle quickly established the first part of his founding: a constitutional republic based on the president's authority, not the parliament's. But one can often resist foreigners more easily than fellow-citizens who serve foreign interests — especially when those foreign interests appeal to parts of every citizen's soul. To resist some aspects of modernity, de Gaulle had to, of course, modernize. This meant facing what he called "the peasant problem," the metamorphosing of "an enormous part of the French agricultural population to industry." The *ethos* of rural France, de Gaulle knew, in some aspects resembled the *ethos* he wanted, and resembled it more than the industrial and commercial *ethos* does. (Montesquieu opposes Plato on this, too: In late modernity, Marx sneers at the "idiocy" of rural life.) However, the active, occasionally spirited aspect of industry and commerce contrasts favorably with the passivity of agriculture. De Gaulle recognized a problem of education here, and also a problem of ethics. In founding a new regime de Gaulle attempted to defend modern economic life from its worst aspects and maximize its best ones. In this, institutions provided a place to stand, but rhetoric and example were the only real tools he had.

Appealing not to the many poor, the moderately prosperous majority or the rich few, but to "the *ensemble* of the nation," he outmaneuvered the professedly (and, in some respects, genuinely) democratic interest-groups and parliamentarians who couldn't publicly reject that appeal. The "consent that renders the laws fecund" had to be free consent, yet he had no intention to serve a majoritarian *telos*. In "a time on all sides solicited by the mediocre . . . I would act for *grandeur*," setting what he called the genius of modernity, its spirited *eros* for progress, discipline, against its mediocrity. "An Oedipus who would make Thebes against the Thebans," Malraux thought. *"L'esprit"* should rule the material; de Gaulle's *esprit* combines Machiavellian spiritedness with culture, the life of the mind and an ethics of magnanimity.*

Moreover, de Gaulle was one of the few moderns who synthesized Machiavellian spiritedness with moderation. This, along with his knowledge of the classics, caused his resemblance to pre-modern figures, particularly the Romans. It enabled him to say that man is a political animal.** And this, in turn, enabled him to espouse a genuine patriotism,*** for he

---

*Malraux reinforced this in the domain of culture. Years before meeting de Gaulle he told a group of Americans that "In the struggle against nature, in the exaltation of the conquest of things by man, resides one of the highest traditions of the West, from *Robinson Crusoe* to the Soviet cinema. Determined as we are to fight in the defense of our reasons for living, we refuse to consider this struggle as a fundamental value" [in *The Nation,* March 20, 1937]. And later: "To the extent that man conquers the earth, he loses his soul, not for amoral reasons, but because a civilization of action is a civilization that engages men only in action" [speech at Chamber of Commerce dinner, Montreal, October, 1963, in *Révue de la Chambre de Commerce Française au Canada,* #573, December, 1963, p. 6]. Malraux would re-connect thought and action, culture and politics, without synthesizing them — as Confucianists and historicists do, in radically different ways.

** . . . [T]he first signs of high value attached to the word *sophrosyne* [moderation] are found only with the growth of the *polis,* whose survival . . . depended on the operation of this form of excellence" [Helen North: *Sophrosyne — Self-Knowledge and Self-Restraint in Greek Literature,* Cornell University Press, Ithaca, 1966, p. 3]. North adds that *temperare,* the roman synonym, includes the sense of time: "the intervention at the right time of a wise moderator" [p. 262]. This is a virtue de Gaulle cultivated in himself and praised in others; recall that, in Malraux's word, de Gaulle strove to "put himself on the side of time, in the measure that time [could] contribute to the success of his designs — less like a military man than like a farmer." "What that is great could come to pass in a short time?" asks Plato's Socrates [*Republic,* Bk. X, 608c, Bloom translation].

***The moderns usually do not; their individualism and/or their economism disinclines them. Marx disdains patriotism, and many of his predecessors (Kant, Smith, Montesquieu, Hobbes) wax cosmopolitan with enthusiasm. Even Machiavelli, who finds it useful to profess patriotism at the close of *The Prince,* thereby inspiring generations of superficial readers, deeply cares only for personal glory, not the glory of his country.

saw that the nation-state is the only political realm available in modernity.

De Gaulle does synthesize early modern spiritedness with the modern form of moderation. In domestic politics he substitutes responsibility and participation for the Machiavellian and modern-economic belief in man-as-instrument. In this he resembled the classics, who think of the citizen as one who rules and is ruled. Gaullist spiritedness does not grow out of resentment, and thus lacks the viciousness of much modern spiritedness, from Machiavelli to the historicists.*

Politically, de Gaulle combined the modern, secular, egalitarian, republican tradition of France with the non-modern, Roman Catholic, authoritarian, monarchic tradition of France. Such criticisms as "There was an inherent contradiction between [de Gaulle's] imperious (or imperial) style and the very notion of participation" reflect the tension between these elements of de Gaulle's founding.** They are tensions the classical political philosophers might not object to, if apprised of the circumstance. For

> . . . there are two mother forms of *polises* from which the rest may be truly said to be derived; and one of them may be called monarchy and the other democracy . . . . Now, if you are to have liberty and the comoination of friendship with wisdom, you must have these forms of government in a measure; the argument emphatically declares that no *polis* can be well governed which is not made up of both.

The Athenian Stranger concludes that because the *demos* constitute the body of the body politic and the monarchy the head, the politic part, monarchy should predominate. (In the *Statesman,* Socrates uses the image of the weaver; the statesman should combine the virtues of moderation and courage in his *polis* by marrying citizens of moderate natures to citizens of courageous natures.) In the *Laws* and in the *Republic,* the statesman guides his *polis* with practical wisdom, although the regime of laws, being second-best, provides a smaller domain for statesmanlike action than the regime of practical wisdom does. De Gaulle, who wanted to maximize that domain as much as possible in a modern regime of laws, found himself in tension with the laws (including his own constitution) several times.

Montesquieu would resolve the democracy-monarchy tension in favor of democracy. He opposes the Roman-imposed central government of France, which he associates with authoritarianism and war. He regards commerce as a decentralized, peaceful activity. De Gaulle, whom Malraux considered a Roman type, centralized in order to make France more genuinely political than it had been, then attempted to decentralize power in such a way as to deny power to those who'd enjoyed it before — that is, in a way consonant with political, not merely economic, life.

---

*Among French writers, Corneille presents a spiritedness that resembles de Gaulle's. His Christian-Platonic psychology presents the human soul's elements as reason, spiritedness and the appetites/passions [see *Polyeucte,* Act IV, 11.1191-1194]. Racine's psychology, in contrast, is purely dualistic, a matter of reason vs. passion; Racine therefore lacks understanding of the political.

One should not simply identify Gaulllist politics with that of the classics, however. Thomas Pangle observes that "'Leadership' refers more to the capacity to guide and control followers than to the capacity to deliberate. Thinking of politics in terms of 'leadership' moves the emphasis away from thought toward force and initiative" [Pangle, *op. cit.,* p. 136]. He goes on to say that this leads to depreciating domestic policy, exalting foreign policy (defense, aggrandizement, glory). In this, de Gaulle resembles an early modern, although one should notice that his foreign policy served the purpose of founding. De Gaulle should appear between the classic and the early moderns on any graph of political psychology.

**And there are tensions within these traditions. Napoleon was a modern authoritarian; both monarchism and participation found defenders among Roman Catholic writers in the late 1800's and early 1900's.

Political life depends on certain virtues. Montesquieu's *L'esprit des lois,* that "massive demonstration of the irreconcilable tension between virtue and freedom," and Plato's *Laws,* wherein the Athenian Stranger contends that "he who imagines he can give laws for the public conduct of *polises,* while he leaves the private life of citizens to take care of itself" makes "a big mistake," both demonstrate the problem de Gaulle faced. Montesquieu solved it by relinquishing all but the most modest of virtues. "Laws excessively good are the source of excessive evil," he contends, while attacking the usury laws devised by the classics, Christians and "schoolmen" who synthesized classicism and Christianity. He praises mediocrity, preferring the self-rule of the many to the rule of the best — or the worst. The self-rule of the many guarantees the many's self-preservation, he believes, and self-preservation, to Montesquieu (following Hobbes and Locke) is the *telos* of government. My physical self-preservation requires, for the most part, the same conditions as your physical self-preservation; Montesquieu thus makes politics egalitarian, de-politicizes politics. Hence his notion of "political virtue," "patriotism," amounts to "the love of equality." Montesquieu admires England's devotion to liberty, the basis of self-preservation, and comfort. De Gaulle admires England only for its custom of rule by law.

Montesquieu's moderation bases itself on the same individualism and fear of death. Convinced that security, self-preservation, dominates human nature, he goes so far as to explain suicide as the result of "a defect of the filtration of the nervous juice," which "prompts us to the desire of ceasing to exist." The "heroic virtues which we admire in the ancients" ("moral virtue as it is directed to the public good," not to self-preservation) "to us are known only by tradition." Given their asserted radical unnaturalness, one must conclude that Montesquieu believes this tradition mythological.

We know that Montesquieu errs, as heroic virtues appear even in late modernity. Perhaps Montesquieu knows they exist but regards them as 'immoral,' undesirable. But he offers a different argument:

> The laws of Minos, of Lycurgus, and of Plato suppose a particular attention and care, which the citizens ought of have over one another's conduct. But an attention of this kind cannot be expected in the confusion and multitude of affairs in which a large nation is entangled.

In this, Montesquieu follows Aristotle, who writes that "Experience shows it is difficult, if not indeed impossible, for a very populous *polis* to secure a general habit of obedience to law." For "order . . . is the one thing which is impossible for an excessive number," and to enforce laws that aim at virtue "the citizens of a *polis* must know one another's character." In theory, one might suggest partial decentralization as a remedy to this, but Montesquieu wants decentralization in order to promote commerce, not heroic virtues. He prefers other virtues.

> Commercial laws, it may be said, improve *moeurs* for the same reason that they destroy them. They corrupt the purest morals. This was the subject of Plato's complaints; and we every day see that they polish and refine the most barbarous.

Commerce brings "a certain exact sense of justice," a mean between strict unselfishness and robbery. This type of justice almost typifies what we mean when we say that something is economical. Montesquieu's mean between a virtue and a vice replaces the Aristotelian mean between two vices.* "Economy" replaces moderation; it is the new moderation.

---

*Nietzsche regards the taking of the mean between a virtue and a vice as the formula for mediocrity. Montesquieu knows this, and praises the mediocrity called moderation. He writes that "We begin to be cured of Machiavelism, and recover from it every day. More moderation has become necessary" [*Spirit of the Laws,* Vol. I Bk. XXI, ch. 20, p. 366]. Precisely: Montesquieu *intends* to formulate a more fearful, unspirited, economic "Machiavelism." Also, compare Montesquieu's "exact sense of justice" with Tocqueville and "self-interest rightly understood" [*Democracy in America,* Volume II, Second Book, chapters VIII and IX].

And if economy succeeds in its own terms, what then? Malraux sees that "if all men become socially liberated, they will find again the problems of the ancient free men." To the extent that economic life has yielded this liberation, these problems have indeed reappeared. Mauriac worries that "the whole of French society reveals preoccupations and tastes that in now way correspond to the notion of greatness its leader incarnates"; these preoccupations include "all the basest stimulations of sexuality and violence." Economy that succeeds corrupts itself, becomes uneconomical, immoderate even by its own modest standards. More profoundly, as Malraux also sees, "The Acropolis is the only place in the world haunted at the same time by mind and by courage," which coexist without reconciliation.* In rediscovering the problems of the ancient free men, modernity rediscovers the problem of the relation between mind, philosophy, and courage. It tries to resolve these problems with the doctrine of historicism.

Religion, in the America of Tocqueville, "is the road to knowledge, and the observance of the divine law leads man to civil freedom." It "directs the customs of the community, and, by regulating domestic life, it regulates the state." Tocqueville departs from Montesquieu in seeing that modern public life hasn't lost the need for religion. He also sees that modernity tries to abolish religion, and recommends that "In those countries in which, unhappily, irreligion and democracy coexist,** philosophers and those in power ought to be always striving to place the objects of human action far beyond man's immediate reach." For "the leaders of modern society would be wrong to seek to lull the community by a state of too uniform and too peaceful happiness, and . . . it is well to expose it from time to time to matters of difficulty and danger in order to raise ambition and to give it a field of action." In Nietzsche's (characteristically) more striking words, "the heroic type, the great *pain bringers* of humanity," "contribute immensely to the preservation and enhancement of the species, even if it were only by opposing comfortableness and by not concealing how this sort of happiness nauseates them." Gaullist patriotism — De Gaulle's insistence on his impersonality, his practice of speaking to the French less of themselves than of France — is as close as a statesman ruling a modernized country can come to the ancient, religiously-based founding, with its ancestor-worship (the *pater* in patriotism, of course, means father, and means it literally to the ancients: father-land) and civic virtue. Fanaticism is the danger here, as Orwell sees: "Whereas Socialism, and even capitalism in a more grudging way, have said to people 'I want to offer you a good time,' Hitler has said to them 'I offer you struggle, danger and death,' and as a result a whole nation flings itself at his feet." Plato would guard against this by instilling not only the zealous piety based on spiritedness but the reverent piety based on fear. (He 'overlooks' another aspect of reverent piety: its basis in a kind of admiration, a sense of the holy.) But Plato knows that spiritedness and fear may become unbalanced without practical wisdom to watch them. The loss of this practical wisdom, noticeable in the spirited Machiavelli and the fearful Hobbes and Montesquieu, may reveal the loss of a more comprehensive, non-practical wisdom, which Plato glimpses. Malraux suggested, in 1955, that "the principal problem of the end of the century will be the religious problem — in a form as unlike any that we know now as Christianity was from the religions of antiquity." It is a problem that both religious and philosophic men would consider. Malraux, who echoes

---

*Aristotle agrees, contending that the Greeks combine intelligence with spiritedness, that the Europeans have spiritedness without intelligence and the Asians intelligence without spiritedness.

**Many of the modern philosophers and their allies attempt to advance democracy and subvert religion simultaneously. Early in modernity, given the association between church and state, this must have seemed a coherent enterprise. But in view of the nature of religious faith, especially Christian faith, it was a paradoxical one. The *demos* as a group often care more for religion than rulers as a group. Perhaps these philosophers wanted to make the *demos* more congenial to modern philosophers. They surely succeeded in making philosophy more congenial to the *demos*.

Nietzsche's depreciation of "little reason," senses the epistemological labyrinth here. Plato, who knows that labyrinth as well as anyone, regards wisdom as knowledge not of the *empeiria* but of the *eidos;* the unwise believe the apparent real.

But for the benefit of the domain of practice, one must ask, with Plato: can virtue be taught? Mauriac assumes so. The Athenian Stranger observes, drily, that "there is no great inclination or readiness on the part of mankind to be made as good, or as quickly good, as possible." One does not teach virtue as one teaches geography because virtue has little to do with information. Nor does one teach it exactly as one teaches more general subjects, by compelling the student to turn away from appearance and turn toward the *eidos* until he's able to endure looking at the *eidos*. This "turning around" of the soul might prepare some for virtuous action, but not all who perceive the *eidos* necessarily stop loving appearance, and few perceive the *eidos* in the first place. To 'teach' virtue, the Athenian Stranger would compel a youth to face both pain (as in Sparta) and pleasure (as in Athens), and learn that they are "foolish and antagonistic counselors." As the youth grows he gradually abandons their counsel, listening instead to the laws. In regard to the laws, "the best way of training the young is to train yourself at the same time; not to admonish them but to be always carrying out your own admonitions in practice."

In addition to the use of example, at which de Gaulle usually excelled, one must present one's admonitions with care. Example enhances the authority of the one who admonishes, but so can memory. Malraux knows of the link between authority and memory. Authority comes from the need "to act *ensemble,*" and that need arises from shared sentiments, principles and memories. Thus Malraux writes that de Gaulle incarnated dreams that existed before he did, that he "render[ed] France near and convincing." The Greek word for making-near, making-present, is *anamnesis* — literally, not-forgetting. *Anamnesis* is Malraux's most important artistic technique in *Le miroir des limbes;* it also dominates what de Gaulle considered Malraux's finest speech, his speech on the occasion of the transfer of Jean Moulin's ashes to the Pantheon. In it Malraux remembers, and causes French youth, unborn when Moulin lived, to 'remember' *with him,* fraternally, the life of the greatest resistance hero. He remembers Moulin's understanding that de Gaulle compelled others to remember France, caused France to be present even after Hitler's troops overran Paris. France's presence made unity possible — a unity not only of thought but of practical action against a powerful enemy. In organizing the Resistance, in giving it unity in practice, Moulin "was the Carnot of the Resistance" — another remembering, parallel vision.

After de Gaulle named Moulin President of the Committee of Coordination of the Resistance, what Malraux calls "the prehistory" of the Resistance "had ended." But the "prehistory," as Malraux recounts it, was on the 'level' of what one ordinarily regards as history; Malraux narrates it, and associates its protagonist with a historical figure, Carnot. "Before [the Resistance] had fought as an army does, in the face of victory, death or captivity."

> It now began to discover the world of concentration camps, the certitude of torture. It was then that it began to fight in the face of Hell.

Malraux henceforth minimizes narration and elevates his parallel vision to the domain of myth. He quotes Moulin's sister, who said that after his capture "his Calvary began." "Understand well that during the several days when he could have talked . . . the destiny of the Resistance was suspended on the courage of this man," the one who knew its secrets. Moulin, the parallel of Christ, endured torture in the shadows and thereby saved his "brothers in the order of the Night": a harrowing of Hell, sacrifice in the service of fraternity.

Malraux ends by synthesizing the mythological and historical domains. He remembers Carnot, Hugo, Jaurès (also buried in the Pantheon, hence present) and associates them with Moulin. The exordium: "Today, youth, may you think of this man as you would have brought your hands to his poor misshapen face on his last day, to his lips which had not spoken — that day, his was the face of France." Moulin, Christ, the heroes of the Pantheon, France: this parallel vision presents the only civic 'religion' possible in modernity.*

Culture, "the mysterious presence, in each of us, of that which should belong to death," "orients" our fantasy-life, "and orients it 'up' by obliging it to compete with the greatest human dreams." Malraux thus distinguishes it from religion, which acts on the fantasy-life "by its exemplary nature," as in this speech on Moulin. But both religion and culture are makings-present of that which affects our ethical and political life by affecting our dreams.

Memory is not enough. De Gaulle not only made France near, he made it convincing; memory preserves sense-impressions, opinions and knowledge but is not itself knowledge, that which convinces the souls who transcend appearance. Plato's *Meno* demonstrates memory's limitations. A thing of the *polis,* memory metamorphoses as the *polis* does; the oft-decried forgetfulness of the contemporary *demos* reflects the incessant change of democratic life. (The 'forgetfulness' of totalitarians reflects *planned* change.) "Only knowledge of the kind *phronesis* [practical wisdom, wise judgment] seems immune to forgetfulness." Only reason truly binds right opinions to the soul, and the reason which yields practical wisdom yields a kind of knowledge dissimilar to, for example, mathematical knowledge. It is a knowledge lacking the precision of other kinds of knowledge; hence Aristotle warns us, at the beginning of the *Nichomachean Ethics,* that we must not demand of him greater precision than the subject-matter allows. This accounts for the persistance of the problem of civic education, an education that might otherwise stay in the domain of memory, of the public ceremonies of civic religion.

The French educational system became the vehicle of a democratic and parliamentarian ideology during the Third Republic. But its structure, built by Napoleon, reflected his despotic ideology. A political scientist observes that from then on

> . . . the Ministry of Education has dictated to teachers from the Pyrenees to the Rhine exactly what should be taught and when. The authoritarian style of instruction limited opportunities for students to learn the skills of cooperation and participation associated with one facet of the democratic citizen's role.

Another reflection of the schism between the French state and French society: one reads without surprise that in the new generation of French youth, the generation de Gaulle hoped to see before he died, "neither the sons of the bourgeoisie nor the sons of the workers . . . retained the Gaullist image of France." In their secondary schools they learned little that was concrete ("abstract and rhetorical formation" overbalanced "all other modes of instruction"); they acquired no habits of deference ("One is astonished that boys of twenty want to reconstruct society, but they are asked, when they are fifteen years old, what they think of love in Racine; when they are sixteen years old they have refuted the philosophy of Kant after

---

*St. Augustine and St. Bernard, both of whom Malraux admired, developed this technique. As the scholar Dennis Quinn explains, through the use of analogy or typologies (Adam, for example, is the "type," the prefiguration, of Christ) a Christian rhetorician would cause his listener to *remember* himself in a Biblical figure. Preaching on the theme of sin, for example, the rhetorician would remind his listener of Adam: thus causing the listener "to remember himself, to become aware of the burden of sin" by learning of his own Adamic sinfulness. He would then learn that "Christ enacts man's tragedy with absolute perfection" — that Christ, too, is himself if he accepts Him. Finally, the sinner would see that he "owes Christ an agony; he must suffer for his sin through repentance," then escape the wages of that sin (eternal death) in Christ — unite with Him. The rhetorician thus conceives of his sermon "not as exhortation but as action," as the re-enactment of "the spiritual dialectic which the (psalm's) verses in their very structure embody." [Dennis Quinn: "Donne's Christian Eloquence," in *Seventeenth Century Prose — Modern Essays in Criticism,* Stanley E. Fish, editor, Oxford University Press, New York, 1971, pp. 369-370.] To Malraux, of course, Christ belongs to the domain of myth; one's 'salvation' depends on courageous practical action and unity more than on spiritual action and union.

three months of philosophy class");* they developed no patriotism (their course of study formed "intellectuals more than citizens").

De Gaulle knew this. Regarding educational reform as more difficult than other kinds because it involves ideological as well as economic interests, he observed that no institution can be truly reformed if its members do not consent — "unless by making a *tabula rasa* by dictatorship or revolution." He might have added that the Algerian struggle, also involving ideological as well as economic interests, raised the question of immediate national survival, thus inclining the French to follow de Gaulle; education could provoke no equivalent feeling of urgency.

De Gaulle wanted French youth to receive "not only instruction, but also education which is the foundation of the value of a people." As early as 1949 he proposed that the government give credits to families, who would then choose the school they wanted their children to attend; the French family was to be the basis for the return to "moral health" in France. When done, this program strengthened the Roman Catholic schools, whose patrons were among de Gaulle's constituencies. De Gaulle thereby used a modern device against modernity. Locke and Rousseau both emphasize private education, partly in order to undermine the traditional religious schools and partly as a reflection of their individualism.** De Gaulle found himself in the opposite circumstance — with a dominant secular education that failed to provide an adequate civic education — and acted appropriately. He understood that along with scientific and technical instruction, pure thought — expressed by philosophy, defended by letters, illustrated by the arts — and ethics must inspire the most learned Frenchmen. He went so far as to tell a group of scientists to elevate their thought to France. He lacked the power to use curriculum to sufficiently insist upon this combination of disinterested nonpolitical contemplation and patriotism.

He thought of himself as a teacher, having first taught himself by assuming the persona of the leader, then assuming France: character in the individual, grandeur in the country. He would educate the French not by asking them all to become men of character and to assume France but to assume true Frenchness by means of participation. Participation would educate men to be citizens, not mere individuals, economic beings. De Gaulle's means for arriving at participation were rhetoric (speaking to the French less of themselves than of France), actions (foreign and domestic) and institutions (a certain kind of education for children, certain kinds of cultural, political and economic arrangements for adults). For Plato, the rule of law is second-best; for de Gaulle, knowing the French resistance to the rule of law, a people animated by national passion is second-best. Rule by a moderate and courageous elite is best, as it brings practical wisdom, what he calls "good sense."

Montesquieu would have told de Gaulle that whereas both the ancients and the moderns encourage virtue and constancy of belief, in the *polis* these were "never effaced by contrary impressions," while in modernity youth receives three educations: by parents, by masters, by the world. The latter effaces the work of the others. "This, in some measure, arises from the contrast we experience between our religious and worldly engagements, a thing unknown to the ancients."

Had de Gaulle wielded the power to truly reform French education, he would have done well to consult older writers. Aristotle thinks that "the legislator should make the education of

---

*Plato's Socrates recommends withholding the study of dialectic from the young because they use it as puppies use new teeth — to tear things. [Plato: *Republic,* Bk. VII, 539b, Bloom translation, Basic Books, New York, 1970.]

**In Locke we see the paradox of a civic education based on individualism. See Robert H. Horwitz's informative essay, "John Locke and the Preservation of Liberty: A Perennial Problem of Civic Education," in *The Moral Foundations of the American Republic,* Robert H. Horwitz, editor, University Press of Virginia, Charlottesville, 1977.

the young his chief and foremost concern." He must know the *telos* he aims at. Aristotle regards war as one *telos* of the *polis* ("men who cannot face danger courageously become the slaves of the first to assail them"), but leisure, finally, matters more; "most of the *polises* which make war their aim are safe only while they are fighting." Immoderation, injustice and the lack of practical wisdom endanger men at leisure. Education's *telos*, "like that of art generally, is to copy nature by making her deficiencies good"; while immoderation, injustice and folly have their delights, "the education of a citizen in the spirit of his *politeia* does not consist in his doing the actions in which the partisans of oligarchy, or the adherents of democracy delight" but "in his doing the actions by which an oligarchy or a democracy will be enabled to survive." De Gaulle wanted a republic, what Aristotle calls a mixed regime; French youth needed education that inclined them toward doing the actions by which a republic would be enabled to survive.

The Athenian Stranger advises that "the soul of the child in his play should be guided to the love of that sort of excellence in which when he grows up to manhood he will have to be perfected." Education, "that training which is given by suitable habits to be the first instinct of virtue in children," requires the use of music and gymnastic in such a way as to artfully identify virtue and pleasure by means of praise and blame. (This does not contradict his observation that physical pleasure and pain are foolish and antagonistic counselors; indeed, the mental pleasure and pain associated with reputation is also a foolish and self-antagonistic counselor in a *polis* wherein the ruling opinions ricochet like errant bullets: the teaching of the *Phaedo.)*

Aristotle also writes of the importance of habituation. Because "we always prefer what we come across first," educators must prevent "an early familiarity with anything that is low," subhuman. Music, which cultivates "the mind at leisure," "provides us with images of states of character — images of anger, and of calm; images of fortitude and temperance, and of all the forms of their opposites . . . ." "[T]o listen to these images is to undergo a real change of the soul," because to "acquire a habit of feeling pain or taking delight in an image is something closely allied with feeling pain or taking delight in the actual reality." The Athenian Stranger derides the regime in which the rulers claim "that music has no truth, and, whether good or bad, can only be judged of rightly by the pleasure of the hearer" as "theatrocracy." Music and the other arts do not merely decorate things, as moderns tend to believe. "The depreciation of music is both a cause and a sign of the difficulty modern education has with the formation of civic sentiment."*

The laws should link the child's education with the 'education' he receives in the world. Law and punishment form part of "the nurture and education of the living soul of man." "Laws are partly framed for the sake of good men, in order to [educate] them on how they may live on friendly terms with one another, and partly for the sake of those who refuse to be [educated] . . . ." Laws provide the conditions of friendship among those who participate in actions aimed at fulfilling the *telos* of the *polis,* while excluding those who refuse to participate and thus refuse that friendship.

Modernity fails to cultivate practical wisdom in its statesman. So did antiquity. Some religious men and all modern historicists predict that human nature itself will metamorphose, and the metamorphosis will bring wisdom. Others think not. "Unless . . . the philosophers rule as kings or those now called kings or chiefs genuinely and adequately philosophize, and political power and philosophy coincide in the same place, while the man natures now making their way to either apart from the other are by necessity excluded, there is no rest from ills for

---

*The writer is Eva T.H. Brann, whose *Paradoxes of Education in a Republic* [University of Chicago Press, Chicago and London, 1979, p. 34] should orient contemporary discussions of this topic. See also Pangle [*op. cit.,* pp. 228-230] on the way modern subjectivism undermines the use of culture in civic education.

Few moderns regard the magistracy of education as the "greatest" in the *polis,* as the Athenian Stranger does [*Laws,* Bk. VI, 765e].

cities, my dear Glaucon, nor I think for human kind, nor will the regime we have now described in speech ever come forth from nature, insofar as possible, and see the light of the sun." Knowing something of the nature of *logos* and of its peculiar relationship to the world, we can almost say, with a historian, that "the brilliant failures of great men to achieve their ideals form the best treasures of nations."

APPENDIX

DE GAULLE'S MILITARY EPISTEMOLOGY:
A NOTE ON *LE FIL DE L'ÉPÉE*

Because the character of contingency is essential to the action of war, Heraclitus and Bergson are the relevant epistemologists. Bertrand Russell found the latter's activity-oriented metaphysic "becoming in a cavalry officer, but not in a philosopher"; de Gaulle, no philosopher, but sufficiently like one to eschew pacifism, might have taken the compliment while reserving judgment on the insult.

On the philosophic level, Russell formulates, among several criticisms of Bergson, two just ones. He remarks that Bergson's conception of number as spatial confuses numbers of objects (twelve phiilosophers, for example) with number (the number twelve) and Number (the idea); he might have cited Plato's observation that mathematics is inferior to philosophy in its 'abstraction' — but Russell prefers not to go that far. Russell also remarks that Bergson tends to visualize "successions as spread out on a line": an idiosyncrasy that causes him to criticize mathematics for specifying not an object's movements but only some of the points through which it moves. For the mathematical approach Bergson would substitute his concept of "duration," which is based on our perception of movement as continuous. Russell's essentially just criticism might be restated more simply by remarking that Bergson commits the error of gradualism: assuming that the *practically* "indivisible continuity of change" precludes the discernment of points that may, for reason of another kind of practicality, be 'frozen' for measurement's sake. Were this mathematical 'freezing' invalid, it would fail when applied to Bergsonian reality. But it doesn't; engineering works.

Moreover, gradualism assumes an egalitarianism of time and space: one point on the curve is held to be no more significant than another. This is true in the sense that to alter one point in a curve is to make a new curve; it is false in the sense that, practically considered, extremities count more than non-extremities — as any driver knows. This suggests a more important criticism: Bergson tends to neglect structure — the skeleton under the surface of things, where delineation of extremes counts very much — because he is enamored of flow, which he associates with freedom.

Russell ends by charging Bergson with confusing the subject and the object, the act of knowing with the object known. To do this he ignores the concept Bergson calls "intellectual sympathy." Analysis "express[es] a thing as a function of something other than itself," mathematicians do it. (Some mathematicians, following Plato, would reply that this "something other" is in fact closer to the thing's true nature than is the physical thing itself.) But "intellectual sympathy" is that "by which one places oneself within an object in order to coincide with what is unique in it and consequently inexpressible." The inexpressibility of reality accounts for Bergson's frequent use of metaphor, which disturbs Russell. However, the real 'proof' of Bergson's thesis isn't metaphor; it is experience. Those of us who have had this experience of self-transferrence (Mr. Russell, despite his paeans to "universal love" — so prominent in his chapter on Nietzsche — evidently hasn't) see Bergson's point. Reality, Bergson contends, is not constructed (as in subjectivism) or reconstructed (as in objectivism) but "touched, penetrated, lived."

The rule of science is the one posited by Bacon: obey in order to command.
The philosopher neither obeys nor commands: he seeks to be at one with nature.

Modern science, adopting the Roman metaphor of law to describe nature (Plato and Aristotle rarely if ever use that metaphor), does indeed try to obey in order to command, to conquer. The Bergsonian philosopher attempts to revive an older ideal, common to West and East.*

---

*In this sense Russell's claim that Bergson is purely modern is false, as is his worry that Bergsonian philosophy contains no harmony, only conflict. Russell scares himself too easily when conflict appears or seems about to appear.

But this one-ness does not have one-ness-with-Being as its end. Bergson's nature is active, simply, and not, as older philosophers had it, activity tending toward rest. Instinct is for using and intelligence is for making. Instinct is "intellectual sympathy," and intuition is instinct made "disinterested, self-conscious, capable of reflecting upon its object and of enlarging it indefinitely" by intelligence. This is de Gaulle's epistemology, also; the defense of force rests on the fact Nietzsche observed: that nature's force 'creates' as well as destroys. By intuition, de Gaulle writes, "We participate in what it is possible to find [in nature] of obscure harmony." If intelligence attributes to nature a definition and coherence it may not actually possess, this apparently serves the military leader nonetheless, although it also makes error possible. The nature of war, abstracted from politics, is unquestionably active; Bergsonian epistemology makes sense on the battlefield.

For a military leader, the 'proof' of his intuition's accuracy is the result on the battlefield (although, as de Gaulle noticed in *La discorde chez l'ennemi,* fortune may consecrate faulty plans; he thus avoids vulgar historicism). For Bergson, I have suggested, 'proof' is experience; Bergson almost claims otherwise: "Dialectic is necessary to put intuition to the proof; necessary also in order that intuition break itself up into concepts and so be propagated to other men . . . ." But he continues:

> . . . all [logic] does, often enough, is to develop the result of that intuition which transcends it. The truth is, the two procedures are of opposite direction: the same effort, by which ideas are connected with ideas, causes the intuition which the ideas were storing up to vanish. The philosopher is obliged to abandon intuition, once he has received from it the impetus, and to rely on himself to carry on the movement by pushing the concepts one after another. But he soon feels he has lost foothold; he must come into touch with intuition again; he must undo most of what he has done. In short, dialectic is what ensures the agreement of our thought with itself. But by dialectic — which is only a relaxation of intuition — many different agreements are possible, while there is only one truth. Intuition, if it could be prolonged beyond a few instants, would not only make the philosopher agree with his own thought, but also all philosophers with each other.

A scholar has written that de Gaulle's "instinct" or "intuition" isn't truly Bergsonian; "what he was really talking about was not an 'ineffable' mystical and aesthetic experience, but the well-informed hunches of the acting pragmatist." De Gaulle lacked *mystique,* it is true (except for the well-calculated kind), but how effable is what he calls "intuition"? The well-informed hunches of the acting pragmatist may not be so easy to express; they were surely difficult to convey satisfactorily to most of de Gaulle's ranking officers. The difference between Bergson's epistemology and de Gaulle's military epistemology has less to do with effability than with the possibility of observing results; Bergsonian 'proof' is experienced or not experienced by each individual who considers his thesis, whereas Gaullist 'proof' comes on the battlefield. In view of the second World War, one could accept de Gaulle's military application of Bergsonism while doubting its metaphysical accuracy.

De Gaulle's military epistemology, an anti-dogmatism, underlies his advocacy of mobile warfare. More important, it tends toward a politics of deed as much if not more than a politics of speech, a politics of executive, not parliamentary, rule. For de Gaulle, *logos* does not apprehend nature; intuition does — intuition, which is vitiated by excessive speech. If Aristotle found the human potentiality for politics in the human capacity for speech, de Gaulle, living at the end of Europe's parliamentary age, sees that too much speech, speech uncorrected by knowledge of, acknowledgment of, the reality of force is an invitation to inhumanity. Aristotle did not intend his disciples to be parliamentarians; with de Gaulle's epistemology, they could not be. The problem of the disjunction between speech and action — posed best by Plato, whose regime-in-speech is evidently not a programme for action, and denied by Marx, who would subordinate speech to action — reappears in this century with a persistence that tempts one to think the problem to be as perennial as human nature. Bergsonism freed de Gaulle's hand to act without freeing it to act in any way: which leads to Gaullist ethics.

NOTES

The page-numbers on the left side of the page are the pages in the text. They are followed by the lines on each page where quoted material appears and by the first few words of that quoted material. The numbers in parentheses are the page-numbers on which the quoted material appears in the source; on those occasions when the source is available in French and in English translation, the first number refers to the French edition and the second, italicized, number refers to the translation.

*

FIRST PART, Chapter 1: *La discorde chez l'ennemi* (1924)

(All references, unless otherwise noted, are to *La discorde chez l'ennemi,* Editions Berger-Levrault, Paris, 1924, "Le Livre de Poche" edition, printed by Brodard et Taupin, Paris, 1973.)

Page 3:

ll.26-32: "it is possible . . . ." (7)
l.37: "did not diminish . . . . " (8-9)
ll.39-40: "taste for inordinate . . . . " (9)
ll.41-43: "far from combatting . . . . " (9)

Page 4:

ll.3-12: "far from combatting . . . . " (9)
ll.13-15: "philosophy of war . . . . " (9)
ll.18-23: "This study will . . . . " (10)
ll.31-33: "The Greek genius . . . ." (André Malraux: "The Painting of Galanis," preface to a catalogue of Galanis' paintings, dated March 18, 1922, reprinted in *Malraux Miscellany,* vol. 1, no. 2, 1969.)
ll.35-41: "In the French-style garden . . . ." (10)

Page 5:

ll.19-29: "the indiscipline of von Kluck . . . ." (8)
ll.36-41: "admitting, *a priori* . . . . " (15)
l.42, *p. 6,* ll.1-3: "By virtue of . . . . " (16)

Page 6:

ll.7-8: "All military Germany . . . ." (18)
l.10: "totally personal conception . . . . " (19)
ll.11-12: "The systematic inertia . . . . " (20)
ll.12-13: "the system of Moltke . . . . " (20-21)
ll.16-19: "It was from Nietzsche . . . . " (21)
ll.20-21: "exaggerated their . . . . " (21)
ll.24-26: "sick, and considered . . . . " (22)
l.29: "certain other means . . . . " (23)
ll.30-34: "like the illustrious . . . . " (24)
ll.35-37: "the strategical surprise . . . . " (26)
ll.39-41: "German military history . . . . " (26)
ll.42-43: "in war, apart . . . . " (14)
ll.43-44: "this obsession . . . . " (14)

Page 7:

ll.2-3: "tenacious struggle between . . . . " (29)
ll.4-5: "essentially a Junker . . . . " (30)
ll.6-7: "entire life was . . . . " (31)

178

11.13-16: "produced a profound . . . . " (157)
11.25-29: "A sort of . . . . " (162)
 1.30: "moment to galvanize . . . . " (162)
11.31-32: "had deprived the . . . . " (163)
11.33-36: "the Government of Berlin . . . . " (167)
11.37-38: "at the hour . . . . " (168)
11.38-39: "at the same . . . . " (169)
 1.42: "the most complete . . . . " (170)
11.45-47: "As always . . . . " (171)

Page 13:

 1.1: "abandoned themselves . . . . " (171)
11.1-3: "Each one knew . . . . " (172)
11.6-7: "Nothing, no one . . . . " (178)
11.7-9: "the life of . . . . " (179)

FIRST PART, Chapter 2: Moderation (Nietzsche contra Plato): Reflections on *La discorde chez l'ennemi*

Page 15:

(no quotations not previously cited)

Page 16:

11.7-11: "the eruption of madness" . . . . (Nietzsche: *The Gay Science,* Walter Kaufmann translation, Random House, New York, 1974, Book II, sec. 76, p. 131)

11.13-15:"Hatred of mediocrity . . . . " (Nietzsche: *The Will to Power,* Walter Kaufmann and R.J. Hollingdale translation, Random House, 1968, Book IV, sec. 893, p. 476)

11.19-24: "What? Does life . . . . " (Nietzsche: *Thus Spoke Zarathustra,* Second Part, "On the Rabble," in *The Portable Nietzsche,* edited/translated by Walter Kaufmann, Viking Press, New York 1954, p. 209)

11.25-26: "*Nausea* over man . . . . " (Nietzsche: *Ecce Homo,* "Why I Am So Wise," in *Basic Writings of Nietzsche,* edited/translated by Walter Kaufmann, Modern Library, New York, 1968, p. 690)

 1.32: "though it be called . . . . " (*Zarathustra,* in *The Portable Nietzsche, op. cit.,* p. 282)

 1.32: "Aristotelianism of morals" (*Beyond Good and Evil,* "Natural History of Morals," sec. 198, in *Basic Writings of Nietzsche, op. cit.,* p. 299)

Page 17:

11.2-3: "public spirit, benevolence . . . . " (*ibid.,* p. 299)

11.4-5: "*imprudently*" . . . . (*Beyond Good and Evil,* in *Basic Writings of Nietzsche,* p. 315)

11.7-10: A scholar has observed . . . . (Werner J. Dannhauser: *Nietzsche's View of Socrates,* Cornell University Press, Ithaca and London, 1974, p. 202)

11.14-15: "And only those . . . . " (*The Gay Science, op. cit.,* p. 55)

 1.18: "your ears . . . . " (*Zarathustra,* in *op. cit.,* p. 151)

11.20-22: " . . . it harms your . . . . " (*ibid.,* p. 151)

11.24-26: "Hourly, they are . . . . " (*ibid.,* p. 284)

Page 18:

 1.2: "all truths . . . . " (*ibid.,* p. 228)

11.4-5: "Not every word . . . . " (*ibid.,* p. 400)

11.7-9: "Those who can . . . . " (*Ecce Homo,* in *op. cit.,* p. 674)

11.14-15: "Culture owes . . . . " (*Human, All-too-Human,* sec. 465, in *The Portable Nietzsche,* p. 61)

1.24: "great politics" (*Ecce Homo,* in *op. cit.,* p. 783)
   1.24: "civic mediocrity" (*Beyond Good and Evil,* in *ibid.,* p. 77)
11.26-27: "All community . . . . " (*ibid.,* 416)

Page 19:

11.3-6: "peace from . . . . " (*ibid.,* p. 263)
11.18-19: "The concept of . . . . " (*Ecce Homo,* in *ibid.,* p. 783)
11.19-20: "an end to that . . . . " (*Beyond Good and Evil,* in *ibid.,* p. 307)
11.22-23: "the life that . . . . " (*Zarathustra,* in *op. cit.,* p. 216)
11.23-25: "social or herd nature" (*The Gay Science, op.cit.,* p. 299)
  1.37: "*primordial fact* . . . . " (*Beyond Good and Evil,* in *op. cit.,* p. 394)
11.39-41: "is *essentially* . . . . " (*ibid.,* p. 393)
11.42-44: "wasteful beyond measure . . . . " (*ibid.,* p. 205)

Page 20:

11.5-8: " . . . [A]t the bottom . . . . " (*Beyond Good and Evil,* in *op. cit.,* p. 352)
11.18-19: "One ought to . . . . " (*Zarathustra,* in *op. cit.,* p. 202)
11.23-25: "Will nothing . . . . " (*ibid.,* p. 401)
11.29-30: "a certain kind . . . . " (Plato: *The Republic,* Allan Bloom translation,
     Basic Books, New York and London, 1968, 430e, p. 109)
  1.39: "is like a . . . . " (*ibid.,* 431e, p. 110)
11.40-44: " . . . it's unlike courage . . . . " (*ibid.,* 432a, p. 110)
11.45, *p. 21,* 1.1: A scholar has observed . . . . (Allan Bloom, *ibid.,* p. 452,
     note #31)

Page 21:

11.8-11: "For all these . . . . " (Plato: *Statesman,* 284a, Benjamin Jowett
     translation, in *The Dialogues of Plato,* Oxford University Press, Oxford,
     University Press, Oxford, 1964, volume III, p. 497)
  1.13: "everything is overthrown" (Plato: *Laws,* 691c in *The Dialogues of Plato,*
     ibid., volume IV, p. 260)
11.15-16: "tuned to the . . . . " (*The Republic, op. cit.,* 412a, p. 90)
11.28-30: "[W]hen the feeling . . . . " (Plato: *Phaedo,* 83c Benjamin Jowett
     translation, *op. cit.,* volume I, p. 439)

Page 22:
(None)

SECOND PART, Chapter 3: *Le fil de l'épée (1932)*

(All references, unless otherwise noted, are to *Le fil de l'épée,* Berger-Levrault, Paris, 1944,
"Le Livre de Poche" edition, Paris, 1973, and to *The Edge of the Sword,* Gerard Hopkins
translation, Criterion Books, New York, 1960.)

Page 25:

11.11-14: "The more he . . . . " (Aidan Crawley, *De Gaulle,* The Bobbs-Merrill
     Company, Inc., Indianapolis and New York, 1969, p. 53)
  1.22: "a self-portrait in anticipation" (Stanley Hoffmann, *Decline or Renewal?*
     France Since the 1930's, The Viking Press, New York, 1974, p. 217)
  1.25: "*Être grand* . . . . " (p. 7, *7*)

Page 26:

11.2-5: "Incertitude marks . . . . " (p. 7, *7*)
11.8-14: "The ambiance . . . . " (p. 8,*8*)
11.14-16 "only the blood . . . . " (9, *8*)
11.20-23: "only too easily . . . . " (9, *8*)
11.24-25: "international order" (9, *8*)

11.26-28: "temporarily made wiser . . . . " (9, *8-9*)
11.31-34: "Without disavowing . . . . " (9, *9*)
1.38: "Whatever direction . . . . " (10, *9*)
11.39-41: "Without force . . . . " (10, *9*)
11.42-45: "Shield of masters . . . . " (10, *9-10*)

Page 27:

11.3-11: "In truth . . . . " (11, *10*)
1.18: "the general harmony" (11, *10*)
11.20-23: "power escapes . . . . " (11, *10*)
11.23-24: "to restore . . . . " (11-12, *10*)
1.35: "the action of . . . . " (13, *15*)
11.37-39: "In war . . . . " (14, *16*)
11.44-45: "elaborating in advance . . . . " (15-16, *17*)
11.46-47: "in short . . . . " (19, *20*)
1.48, *p. 28,* 11.1-2: "a direct contact . . . . " (19-20, *20*)

Page 28:

11.4-7: "We participate . . . . " (20, *20*)
11.12-13: "hope", "fortune" . . . . (21-22, *22*)
11.18-20: "the impression of . . . . " (22, *22*
11.23-24: "elaborates them . . . . " (22, *22*)
11.27-28: "It is why . . . . " (23, *23*)
1.30: "lose the sentiment . . . . " (24, *24*)
11.33-35: "It is true . . . . " (25, *24*)

Page 29:

11.13-21: "who formerly did not . . . . " (Xenophon, *Memorabilia,* Book III,
          chapter 5.)
11.32-33: "depression of spirits" (26, *25*)
11.33-36: "deduce the conception . . . . " (27, *26*)
11.38-41: "In fact . . . . " (28, *26-27*)
11.42-44: "This is why . . . . " (28, *27*)
11.47-48: "to the point of . . . . (31, *29*)
11.49-50 "the absence or . . . . " ')32, *30*)
1.51, *p. 30,* 1.1: "the spirit of enterprise . . . . " (32, *30*)

Page 30:

11.3-4: "but it does not . . . . " (33, *31*)
11.5-10: "It is in . . . . " (33-34, *31*)
11.15-16: "The profound motive . . . . " (35, *32*)
11.24-21: "Today, it is . . . . " (36, *33*)
11.32-33: "powerful personalities . . . . " (34, *37*)
11.38-40: "Our times . . . . " (38, *34*)
1.42: "The smell . . . . " (39, *35*)
11.45-46: "powerful life . . . . " (39, *35*)

Page 31:

11.8-9: "rather ostentatious . . . . " (41-42, *37*)
11.14-16: "efficacy". . . . " (46, *40-41*)
11.19-23: "The man of character . . . . " (46-47, *41*)
11.24-25: " . . . the man of character . . . . " (47, *41*)
11.27-28: "the supreme element . . . . " (47, *42*)
11.30-34: "This property . . . . " (48, *42*)
1.35: "the austere joy . . . . " (48, *42*)
1:42: "but in action . . . . " (48, *42*)
11.44-48: "Reciprocally . . . . " (49, *43*)

11.19-20: "The most just glory . . . . " (152, *124*)
11.24-27: "chance", "inspire" . . . . (153, *125*)
11.19-31: "personified all . . . . " (154, *126*)
11.44
11.44-46: "one could conceive . . . . " (155, *126-127*)

Page 38:

11.1-5: "One does nothing . . . . " (156-157, *127-128*)

Page 39:

(None)

SECOND PART, Chapter 4: Character and Magnanimity: Reflections on *Le fil de l'épée*

Page 41:

11.25-26: "thinks himself worthy . . . . " (Aristotle, *Nichomachean Ethics,* 1123b,
    Richard McKeon translation, *The Basic Works of Aristotle,* Random House,
    New York, 1941, p. 991.)
1.29: "both commoner . . . . " (*ibid.,* 1125a, p. 995)
11.31-32: "that which we . . . . " (*ibid.,* 1123b, p. 991)
11.34-35: "And greatness . . . . " (*ibid.,* 1123b, p. 992)
11.35-37: "it would be . . . . " (*ibid.,* 1123b, p. 992)
11.38-39: "towards wealth . . . . " (*ibid.,* 1124a, p. 992)
11.41-45, *P. 42,* 11.1-2: " . . . at honors . . . . " (*ibid.,* 1124a, p. 992)

Page 42:

11.3-4: "the [magnanimous] . . . . " (*ibid.,* 1124b, p. 993)
11.4-5: "a sort of . . . . " (*ibid.,* 1123b, p. 992)
11.7-9: "run into . . . . " (*ibid.,* 1124b, p. 993)
11.10-12: "for what people . . . . " (*ibid.,* p. 994)
11.14-15: "he is apt . . . . " (*ibid.,* 1124b, p. 993)
11.16-18: "to hear of . . . . " (*ibid.,* 1124b, p. 993)
11.20-23: One of Aristotle's translators . . . . (Martin Ostwald, translator and
    editor of *Nichomachean Ethics,* Bobbs-Merrill Company, Inc.,
    Indianapolis and New York, 1962, p. 97, notes #23 and #24. The quotation
    of Thetis's entreaty is Richmond Lattimore's: *Iliad,* I, 11.503-504,
    University of Chicago Press, Chicago and London, 1951, p. 72)
11.27-29: Another scholar . . . . (Harry V. Jaffa, "The Conditions of Freedom,"
    in *The Conditions of Freedom — Essays in Political Philosophy,* The
    Johns Hopkins University Press, Baltimore and London, 1975, p. 233)
11.32-37: "towards people who . . . . " (Aristotle, *Nichomachean Ethics,* Richard
    McKeon translation, *op. cit.,* 1124b, p. 993)
11.39-40: "Nor is he . . . . " (*ibid.,* 1125a, p. 994)
11.44-45: "who thinks . . . . " (*ibid.,* 1125a, p. 994)
11.47-48: "One shudders . . . . " (Bertrand Russell, *A History of Western
    Philosophy,* Simon and Schuster, New York, 1945, p. 176)

Page 43:

11.2-4: "largely depend . . . . " (*ibid.,* p. 176)
1.15: Paul Eidelberg argues . . . . (Paul Eidelberg, *A Discourse on
    Statesmanship: The Design and Transformation of the American Polity,*
    University of Illinois Press, Urbana, Chicago and London, 1974, see
    especially pp. 241-276)
1.16: "promoting the public . . . . " (ibid., p. 260)

Page 44:

(None)

(All references, unless otherwise noted, are to *Vers l'armée de métier,* Editions Berger-Levrault Paris, 1934, Le Livre de Poche edition, Paris, 1973, and to *The Army of the Future,* no tranlator listed, forward by Walter Millis, J.B. Lippincott Company, Philadelphia and New York, 1941.)

Page 47:

      11.16-17: "examin[ing] what role . . . . " (*Role des Places Françaises,*" *Revue militaire française,* #54, December 1, 1925. Reprinted in *Trois Études,* Editions Berger-Levrault, Paris, 1925, republished by Plon, Paris, 1973, (Le Livre de Poche), p. 75)

      11.20-21: "technique" and "on the means . . . . " (*ibid.,* p. 75)

      11.31-32: "To the French . . . . " (5, *omitted from translation*)

      1.41, *p. 48,* 1.1: "As the viewing . . . . " (11, 15)

Page 48:

      11.2-3: "terrible breach . . . . " (11, *15*)

      11.5-6: "Vanquisher at one point . . . . " (12, *16*)

      11.6-8: "each time . . . . " (13, *18*)

      11.12-13: "mortgaged" and "for which . . . . " (13, *17*)

      11.14-15: "in the people . . . . " (13, *17*)

      11.18-21: "To establish . . . . " (17, *22*)

      11.23-25: "the opposition of . . . . " (19, *24*)

      11.27-28: "sublime and glaucous . . . . " (19, *24*)

      11.29-30: "by a traditional . . . . " (20, *25*)

      11.31-32: "this menace . . . . " (21, *26*)

      11.35-36: "recent and suspicious . . . . " (23, *29-30*)

      11.37-40: "a new international . . . . " (23, *30)*

      11.41-42: "a thousand practical . . . . " (24, *30*)

      11.45-50, *p. 49,* 11.1-2: " . . . time passes . . . . " (24, *30*)

Page 49:

      1.3: "nostalgia for danger" (24, *30*)

      11.6-8: "plenty of passion . . . . " (26, *34-35*)

      11.10-12: "All there is . . . . " (28, *37*)

      1.16: "a military people" (30, *38*)

      11.21-22: "To build . . . . " (32, *41*)

      11.23-26: "that mark . . . . " (33, *42*)

      11.29-30: "No French security . . . . " (33, *43*)

      11.32-34: "the machine . . . . " (37-38, *47-48*)

      11.36-38: "By being riveted . . . . " (40, *50*)

      11.40-42: "the army . . . . " (41, *52*)

      1.46: "nothing prevails . . . . " (41, *52*)

Page 50:

      11.1-2: "Here come . . . . " (42, *53*)

      11.4-7: "the notion . . . . " (43, *54*)

      11.10-11: "accorded so well . . . . " (44, *55*)

      1.12: "quality from deploying . . . . " (44, *56*)

      1.15-16: "As usual . . . . " (46, *58*)

      11.18-20: "and those who wish . . . . " (46, *58*)

      11.24-25: "the ancient . . . . " (48, *60*)

      11.25-26: "behind the *décor* . . . . " (50, *63*)

      1.28: "technical progress." (51, *63*)

      11.31-32: "To be protected . . . . " (53, *65*)

      1.33: "maneuver was restored . . . . . " (55, *68*)

185

Page 56:

        11.1-2: "the conditions in . . . . . " (157, *178*)
        11.7-15: "If this national . . . . " (158,*179*)

THIRD PART, Chapter 6: The Force of War: Reflections on *Vers l'armée de métier*

        1.15: "presupposes discipline" (Max Weber: *From Max Weber: Essays in Sociology,* translated and edited by H.H. Gerth and C. Wright Mills, Oxford University Press, New York, 1946, p. 252, and cited in Neal Wood: "Introduction", *The Art of War* by Nicolo Machiavelli, translated by Ellis Farneworth and revised by Neal Wood, Bobbs-Merrill Company, Inc., Indianapolis, New York and Kansas City, 1963, p. xxxiv.)

Page 57:

        11.22-23: "the most retired . . . . " (Machiavelli: *ibid.,* p. 9)
        11.26-31: " . . . had endeavored . . . . " (*ibid.,* p. 10)
        11.32-33: "desirous of . . . . " (*ibid.,* p. 9)
        1.36, *p. 58,* 11.1-2: " . . . it often happens . . . . " (*ibid.,* p. 11)

Page 58:

        1.7: "good order . . . . " (*ibid.,* p. 12)
        11.7-8: "He that takes . . . . " ((*ibid.,* p. 13)
        11.17-22: "Those . . . who have . . . . " (*ibid.,* p. 25)
        11.26-27: "For it is not . . . . " (*ibid.,* p. 64)
        11.29-31: "And although . . . . " (*ibid.,* p. 79)

Page 59:

        11.21-23: "Just as no . . . . " (*ibid.,* p. 210)
        11.33-34: "Defense appears . . . . " (Carl von Clausewitz, *On War*
                          Michael Howard and Peter Paret translation
                          Princeton University Press, 1976, p. 361)
        1.35: "time which is . . . . " (*ibid.,* p. 357)
        11.38-39: "strictly speaking . . . . (*ibid.,* p. 149)
        11.38-39: "strictly speaking . . . . (*ibid.,* p. 149)
        1.46, *p. 60,* 1.1: "would construct . . . . " (*ibid.,* 374)

Page 60:

        11.5-6 "an impartial student . . . . " (*ibid.,* 282)
        11.23-26: "makes possible . . . . " (Henry Kissinger, *Nuclear Weapons and Foreign Policy,* Harper and Brothers, New York, 1957, p. 9)
        11.28-32 "It is . . . . " (*ibid.,* pp. 132-133)
        11.35-38, *p. 61,* 11.1-6: " . . . the outlines . . . . " (Henry Kissinger: *The Necessity for Choice: Prospects of American Foreign Policy,* Doubleday and Company, Garden City, 1960/1962, p. 6)

Page 61:

        1.10: "still reverse these trends" (*ibid.,* p. 6)

Page 62:

    (None)

FOURTH PART, Chapter 7: *La France et son armée* (1938)

(All references, unless otherwise noted, are to *La France et son armée,* Librairie Plon, 1938, Le Livre de Poche edition, Paris, 1973.)

Page 65:

        11.11-15: "France has been . . . . " (5)

11.8-8: "the deplorable . . . . " (184)
11.9-12: "personifie[d] before History . . . . " (184)
11.13-15: "mingled with war-instinct . . . . " (190-191)
1.19: "Ideology, insouciance . . . . " (196)
11.26-27: "the defense . . . . " (198)
11.29-30: "in the military . . . . " (199)
11.31-32: "democracy had not . . . . " (200)
11.39-41: "The lessons of . . . . " (205)
1.42: "Nothing comes . . . ." (207)

Page 74:

1.1-2: "for better or . . . . " (209)
1.2: "an excellent school . . . . " (210)
11.5-6: "Above all . . . . " (211)
1.7: "which desired peace . . . . " (211)
11.11-14: "political struggles . . . . " (215-216)
11.16-18: "A sort of doubt . . . . " (216)
1.20: "disdained" (216)
11.22-23: "the superiority . . . ." (220)
11.24-25: "the army itself . . . . " (221)
11.25-26: "will to vanquish" (222)
1.28: "under the pretext . . . . " (223)
1.32: "moderation does not . . . . " (228)
11.34-35: "the inclination of . . . . " (230)
11.37-39: "brought to conscious . . . . " (233)
11.40-41: "solicitude replaced . . . . " (234)
1.44: "The Great War . . . . " (241)
11.45-47, *p. 75,* 11.1-2:" . . . the regime . . . . " (241-242)

Page 75:

11.3-4: "Like other . . . ." (242)
11.6-11: the ubiquity . . . . " (242)
11.6-11: "the ubiquity . . . . " (242)
11.12-13: "first shock . . . . " (244)
11.17-19: " . . . reports, histories . . . . " (249)
1.20: "precipitous retreat" (250)
11.21-22: Such is the . . . . " (250)
11.22-24: "the doctrines of . . . . " (251)
11.29-30: "For the first time . . . . " (254)
11.30-32: "poison of defeat . . . . " (254-255)
11.39-48: "Implacable, gloomy . . . . " (267-268)

Page 76:

1.4: "turned into indiscipline" (274)
11.5-7: "Passing through the . . . . " (276)
11.9-10: "Assuredly, the political . . . . " (279)
11.14-15: "the reason of France . . . . " (280)
11.15-16: "the reason of France . . . . " (280)
11.16-18 "alternating methodical attack . . . . " (281)
11.21-24: "tyrant, victim or . . . . "(284)

FOURTH PART, Chapter 8: War and Politics: Reflections on *La France et son armée*

Page 76

1.13: "a part of . . . . " (Carl von Clausewitz, *On War,* edited and translated by Michael Howard and Peter Paret, Princeton University Press, Princeton,

1976, p. 149)

11.13-14: "is nothing but . . . . " (*ibid.*, p. 69)

11.15-16: "once the expenditure . . . . " (*ibid.*, p. 92)

11.18-20: "the transformation of . . . . " (*ibid.*, p. 610)

11.22-23: . . . is the womb . . . . " (*ibid.*, p. 149)

11.27-29: "Is war not . . . . " (*ibid.*, p. 605)

Page 78:

11.10-11: "[A]n endless and . . . . " (Montesquieu: *Considerations on the Causes of the Greatness of the Romans and their Decline,* David Lowenthal translation, Cornell University Press, Ithaca, 1965/1968, p. 27)

1.12: "constancy and valor . . . . " (*ibid.*, p. 28)

11.12-13: "the virtue which . . . . " (*ibid.*, p. 36)

11.18-19: "no country in . . . . " (*ibid.*, p. 40)

11.20-21: "produce" . . . "causes" . . . "great changes" (*ibid.*, p. 26)

1.45, *p. 79,* 1.1: "always made war . . . . " (*ibid.*, p. 45)

Page 79:

11.13-15: "Rome was saved . . . . " (*ibid.*, p. 50)

11.20-21: "Nature has given . . . . " (*ibid.*, p. 61)

Page 80:

11.2-6: "Here, in a word . . . . " (*ibid.*, p. 169)

1.19: "the weakness . . . . " (Thucydides: *The Peloponnesian War,* R. Crawley translation, The Modern Library, New York, 1934, p. 4)

1.21: "consequently neither built . . . . " (*ibid.*, p. 4)

11.22-23: "the great aim . . . . " (*ibid.*, p. 12)

1.24: "inevitable" (*ibid.*, p. 15)

11.28-30: "[Y]ou alone wait . . . . " (*ibid.*, p. 39)

11.32-34: [C]onstant necessities . . . . " (*ibid.*, p. 41)

Page 81:

11.15-16: "in the panic . . . . " (*ibid.*, p. 455)

11.20-22: "In education . . . . " (*ibiid.*, p. 104)

11.22-24: "the palm of . . . . " (*ibid.*, p. 105)

1.27: "painful discipline" (*ibid.*, p. 104)

11.31-33: "this offering of . . . . " (*ibid.*, p. 107)

1.36: "a constitutional love . . . . " (*ibid.*, p. 358)

1.40: "to frighten . . . . " (*ibid.*, p. 361)

11.47-48: "A man can . . . . " (p. 382)

Page 82:

11.8-9: "the spirit of . . . . " (Montesquieu: *The Spirit of the Laws,* Thomas Nugent translation, Volume I, Book IX, chapter 2, Hafner Press, New York, 1949, pp. 127-128)

11.11-12: "If . . . a state of . . . ." (Alexis de Tocqueville: *Democracy in America,* The Second Part, Third Book, chapter 21, Henry Reeve, Francis Bowen and Phillips Bradley translation, Vintage Books, New York, 1945. p. 266)

11.13-18: "The ever increasing . . . . " (*ibid.*, chapter 22, p. 279)

1.22: "endanger the freedom . . . . " (*ibid.*, chapter 22, p. 284)

11.26-27: "Teach the citizens . . . . " (*ibid.*, chapter 22, p. 285)

11.29-34: "Among the ancients . . . . " (*ibid.*, chapter 25, p. 296)

11.39-43: "If the love . . . . " (*ibid.*, chapter 24, Appendix X, pp. 385-386)

11.44-45: "Nothing is more . . . . " (*ibid.*, p. 386)

Page 83:

      11.2-3: "the manliness . . . . " (*ibid.,* p. 386)
      11.5-9: "It should never . . . . " (*ibid.,* chapter 26, p. 301)
      11.14-18: "among [such] nations . . . . " (*ibid.,* chapter 24, p. 291)

FIFTH PART, Chapter 9: *Mémoires de guerre* (1954, 1956, 1959)

(All references, unless otherwise noted, are to Charles de Gaulle: *Mémoires de guerre,* in three volumes. Volume I is titled *L'Appel* (Librairie Plon, Paris, 1954, Le Livre de Poche edition printed by Brodard et Taupin, Paris, 1971). Volume II is titled *L'Unité* (Librairie Plon, Paris, 1956, Le Livre de Poche edition printed by Brodard et Taupin, Paris, 1966). Volume III is titled *Le Salut* (Librairie Plon, Paris, 1959, Le Livre de Poche edition printed by Brodard et Taupin, Paris, 1967).

The second, italicized references are to the American translation: *War Memoirs,* in three volumes. Volume I is titled *The Call to Honour,* (Jonathan Griffin translation, The Viking Press, New York, 1955). Volume II is titled *Unity* (Richard Howard translation, Simon and Schuster, New York, 1959). Volume III is titled *Salvation* (Richard Howard translation, Simon and Schuster, New York, 1960).

Page 87:

      11.4-16: "All my life . . . . " (I, 5, *3*)
      11.30-32: "attraction, but also . . . . " (I, 6, *4*)
      11.34-35: "Hollow ideologies" . . . . (I, 6, *4*)
      11.37-38: "rejected grandeur . . . . " (I, 7, *5*)

Page 88:

      1.4: "consumed and paralyzed" (I, 8-9, *6*)
      11.6-7: "the fixed and . . . . " (I, 9, *7*)
      11.8-10: "Such a conception . . . . " (I, 10, *8*)
      11.14-16: "the state of mind . . . . " (I, 10, *8*)
      1.28: "the sad homage . . . . " (I, 25, *22*)
      11.29-32: "our organization . . . . " (I, 26, *22*)
      11.32-33: "in these successive . . . . " (I, 30, *27*)
      11.34-35: "the ultimate warning . . . . " (I, 31, *27*)
      1.38: "*attentisme*" (I, 32, *28*)
      11.40-42: "Conforming to habits . . . . " (I, 35, *31*)
      11.44-46: " . . . to what point . . . . " (I, 35, *31*)

Page 89:

      1.4: "had espoused the system" (I, 38, *33*)
      11.6-8: One can say . . . . " (I, 40, *35-36*)
      11.12-15: "The crumbling of . . . . " (I, 47, *43*)
      11.23-25: "To take action . . . . " (I, 55, *51*)
      11.28-32: "The regime, without . . . . " (I, 55, *52*)
      11.39-42: "a cordial reserve . . . . " (I, 71, *65*)

Page 90:

      11.1-2: "It appeared to . . . . " (I, 76, *70*)
      1.4: "untainted man" (I, 77, *71*)
      11.11-14: "In the judgment . . . . " (79, *73*)
      1.15: "Old age is . . . . " (I, 79, *73*)
      11.21-25: "But that implied . . . . " (I, 86, *79*)
      11.30-41: "It is necessary . . . . " (I, 86-87, *79-80*)
      11.45-46: "The departure took . . . . " (I, 87, *80*)
      1.47: "Pursue the war? . . .) (I, 88, *81*)

Page 91:

11.1-2: "For me . . . . " (I, 88, *81)*
11.3-5: "the disgust . . . . " (88, *81)*
11.10-14: "But this very . . . . " (I, 89-90, *82-83)*
11.19-21: "all limited . . . . " (I, 90, *83)*
11.24-26: "France is not alone . . . . (I, 331-332, *83-84)*
11.27-28: "Crushed today . . . . " (I, 331-332, *83-84)*
11.32-35: "In proportion that . . . . " (I, 90, *84)*
1.37: A historian . . . . (Milton Viorst, *Hostile Allies — FDR and de Gaulle,* The Macmillan Company New York, 1965, 27.)
11.38-41: "Before the confusion . . . . " (De Gaulle: *Discours et Messages,* Volume I, *Pendant la guerre,* Librairie Plon, Paris, 1970, Le Livre de Poche edition printed by Brodard et Taupin, Paris, 1974,) p. 5)
11.43-44: "not one public . . . . " (I, 93, *87)*
11.45-47: "Before the frightening . . . . " (I, 94, *88)*

Page 92:

1.5: "But there is not . . . . " (I, 94, *88)*
1.11: "elite" (I, 101, *94)* I,
1.20: "remake an army . . . . " (114, *106)*
1.22: "links of community" (114, *106)*
11.32-34: "vast collision" . . . . (122-123, *114)*
11.38-40: "the reactions to . . . . " (138, *128)*
11.47-48, *P. 93,* 11.1-4: "The fact of . . . . " (I, 141, *130-131)*

Page 93:

11.11-12: "this great war . . . . " (*Discours et Messages, op. cit.,* August 3, 1940, p. 24)
1.14: "Events impose on me . . . . " (*ibid.,* October 27, 1940, p. 40)
11.19-21: "So harsh were . . . . " (I, 152, *141)*
11.28-33: " . . . I spoke myself . . . . " (I, 167, 154-*155)*
1.39: "propaganda had . . . . " (I, 168, *155)*

Page 94:

11.13-16: "The majority . . . . " (I, 213, *196)*
1.27: "decisive shock" (I, 227, *209)*
11.33-34: "At bottom, what . . . . " (228, *210)*
11.38-39: "I have confidence . . . . " (234, *217)*
11.41-47: "I obviously did not . . . . " (I, 242-243, *224-225)*

Page 95:

11.5-8: "In M. Molotov . . . . " (I, 247-248, *229)*
11.16-17: "incline himself before . . . . " (I, 251, *233)*
11.21-35: " . . . quite aware of . . . . " (quoted in Claude Mauriac: *The Other de Gaulle de Gaulle — Diaries 1944-1954,* Moura Budberg, and Gordon Latta translation, The John Day Company, New York, 1973, pp. 194-195)
11.39-42: "To speak truly . . . . " (I, 264, *244)*
11.48-49: "Greek philosophy . . . . " (*Discours et Messages, op. cit.,* p. 128)

Page 96:

11.1-4: "National liberation . . . . " (*ibid.,* p. 192)
11.17-18: "to establish their . . . . " (I, 289, *268)*
11.19-20: "In the incessant . . . . " (I, 290, *269)*
1.23: "Before philosophizing . . . . " (I, 290, *269)*
11.27-29: "To my mind . . . . " (I, 292, *270)*
11.32-35: "The Resistance . . . . " (I, 296, *275)*
11.36-40: "direct a great . . . . " (I, 297, *275)*

Page 97:

    11.7-9: "In his justice . . . . " (I, 318, *294*)
    11.10-13: "In enterprises in . . . . " (I, 318, *294*)
    11.37-38: "You should know . . . . " (II, 22, *17*)
    11.40-44, *p. 98,* 11.1-10: "a *politique* is . . . . " (37, *31*)

Page 98:

    11.13-15: "A *politique* is . . . . " (37, *31*)
    11.18-20: " . . . it was by bluff . . . . " (Claude Mauriac: *The Other de Gaulle, op. cit.,* p. 214)
    11.27-29: "You are not France!" . . . (II, 44, *38-39*)

Page 99:

    1.6: "temporary expedient" (II, 84, *74-75*)
    11.7-9: "[I]n great moments . . . . " (II, 84, *75*)
    11.22-25: "the most high ambitions" . . . . (II, 97-98, *88*)
    11.31-33: "This prelate . . . . " (II, 116, *105-106*)
    11.36-37: "it was indeed . . . . " (II, 119, *108*)
    11.37-38: "all would pass . . . . " (II, 120, *109*)

Page 100:

    11.7-8: "during this time . . . . " (II, 148, *136*)
    11.9-11: "It is necessary . . . . " (II, 149, *136*)
    11.14-18: "A sort of tide . . . . " (II, 150, *137-138*)
    11.23-36: "*Envers et contre tout* . . . . " (II, 154, *141*)
    1.39: "de Gaulle had won . . . . " (II, 155, *141*)
    11.44-46: "a manner one . . . . " (II, 178, *163*)

Page 101:

    11.10-11: "sounding their souls . . . . " (II, 188, *172*)
    1.13: "demagogy" (II, 192, *175-176*)
    11.20-21: "to let justice . . . . " (II, 190, *174*)
    11.30-31: "As long as . . . . " (II, 210, *193*)
    11.35-41: "The confrontation . . . . " (II, 212, *195*)

Page 102:

    11.7-10: "Many had the . . . . " (II, 223, *205*)
    11.19-21: "Diplomacy, under the . . . . " (II, 229, *211*)
    1.23: "political" (II, 232, *214*)
    11.25-26: "Christian, Latin, European" (II, 237, *219*)
    11.28-29: "before the exactions . . . . " (II, 254, *234*)
    11.33-34: "the intentions of . . . ." (II, 261, *240*)
    11.41-42: "The proof was given . . . . " (II, 283, *261*)

Page 103:

    11.4-8: "The proposals of . . . . " (II, 294, *271*)
    11.9-11: "I never knew . . . . " (II, 295, *272*)
    11.12-13: "As is human . . . . " (II, 292, *269*)
    11.19-30: "That our army . . . . " (II, 299-300, *276-277*)
    11.33-35: "Politics, diplomacy . . . . " (II, 350, *323*)
    11.45-46: "spoke, then, some . . . . " (II, 361, *334*)

Page 104:

    11.12-14: "I had myself . . . . "(II, 370, *341-342*)
    11.16-19: "one of those . . . . " (II, 378-379, *350*)
    11.23-24: in private conversation . . . . (See Claude Mauriac: *The Other de Gaulle op. cit.,* pp. 223-224]
    11.35-40: "One could believe . . . . " (II, 391, *361-362*)

Page 113:

      ll.4-5: "how many hours . . . . " (III, 336, *329*)

      ll.7-8: "As all recommences . . . . " (III, 336, *329*)

      ll.9-10: "the marvellous return . . . . " (III, 337, *330*)

      ll.12-14: "but revived century . . . . " (III, 337, *330*)

      l.17: "new ardors" . . . . (III, 337, *330*)

      ll.19-20: "ultimately, the great . . . . " (Stanley Hoffmann, *Decline or Renewal? France Since the 1930's,* The Viking Press, New York, 1974, pp 200-201)

      ll.29-32: "was an attitude . . . . " (*ibid.,* p. 191)

      ll.33-35: "triple determination" . . . . (*ibid.,* pp. 191-193)

Page 114:

(None)

FIFTH PART, Chapter 10: Political Foundings: Reflections of *Mémoires de guerre*

Page 115:

      ll.1-2: "the political problem . . . . " (Leo Strauss: *Natural right and History,* University of Chicago Press, Chicago and London, 1953/1968, p. 141. What follows owes much to Strauss's seminal book, although the teachings of the book are applied specifically to the subject at hand: founding. Strauss concerns himself with politics and political philosophy in general. The division of foundings into six types is based on Strauss's classification of political thought.)

      ll.14-15: "The religious idea . . . . " (Numa[!] Denis Fustel de Coulanges: *The Ancient City — A study of the Religion, Laws, and Institutions of Greece and Rome,* Translated anonymously, Doubleday and Company, Garden City, 1955, p. 132)

      l.16: "was always . . . . " (*ibid.,* p. 134)

      ll.18-20: "The *urbs* of . . . . " (*ibid.,* 145)

      ll.21-24: "It was not force . . . . "(*ibid.,* p. 178)

      l.25: "The ancient law . . . . " (*ibid.,* p. 190)

      ll.32-34: "The ruler . . . . "(Aristotle: *Politics,* Ernest Barkes trans., Oxford University Press, London, Oxford, New York, 1969, p. 36. Italics mine.)

Page 116:

      l.1: "religion judiciously used" (Machiavelli: *Discourses on the First Ten Books of Titus Livy,* Christian (!) E. Detmold trans., Modern Library, New York, 1950, p. 154).

      ll.2-4: "In truth . . . . " (ibid., p. 147)

      ll.16-17: "atheism did never . . . . " (Bacon: "Of Superstition," *Essays,* in *Francis Bacon —A Selection of His Works,* Sidney Warhaft, editor, The Odyssey Press, New York, 1965, p. 89)

      ll.29-33: "The great Question . . . . " (John Locke: *First Treatise,* in *Two Treatises of Government,* Peter Laslett, editor, New American Library, New York and Toronto, 1965, p. 257)

      ll.43-44: "It would take . . . . " (Rousseau: *The Social Contract,* in *The Social Contract and Discourses,* G.D.H. Cole trans., E.P. Dutton and Company, New York, 1950, p. 38)

      ll.45-46: "ought to feel . . . . "(*ibid.,* p. 38)

      ll.50-52: "Most peoples . . . . "(*ibid.,* p. 42)

Page 117:

      ll.11-12: "to relinquish . . . . " (Hegel: *Preface to the Phenomenology of Spirit,* Walter Kaufmann trans., Doubleday, Garden City, 1966, p. 12)

11.14-16: "What is rational . . . . " (Hegel: *The Philosophy of Right,* T.M. Knox trans., Oxford University Press, London, Oxford, New York, 1952, 1973, p.11)

11.18-21: "not do this as . . . . " (*ibid.,* p. 245)

11.28-31: "A fundamental difference . . . . " (Hannah Arendt: *The Origins of Totalitarianism,* Meridian Books, New York and Cleveland, 1951, 1958, 1971, p. 6)

11.31-33: "Totalitarian policy . . . . " *ibid.,* p. 462)

Page 118:

1.2: "to make himself popular" (Plutarch: *The Lives of the Noble Greeks and Romans,* "John Dryden" trans., Modern Library, New York, p. 9)

Page 118:

11.5-7: "[T]he nobles . . . . " (*ibid.,* p. 16)

11.9-11: "the minds of the people . . . . " (*ibid.,* p. 23)

11.18-20: "pretention to divine . . . . " (ibid., p. 78)

11.28-29: "a nature made . . . . " (*ibid.,* p. 52)

1.31: "their several forms . . . . " (*ibid.,* p. 51)

11.35-40: "obedience and concord . . . . " (*ibid.,* pp. 51-52)

11.45-46: "a central weight . . . . " (*ibid.,* p. 53)

Page 119:

1.3: "only road to eminence" (*ibid.,* p. 55)

11.3-4: "all needless . . . . " (*ibid.,* p. 56)

11.5-6: "schools of moderation" . . . . (*ibid.,* p. 59)

11.9-10: "manner and form" . . . . (*ibid.,* p. 59)

1.15: "religious terrors" (*ibid.,* p. 80)

1.16: awe and reverence . . . . " (*ibid.,* p. 86)

11.17-18: "the task of bringing . . . . " (*ibid.,* p. 80)

1.18: "The harder task . . . . " (*ibid.,* p. 93)

1.21: "so fit his laws . . . . " (*ibid.,* p. 100)

11.23-24: "[W]hen he was afterwards . . . . " (*ibid.,* p. 105)

1.33: A historian has identified: (Gordon Wood: *The Creation of the American Republic,* University of North Carolina Press, Chapel Hill, 1969)

11.37-38: At least one political scientist . . . . (Robert H. Horwitz: "John Locke and the Preservation of Liberty: A perennial Problem of Civic Education," in *The Moral Foundations of the American Republic,* Robert H. Horwitz, editor, University Press of Virginia, Charlottesville, 1977)

Page 120:

11.9-10: "the rights of the whole . . . . "(Thomas Jefferson: letter to James Madison, September 6, 1789, in *The Life and Selected Writings of Thomas Jefferson,* Adrienne Koch and William Peden, editors, Modern Library, New York, 1944, p. 489)

11.18-19: "good acts . . . . " (Jefferson: letter to Thomas Law, Esq., June 13, 1814, in *ibid.,* p. 638)

11.20-21: "the true fountains . . . . " (Jefferson: "Opinion on the question whether the United States have the right to renounce their treaties with France . . . . " (*ibid.,* p. 318)

Page 121:

11.9-11: "like all natural rights . . . . " (Jefferson: "Opinion upon the question whether the President should veto the Bill, declaring that the seat of the government should be transferred to the Potomac in the year 1790," in *ibid.,* p. 316)

Page 122:

        11.17-20: "may safely and advantageously . . . . " (Jefferson: letter to John Adams, October 28, 1813, in *ibid., p. 633)*

        11.40-41: "the transforming democratic . . . . " (Gordon Wood: "The Democratization of Mind in the American Revolution," in *The Moral Foundations of the American Republic, op. cit.,* p. 128)

Page 123:

        11.3-4: defines a people . . . . (John Jay:*The Federalist Papers, #* 2, New American Library, New York, Toronto, 1961, p. 38)

        11.8-15: "all the existing . . . . " (James Madison: *The Federalist Papers, #49, ibid.,* p. 315)

        11.31-34: "the science of politics . . . . " (Alexander Hamilton: *The Federalist Papers, #9,* p. 72)

        1.37: as Madison observes . . . . (Madison: *The Federalist Papers, #63, ibid.,* pp. 386-387)

        11.42-43: "Experience is . . . . " (Hamilton or Madison: *The Federalist Papers, #20, ibid.,* p. 138)

        1.45: "sacred reverence" (Hamilton: *The Federalist Papers, #25, ibid.,* p. 167)

Page 124:

        11.3-5: "whether societies of men . . . . " (Hamilton: *The Federalist Papers, #1, ibid.,* p. 33)

        11.10-12: "Constitutions of civil government . . . . " (Hamilton: *The Federalist Papers, #34, ibid.,* p. 207)

        1.25: "first principles" (Hamilton: *The Federalist Papers, #31,* p. 193)

        11.34-36: "commodious self-preservation" . . . . Martin Diamond: "Ethics and Politics: the American Way," in *The Moral Foundations of the American Republic, op. cit.,* p. 56)

        11.43-44: "the contemplative intellect: (Paul Eidelberg: *A Discourse on Statesmanship,* University of Illinois Press, Urbana, 1974, p. 138)

Page 125:

        11.12-14: "the evils we experience . . . . " (*Debates on the Adoption of the Federal Constitution in the Convention Held at Philadelphia in 1789; with a Diary of the Debates of the Congress of the Confederation; as Reported by James Madison,* Jonathan Elliot, editor, J.B. Lippincott and Company, Philadelphia, 1845, (hereafter cited as *Elliot's Debates),* p. 136)

        11.14-17: "admitted that we . . . . " (*Elliot's Debates,* p. 136)

        11.18-19: "evils under which . . . . " (*Elliot's Debates,* p. 138)

        11.22-24: "the only defence . . . . " (*Elliot's Debates,* p. 162)

        1.24: "the popular branch" (*Elliot's Debates,* p. 167)

        11.25-26: "a system of government . . . . " (*Elliot's Debates,* p. 109)

        11.28-29: "can admit no cure . . . . " (Madison, *The Federalist Papers, #10, op. cit.,* p. 81)

        11.29-30: "refine and enlarge . . . . " (Madison, *ibid.,* p. 182)

        11.34-35: "who possess . . . . " (Madison, *ibid.,* p. 83)

        1.36: "enlightened statesmen . . . . " (Madison, *ibid.,* p. 80)

Page 126:

        11.2-4: "derives all its powers . . . . " (Madison, *The Federalist Papers, #39,* p. 241)

        11.11-15: "In every community . . . . " (*Elliot's Debates,* pp. 202-203)

        1.35: "reflects" (Lenin: "The 3 Sources and 3 Component Parts of Marxism," (1913), *Selected Works in one volume* [hereafter referred to as *SW* (1)], Progress Publishers, Moscow, 1968, p. 21)

11.37-38: "a direct connection . . . . " (Lenin: *Materialism and Empirio-Criticism, Collected Works,* International Publishers, New York, 1929 [hereafter referred to as *CW* (a)], Volume XIII, p. 31)

11.39-40: The division of . . . . (See Lenin: "On Dialectics," *Notebook, CW* (a), Volume XIII, p. 320)

Page 127:

1.2: "Fideism" . . . . (Lenin: *Materialism and Empirio-Criticism, cw* (a), p. 264)

1.4: (Lenin's metaphor) . . . . (See Lenin: "The Honest Voice of a French Socialist," *CW* (a), Volume XIII, p. 328)

11.9-10: "learn each week . . . . " Book I, p. 80) (Lenin: "Lessons of the Revolution" *CW* (a), XXI)

11.13-14: "our morality . . . . " (Lenin: "Tasks of the Youth Leagues," (1920)

1.19: "capable of . . . . " (Lenin: "One of the Fundamental Questions of the Revolution,"*CW* (a), XXI, I, p. 170)

1.21: Lenin chides . . . . (See Lenin: "The Russian Revolution and Civil War," (Sept. 1917), *CW* (a), XXI, I, p. 230)

1.32: "becomes stronger . . . . " (Lenin: "A Talk with Defenders of Economism," (1901), *SW* (1), p. 49)

11.36-37, *p. 128,* 1.1: "politically conscious" . . . . (Lenin: *ibid.,* p. 46)

Page 128:

11.7-9: To Lenin the vanguard . . . . (See Lenin: "What Is To Be Done?" (1902), (1902), *CW* (a), IV, I, p. 112)

11.28-30: Lenin wrote that . . . . (See Lenin: "Farewell Letter to the Swiss Workers, (April 1917), *CW* (a), XX, I, pp. 85-86)

11.30-31: Lenin regarded . . . . (See Lenin: "The Tasks of the Revolution," (October 1917), *CW* (a), XXI, I, p. 256)

1.32: "aversion to . . . . " (Lenin: *Economics and Politics in the Era of the Dictatorship of the Proletariat,* (1919), *SW* (3), volume 3, p. 274.

11.33-34: Lenin said . . . . (Lenin: "Marxism and Revisionism," (1908), *SW* (1) p. 30)

11.37-39: "institutions of . . . . " (Lenin: *Two Tactics of Social Democracy in the Democratic Revolution,* (1905), *SW* (1), p. 82)

11.39-41: Lenin says . . . . (Lenin: *ibid.,* p. 61)

11.41-43: Lenin sketches . . . Report on the Review of the Programme and on Changing the Name of the Party, (March 8, 1918), *SW* (3), volume 2, p. 607)

11.44-46: "War is a continuation . . . . " (Lenin: Report on the Political Situation, (April-May 1917), *CW* (a), XX, I, p. 207)

11.47-48: the task of . . . . (See Lenin: speech, (October 11, 1914), *CW* (a), XVIII, p. 66)

11.51-52: Lenin writes . . . . (See Lenin: "Marxism and Insurrection," (1917), *SW* (1), p. 361)

Page 129:

11.9-10: In *State and Revolution* . . . . (See Lenin: *The State and Revolution,* (1917), *SW* (1), p. 267)

1.10: State power . . . . (See Lenin: "One of the Fundamental Questions of the Revolution," (Sept. 1917), *CW* (a), XXI, I, p. 165)

11.13-14: "a state of . . . . " (Lenin: "Fear of the Collapse of the Old and the Fight for the New," (December 1917), *Collected Works,* Progress Publishers, Moscow, 1966 (hereafter referred to as *CW* (b), vol. 26, p.401)

11.14-15: "stubborn, desperate . . . . " (Lenin: *ibid.,* pp. 403-404)

1.19: "wither away" (Lenin: *The State and Revolution, SW* (1), p. 283)

ll.23-25: The Russian proletariat . . . . (See Lenin: "On Proletarian Militia,"
(March 1917), *CW* (a), XX, I, p. 50)

ll.25-26: Having done . . . . (Lenin: "The Immediate Tasks of the Soviet
Government," (1918), *SW* (1), pp. 428 & 429)

ll.26-28: At the same . . . . (See Lenin: "'Left-Wing' Communism — An
Infantile Disorder," (1920), *SW* (1), p. 518)

ll.30-34: democracy without parliamentarism . . . . (See Lenin: *The State and
Revolution, SW* (1), pp. 297 & 298)

ll.40-41: "firm" and "ruthless" . . . . (Lenin: "Six Theses on the Immediate
Tasks of the Soviet Government," (May 3, 1918), *SW* (3), volume 2,
p. 683)

1.42: "the discipline of . . . . " (Lenin: Speech at the First Congress of Economic
Councils, (May 26, 1918), *SW* (3)

Page 130:

ll.1-3: *"compelling people* . . . . " (Lenin: "Can the Bolsheviks Retain State
Power?" (1917), *SW* (1), p. 378)

ll.5-6: "We must organise . . . . " (Speech at the First Congress of Economic
Councils, (May 26, 1918), *SW* (3), volume 2, p. 727)

ll.7-10: "fundamental aim" . . . . (Lenin: Declaration of Rights of the working
and Exploited People, *CW* (b), volume 2, p. 423)

ll.12-17: Lenin answered . . . . (See Lenin: Report on Work from the
Countryside, (March 23, 1919), *SW* (3), volume 3, p. 182)

ll.21-23: technologically superior . . . . (See Lenin: "The N.E.P. and the Tasks
of the Political Education Departments," (October 17, 1921), *CW* (b),
volume 33, p. 68)

1.24: "Communism is Soviet power . . . . " (Lenin: Report on the Work of the
Council of People's Commissars, (December 22, 1920), SW (3), volume 3,
p. 512)

1.25: "Purging the Party": (*CW* (b), volume 33, p. 39)

1.28: "Fatal" . . . . (Lenin: "Pages from a Diary," (January 4, 1923,), *CW*
(b), volume 33, p. 465)

ll.29-30: "true, not paper . . . . "(Lenin: Report on the Party Programme,

ll.20-23: (March 19, 1919), *SW* (3), volume 3, p. 162)

Page 131:

ll.18-21: "they should not be . . . . " (Caesar: *Commentaries on the War in
Gaul,* W.A. McDevitte trans., Harper and Brothers, New York, 1887,
Book VII, ch. 29, p. 182)

Page 132:

(None)

SIXTH PART, Chapter 11: *Memoires d'espoir* (1970)

(All references, unless otherwise noted, are to Charles de Gaulle: *Mémoires d'espoir,* Volume
1, *Le Renouveau,* Librairie Plon, Paris, 1970, Le Livre de Poche edition printed by Brodard
et Taupin, Paris, 1972; Volume 2, *L'Effort,* Librairie Plon, Paris, 1971, Le Livre de Poche
edition printed by Broadard et Taupin, Paris, 1972; and to *Memoirs of Hope: Renewal and
Endeavor,* Terence Kilmartin translation, Simon and Schuster, New York, 1971. The first
page-reference is to the French edition, the second to the American edition.)

Page 135:

ll.4-5: "crusader with great ambitions" . . . . (Stanley Hoffmann: *Decline or
Renewal? France Since the 1930's,* Viking Press, New York, 1974, p. 260)

11.18-23: "France comes from . . . . " (7, *3*)
11.26-31: "But, by the geography . . . . " (7, *3*)
11.36-37: "All my life . . . . " (cited in chapter on *Mémoires de guerre*)
11.41-42, *p. 136,* 11.1-2: "Vital necessity . . . . " (8, *3)*

Page 136:

1.3: "received and lost . . . . " (8, *4*)
1.10: "several months after . . . . " (9, *5*)
11.11-12: "[A]s long as . . . . " (10, *5*)
11.13-15: " . . . all the pretensions . . . . " (10, *5*)
1.16: "I must say . . . . " (10, *6*)
11.17-18: "could be parcelled out . . . . " (10, *6*)
1.19: "fractions" . . . . (de Gaulle: *Discours et Messages,* Volume III, Librairie
    Plon, Paris, 1970, Le Livre de Poche edition printed by Brodard et Taupin,
    Paris, 1974, p. 19) (Hereafter abbreviated as *D & M)*
11.20-22: "the instrument of . . . . " (11, *6*)
11.24-26: "held it as necessary . . . . " (11, *6*)
11.32-34: "could not deceive . . . . " (11, *6*)
1.39: "the derisory figures . . . . " (14, *9*)
11.43-44: "satisfy others" (15, *10*)
1.44: "effacement" . . . . (16, *20*)

Page 137:

11.2-4: "it was necessary . . . . " (26, *18-19)*
11.5-6: "a Roman simplification . . . . " (Malraux: *Le Miroir des limbes,* volume
    II, *La corde et les souris,* Librairie Gallimard, Paris, 1976, "Le Livre de
    Poche" edition printed by Brodard et Taupin, Paris, 1976, p. 163, and
    Felled Oaks, Irene Clephane and Linda Asher translation, Holt, Rinehart
    and Winston, New York, 1971, p. 25)
11.10-11: "a profound transformation . . . . " (37, *28*)
11.13-15: "the somewhat mythical . . . . " (39, *30*)
11.15-16: "Eminent dignity . . . . " (40, *30*)
11.27-43: " . . . I saw open . . . . " (46, *35-36*)

Page 138:

1.2: "the State, progress . . . . " (47, *36*)
1.6: "'philosophic'" (*L'Effort,* 154, *378*)
11.13-16: "conjunction" . . . . (*D&M*), III, 86)
11.17-21: "Man, at grips . . . . " (*D&M*, III, 87)
11.24-25: "that new world . . . . " (D&M, III, 87)
11.27-30: "But, at the same time . . . . " (*D&M,* III, 87)
11.36-39: "This [conflict] is why . . . . " (*D&M*, III, 87)
11.40-41: "the development of . . . . " (*D&M,* III, 87)
11.43-44: "has the duty . . . . " (*D&M,* III, 88)
11.44-45: "entusiasm for . . . . " (*D&M,* III, 87)

Page 139:

11.1-2: "Yes! nothing is . . . . " (*D&M,* III, 88)
11.6-14: " . . . the conditions . . . . " (*D&M,* III, 104)
11.15-16: "grandeur" . . . . (*D&M,* III, 104)
11.19-21: "Gentlemen, I would end . . . . " (*D&M,* III, 104)
1.22: "the honor of responsibilities" (*D&M,* III, 104)
11.32-34: "One can think . . . . " (*Le Renouveau,* 49, *37*)
11.37-38: "What a moral trial . . . . " (50, *37*)
1.39: *"espérance"* (50, *37*)
11.43-44: "the attraction . . . . " (51, *38*)

ll.41-42: "create an atmosphere . . . . " (*D&M,* III, 232)

 l.43: "free peoples" . . . . (*D&M,* III, 349)

ll.45-51: "that the ambitions of . . . . " (*D&M,* III, 398)

Page 146:

ll.5-6: "organized cooperation . . . . " (*D&M,* III, 233-234)

ll.7-8: "holds, in relation to . . . . " (*D&M,* III, 238)

ll.13-17: "The ideology . . . . " (323, *256*)

 l.19: "misery and humiliation . . . . " (324, 256)

 l.22: "depends solely on Moscow" (327, *259*)

ll.27-28: "the most important . . . . " (*D&M,* III, 158)

 l.34: "only the appeal . . . . " (342, *270*)

ll.35-37: "my initiative . . . . " (343, *271*)

 l.40: "I kept my distance . . . . " (346, *274*)

Page 147:

ll.1-2: "Always I spke . . . . " (364, *289*)

 l.8: "*métier* [which] blunts . . . . " (365, *290*)

ll.8-11: "But, if I am . . . . " (376, *299*)

ll.20-25: "How to doubt . . . . " (*L'Effort,* 13, *306*)

ll.29-32: " . . . in any time . . . . " (14, *306*)

 l.35: "'the man of the country'" (14, *306*)

 l.42: "political games" (18, *308*)

Page 148:

 l.3: "modification of the Constitution" . . . . (22-23, *311*)

ll.5-6: De Gaulle was obviously correct . . . . " (28, *314*)

ll.10-11: "the principal inspirer" (29, *315*)

ll.12-13: "in sum . . . . " (40, *320*)

ll.14-15: "would have clarified . . . . " (31, *315*)

ll.20-22: "In truth . . . . " (56-57, *329*)

 l.26: "born under the . . . . " (63, *333*)

ll.33-35, *p. 149,* ll.1-2: "the relative" . . . . (80, *341*)

Page 149:

 l.3: "in some irrational crisis" (82, *341*)

ll.4-7: "All the strata . . . . " (82, *342*)

ll.8-26: "Without doubt . . . . " (85-86, *343-344*)

ll.28-29: "Is it not . . . . " (106, *354*)

ll.32-33: "the hurricane of 1968 . . . . " (Hoffmann: *op. cit.,* p. 273)

 l.49: "an incomparable . . . . " (116, *358*)

ll.51-52: "in all my sayings . . . . " (116, *359*)

Page 150:

 l.3: "political" . . . . (116, *359*)

 l.4: "utilitarian . . . . " (117, *360*)

ll.8-11: "a dull and passive resistance" . . . . (123-124, *363*)

 l.16: "modern life . . . . " (128, *366*)

ll.27-28: "solidity" . . . . (144-*374*)

ll.30-35: " . . . in the interior . . . . " (144, *374*)

ll.41-43: "but how could I . . . . " (146-147, *376*)

Page 151:

ll.1-3: "'political'" . . . . (154, *378*)

ll.17-18: "the capital fact . . . . " (*D&M,* IV, 370)

ll.18-19: "temptation of renouncement" . . . . (D&M, IV, 369)

ll.20-22: "this strange passion . . . . " (*D&M,* IV, 219 & 220) l.26: "scientific, technical . . . . " (*D&M,* IV, 240)

ll.28-29: "the most expensive . . . . " (*D&M,* IV, 207)

ll.30-32: "the superior interest . . . . " (D&M, IV, 409)

ll.38-40: "Any system . . . . " (*D&M,* IV, 97)

l.42: "*Vive le Québec libre!*" (D&M, V, 207)

Page 152:

l.5: "the banner of . . . . " (D&M, IV, 129)

ll.7-10: "Europe remembers . . . . " (C.L. Sulzberger: *An Age of Mediocrity,* Macmillan and Company, New York, 1973, p. 146)

ll.11-12: "the monolithism of . . . . " (*D&M,* IV, 234)

ll.13-14: "it is too late . . . . " (D&M, V, 365)

ll.18-21: "No problem . . . . " (Claude Mauriac: *The Other de Gaulle,* Moura Budberg and Gordon Latta translation, The John Day Company, New York, 1973, p. 287)

l.29: "the first of . . . . "(*D&M,* V, 215)

ll.30-31: "for independence . . . . " (D&M, V, 218)

ll.36-37: "What is the primary . . . . " (Sulzberger: *An Age of Mediocrity, op. cit.,* p. 189)

ll.38-42: "One must draw . . . . " (*ibid.,* p. 189)

Page 153:

ll.10-14: "[Chateaubriand] knew that France . . . . " (Maurice: *op. cit.,* p. 232)

l.20: "is freedom *from* . . . . " (Hoffmann: *op. cit.,* p. 146)

ll.22-25: " . . . the people are . . . . " (Mauriac: *op. cit.,* p. 185)

ll.31-32: "the envious, the cudkolds . . . . " (*ibid.,* p. 169)

ll.37-39: "Frenchmen have nothing . . . . " (Phillippe Alexandre: *The Duel: de Gaulle and Pompidou,* Elaine P. Halperin translation, Houghton Mifflin Company, Boston, 1972, p. 122)

ll.40-45: "what embarrasses me . . . . " (François Mauriac: *De Gaulle,* Richard Howard translation, Doubleday and Company, Garden City, 1966, p. 60)

Page 154:

ll.1-4: "We must have . . . . " (*ibid.,* pp. 96-97)

ll.11-12: "on a very elevated level" (*D&M,* IV, 433)

l.14: "economic and social epoch" (*D&M,* IV, 433)

ll.15-16: "That is very convenient . . . . " (*D&M,* IV, 434)

ll.18-19: "these excessive systems" (*D&M,* IV, 339-340))

ll.21-22: "unprecendented transformations" . . . . (*D&M,* V, p. 328)

l.24: "colossal" (*D&M,* V, 328)

ll.25-33: "against all authority" . . . . (*D&M,* V, 328-329)

l.36: "is an *esprit* . . . . " (*D&M,* IV, 168)

ll.37-38: "a day shall come . . . . " (*D&M,* V, 268)

l.42, *p. 155,* l.1: "rejected . . . an abusive capitalism . . . . " (*D&M,* V, 174)

Page 155:

ll.3-9: "In our epoch . . . . " (D&M, IV, 104)

ll.14-15: "participat[ing] actively . . . . " (*D&M,* V, 417)

ll.23-27: "must not be . . . . " (*D&M,* V. 251)

ll.31-36: "changes the condition . . . . " (*D&M,* V, 330)

Page 156:

ll.2-7: "conjugated" . . . . (*D&M,* V, 33)

ll.15-21: "Even as the French . . . . " (*D&M,* V, 33)

ll.34-35: "France is one . . . . " (*D&M,* IV, 210)

ll.37-39: "The purpose . . . . " (*D&M,* IV, 210)

11.40-42: "The law of our epoch . . . . " (*D&M,* IV, 213)

11.47-48,*p. 157,* 1.1: "danger of destruction . . . . " (*D&M, IV, 213*)

Page 157:

    1.13: "General de Gaulle . . . . " (Alexandre: *The Duel, op, cit.,* p. 263)

    11.26-27: "We defeated Vichy . . . . " (*ibid.,* p. 309)

SIXTH PART, Chapter 12: Founding and education: Reflections on *Mēmoires d'espoir*

Page 159:

    1.1: "All revolutions . . . . " (George Orwell: *The Collected Essays, Journalism and Letters of George Orwell,* Harcourt, Brace and World, New York, 1968, vol. 3, p. 244)

    11.11-16: "the natural means" . . . . (Montesquieu: *The Spirit of the Laws,* Thomas Nugent translation, Hafner Press, New York, 1949, Vol. 1, Bk. XIX, ch. 14, pp. 299-300)

Page 160:

    1.7: "trust presupposes . . . . " (Leo Strauss: *Natural Right and History,* University of Chicago Press, Chicago and London, 1953, 1968, p. 131)

    1.15: "mandate" from "natural legitimacy" (De Gaulle: radio address, January 29, 1960, *Discours et messages,* III, p. 180)

    11.20-22: "Must a givernment . . . . " (Abraham Lincoln: "Message to Congress in Special Session," July 4, 1861, *Collected Works,* Rutgers University Press, New Brunswick, 1953, vol. IV, p. 426)

    1.22: "Democracies never attack . . . . " (in Claude Mauriac: *The Other de Gaulle,* Moura Budberg and Gordon Latta translation, The John Day Company, New York, 1973, April 2, 1946, p. 176)

    11.23-25: "Democracy . . . has two excesses . . . . " (Montesquieu: *op. cit.,* Vol, I, Bk. IX, ch. 3, p. 128)

    11.29-31: "questioned the integration . . . . " (Harold Macmillan: *Pointing the Way,* Harper and Row, New York, Evanston, San Francisco, London, 1972, p. 88)

Page 161:

    11.5-7: "The problem here . . . . " (Stanley Hoffmann: *Decline or Renewal? France Since the 1930's,* Viking Press, New York, 1974, p. 435)

    11.8-7: "but one single state" . . . . (Montesquieu: *op. cit.,* Vol. I, Bk. XX, ch. 23, p. 328)

    11.12-15: "In modern times . . . . " (Adam Smith: *The Wealth of Nations,* Modern Library, New York, 1937, 1965, p. 6

    11.29-34: A scholar . . . . (Edward L. Morse: *Foreign Policy and Interdependence in Gaullist France,* Princeton University Press, Princeton, 1973, pp. 188-189)

Page 162:

    11.7-8: "the peasant problem" (De Gaulle: *Discours et messages,* IV, p. 437)

    11.23-24: "An Oedipus . . . . " (Malraux: *Le Miroir des limbes, op. cit.,* p. 166,*26*)

Page 163:

    11.10-11: "There was an inherent . . . . " (Hoffmann: *op. cit.,* p. 250)

    11.13-18: " . . . there are two . . . . " (Plato: *Laws,* Benjamin Jowett translation, Book III, 693d-693e)

    1.31: whom Malraux considered a roman type . . . . (See C.L. Sulzberger: *An Age of Mediocrity,* Macmillan, New York, 1973, p. 300)

Page 164:

    11.1-2 "massive demonstration . . . . " (Thomas L. Pangle:*Montesquieu's Philosophy of Liberalism,* University of Chicago Press, Chicago and London, 1973, p. 5)

    11.3-5: "he who imagines . . . . " (Plato: *Laws, op. cit.,* Bk. VI, 780a)

    11.6-7: "Laws excessively good . . . . " (Montesquieu: *op. cit., Vol. I, Bk. XXII, ch. 21. p. 397)*

    11.3-5: "he who imagines . . . . " (Plato: *Laws, op. cit.,* Bk. VI, 780a)

    11.6-7: "Laws excessively good . . . . " (Montesquieu: *op. cit.,* Vol. I, Bk. XXII, ch. 21. p. 397)

    1.14: "political virtue" . . . . (*ibid.,* p.lxxi

    11.19-20: "a defect of . . . . " (*ibid.,* Vol I, Bk. XIV, ch. 12, p. 231)

    11.20-22: "heroic virtues . . . . " (*ibid.,* Vol I, Bk. III, ch. 5, p. 23)

    11.4-7: "The laws of Minos . . . . " (*ibid.,* Vol. I, Bk. IV, ch. 7, p. 37)

    11.31-34: "Experience shows . . . . " (Aristotle: *Politics,* Ernest Barker translation Oxford University Press, Oxford, London, New York, 1946, 1969, Bk. VII, ch. 4, p. 291)

    11.37-40: "Commercial laws . . . . " (Montesquieu: *op. cit.,* Vol. I, Bk. XX, ch. 1, p. 316)

    1.18: "a certain exact sense of justice" (*ibid.,* Vol. I, Bk. XX, ch. 2, p. 317)

Page 165:

    1.2-3: "if all men become . . . . " (Malraux: *La corde et les souris, op. cit.,* p. 29)

    11.5-7: "the whole of French . . . . " (Francois Mauriac: *De Gaulle,* Richard Howard translation, Doubleday and Company, Garden City, 1966, p. 60)

    11.9-10: "The Acropolis . . . . " (Tocqueville: *Democracy in America,* Henry Reeve, Francis Bowen, and Phillips Bradley translation, Vintage Books, New York, 1945, Vol. I, pp. 314-315)

    11.17-18: "In those countries . . . . " (*ibid.,* Vol. II, p. 159)

    11.19-22: "the leaders of . . . . " (*ibid.,* Vol. II, p. 262)

    11.23-26: "the heroic type . . . . " (Nietzsche: *The Gay Science, Walter Kaufmann translation, Vintage Books, New York, 1974, Bk. IV, p. 253)*

    11.31-33: "Whereas Socialism . . . . " (George Orwell: *op. cit.,* vol. 2, p. 14)

    40-41: "the principal problem . . . . " (Malraux: "Replies to 13 Questions," (interview), *Partisan Review,* Spring 1955, p. 170)

Page 166:

    11.5-7: "there is no . . . . " (Plato: *Laws, op. cit.,* Bk. IV, 718d)

    1.10: "turning around" (Plato: *Republic, op. cit.,* Bk. VII, 518c-519b)

    1.14: "foolish and antagonistic counselors" (Plato: *Laws, op. cit.,* Bk. V, 644c)

    11.15-17: "the best way . . . . " (*ibid.,* Bk. V, 729c)

    1.21: "to act *ensemble*" (Malraux: *Antimemoires,* Gallimard, Paris, 1972, p. 258; *Anti-Memoirs,* Terence Kilmartin translation, Holt. Rinehart and Winston, New York, 1967, p. 170)

    1.23: "render[ed] France near . . . . " (Malraux: *La corde et les souris, op. cit.,* p. 287)

    11.32-33: "was the Carnot . . . . " (Malraux: Transfert des cendres de Jean Moulin au Pantheon," in *Oraisons funebres,* Gallimard, Paris, 1971, p. 126)

    1.35: "the prehistory" . . . . (*ibid.,* p. 129)

ll.40-41: "it now began . . . . " (*ibid.,* p. 129)
ll.43-45: "his Calvary began" . . . . (*ibid.,* p. 133)
ll.46-47: "his brothers in the order . . . . " (*ibid.,* p. 136)
ll.50-51, *p. 167,* l.1: "today, youth . . . . " (*ibid.,* p. 137

Page 167:

ll.3-6: "the mysterious presence . . . . " (Malraux: "Address at the French
Institute in New York," May 15, 1962, in Charles Blend: *Andrē Malraux:
Tragic Humanist,* Ohio State University Press, Columbus, 1963, p. 244)
ll.13-14: "Only knowledge of the kind . . . . " (Jacob Klein: *A Commentary on
Plato's Meno,* University of North Carolina Press, Chapel Hill, 1965,
p. 248)
ll.25-28: " . . . the Ministry of Education . . . . " (John S. Ambler: *The
Government and Politics of France,* Houghton Mifflin Company, Boston,
1971, p. 42)
ll.31-32: "neither the sons of . . . . " (Raymond Aron: *La revolution
introuvable,* Librairie Artheme Fayard, Paris, 1968, p. 152)
ll.33-36, *p. 168,* ll.1-2: "abstract and rhetorical formation" . . . . (*ibid.,*
pp. 122-123)

Page 168:

ll.5-6: "unless by making . . . . " (cited previously)
ll.10-11: "not only instruction . . . . " (De Gaulle: *"Discours prononce a Lille,"*
February 12, 1949, *Discours et messages,* Vol. II, p. 270)
ll.37-38: "never effaced . . . . " (Montesquieu: *op. cit.,* Vol. I, Bk. IV, ch.
4, p. 33)
ll.39-41: "This, in some measure . . . . " (*ibid.,* p. 33)
l.43, *p. 169,* l.1: "the legislator should . . . . " (Aristotle: *op. cit.,* Bk. VIII,
ch. 1, p. 332)

Page 169:

ll.2-3: "men who cannot face . . . . " (*ibid.,* Bk. VII, ch. 15, p. 321)
ll.3-4: "most of the *polises* . . . . " (*ibid.,* Bk. VII, ch. 14, p. 320)
ll.5-6: "like that of art . . . . " (*ibid.,* Bk. VII, ch. 17, p. 331)
ll.7-10: "the education of . . . . " (*ibid.,* Bk. V, ch. 9, p. 233)
ll.13-15: "the soul of . . . . " (Plato: *Laws, op. cit.,* Bk. I, 643d)
ll.15-16: "that training which . . . . " (*ibid.,* 653b)
ll.21-22: "we always prefer . . . . " (Aristotle: *op. cit.,* Bk. VIII, Ch. 5, p. 343)
l.23: "the mind at leisure" (*ibid.,* Bk. 3, p. 336)
ll.23-27: "provides us with images . . . . " (*ibid.,* Bk. V, pp. 343-344)
ll.28-32: "that music has . . . . " (Plato: *Laws, op. cit.,* Bk. I, 701a)
l.34: "the nurture and . . . . " (*ibid.,* Bk. IX, 874d)
ll.35-37: "Laws are partly framed . . . . " (*ibid.,* Bk. IX, 880d-880e)
ll.42-45, *p. 170,* ll.1-3: "Unless . . . the philosophers rule . . . . " (Plato,
Republic, op. cit., Bk. V, 473d-473e)

Page 170:

ll.4-5: "the brilliant failures . . . . " (Theodore Mommsen: *The History of
Rome,* edited and translated by Dero A. Saunders and John H. Collins,
Meridian Books, Cleveland and New York, 1958, p. 523)

APPENDIX: De Gaulle's Military Epistemology: A note on *Le fil de l'ēpēe*

Page 173:

l.3: "becoming in a cavalry . . . . " (Bertrand Russell: *A History of Western*

Philosophy, Simon and Schuster, New York, 1945—1966, p. 800)

1.11: "successions as . . . . " (Russell: *ibid.,* p. 803)

1.16: "indivisible continuity . . . . " (Bergson: *A Study of Metaphysics: The Creative Mind,* translated by Mabell L. Andison, Littlefield, Adams and Company, Totowa, N.J. 1970, p. 149)

1.29: "express[es] a thing . . . . " (Bergson: *An Introduction to Metaphysics,* T.E. Hulme translation, The Bobbs-Merrill Company, Inc., Indianapolis and New York, 1955, p. 24)

11.23-33: "by which one . . . . " (Bergson: *ibid.,* pp. 23-23)

1.36: "universal love" (Russell: *op. cit.,* p. 773)

1.39: "touched, penetrated, lived" (Bergson: *Matter and Memory,* translated by Nancy Margaret Paul and W. Scott Palmer, George Allen and Unwin, Ltd., London, 1951, p. 75)

11.40-41: "The rule of . . . . " (Bergson: *A Study in Metaphysics: The Creative Mind, op. cit.,* p. 126)

Page 174:

11.5-6: "disinterested, self-conscious . . . . " (Bergson: *Creative Evolution,*
Arthur Mitchell translation, Henry Holt and Company, New York, 1911, p. 176)

11.16-18: "Dialectic is . . . . " (Bergson: *ibid.,* p. 238)

11.19-31: " . . . all [logic] does . . . . " (*ibid.,* p. 238)

11.32-34: "what he was really . . . . " (Monique Clague: "Conceptions of Leadership — Charles de Gaulle and Max Weber," *Political Theory,* volume 3, number 4, November 1975, p. 426)

Page 175:

(None)

INDEX OF NAMES